TROTSKY
THE PASSIONATE
REVOLUTIONARY

Dedication

For all those who believe that, despite 'hell-black nights', another – kinder and fairer – world is possible.

TROTSKY
THE PASSIONATE
REVOLUTIONARY

ALLAN TODD

PEN & SWORD
HISTORY

AN IMPRINT OF PEN & SWORD BOOKS LTD.
YORKSHIRE - PHILADELPHIA

First published in Great Britain in 2022 by
PEN AND SWORD HISTORY
An imprint of
Pen & Sword Books Ltd
Yorkshire – Philadelphia

ISBN 978 1 39901 076 4

Typeset in Times New Roman 11/13.5 by
SJmagic DESIGN SERVICES, India.
Printed and bound in the UK by CPI Group (UK) Ltd.

Pen & Sword Books Limited incorporates the imprints of Atlas, Archaeology,
Aviation, Discovery, Family History, Fiction, History, Maritime, Military, Military
Classics, Politics, Select, Transport, True Crime, Air World, Frontline Publishing,
Leo Cooper, Remember When, Seaforth Publishing, The Praetorian Press,
Wharncliffe Local History, Wharncliffe Transport, Wharncliffe True Crime and
White Owl.

For a complete list of Pen & Sword titles please contact
PEN & SWORD BOOKS LIMITED
47 Church Street, Barnsley, South Yorkshire, S70 2AS, England
E-mail: enquiries@pen-and-sword.co.uk
Website: www.pen-and-sword.co.uk

Or

PEN AND SWORD BOOKS
1950 Lawrence Rd, Havertown, PA 19083, USA
E-mail: Uspen-and-sword@casematepublishers.com
Website: www.penandswordbooks.com

Contents

Acknowledgements   vi

A Note on Usages   vii

Family Tree   ix

Main Characters   x

Introduction: Against the Stream   xiii

Chapter 1   The Young Trotsky, 1879–1896   1

Chapter 2   Revolution, Love and Exile, 1897–1902   17

Chapter 3   Escape, Splits and Revolution, 1902–06   33

Chapter 4   The Vienna Years, 1907–13   52

Chapter 5   War and Internationalism, 1914–17   70

Chapter 6   Revolution and Civil War, 1917–19   84

Chapter 7   The Commissar in Power, 1920–23   105

Chapter 8   Fighting Against His Time, 1924–28   126

Chapter 9   Prophet Without a Home, 1929–36   150

Chapter 10   Love and Death in Mexico, 1937–40   175

Conclusion: Legacy   194

Bibliography/Further Reading   201

Endnotes   203

Index   220

Acknowledgements

Work on this book started at the end of August 2020, just a few days after the 80th anniversary of Trotsky's death in Mexico City, on 21 August 1940, following a dramatic and ultimately successful assassination attempt the previous day.

I would like to thank Jacqui Petrie, Ken and Di Barrell, Chrissie Parfitt, Ian Rycroft, Paul Wilmott, Tony Lywood – and two of my ex-History students, Nicky Barrell and Patrick Fitzgerald – for kindly reading, and offering constructive criticism on early drafts of various chapters.

Thanks are also due to Chris Evan Brown for shaping my proposal, and to Claire Hopkins, Laura Hirst and the rest of the team at Pen & Sword for pre-publication improvements. Thanks are also due to Thomas Bohm, of Design, Illustration & Typesetting, for his skill – and patience! – in drawing up the Family Tree and the various maps.

Any remaining faults and errors are down to me.

I would also like to thank our daughters, Megan and Vanessa, and our grandchildren, Alexander and Emilia, for their support and encouragement – especially over the past eleven years, and during what was a difficult year for so many.

And finally, I owe a huge debt of gratitude to Cyn who, for Christmas 1972, bought me Wyndham and King's *Trotsky: A Documentary* – which, 50 years later, helped me shape and complete this book.

Allan Todd
June 2021
Keswick

A Note on Usages

Names

(a) Trotsky's name was Leon Davidovitch Bronstein; but 'Trotsky' is the name by which he is known to History, so to avoid confusion with any of the other members of his family, he will be referred to as 'Trotsky' throughout the book.
(b) As will become apparent, most Russian first names have several diminutives which were used by family and friends. Trotsky was frequently referred to as 'Lev' or 'Lyova'; whilst Natalya Sedova was often called 'Natasha'.

Dates

Russian History is complicated by the fact that, before February 1918, Russia used the Julian calendar, which was thirteen days behind the Gregorian calendar used in the rest of Europe. Three months after the November Revolution of 1917, Soviet Russia adopted the Gregorian calendar – the introduction of which was overseen by Trotsky. This is why the March and November Revolutions of 1917 are referred to in some books as the 'February' and 'October' Revolutions. To avoid any (mathematical) confusions, this book uses the Gregorian calendar throughout – including for the years before 1918.

Soviet/Soviets

Twentieth century Russian history is littered with Soviets. Unless otherwise stated, where 'Soviet' is used in the singular, it refers to the Petrograd Soviet; where 'Soviets' is used, it refers to the All-Russian Congress of Soviets.

Dictatorship of the Proletariat

The term 'dictatorship' – when used in this Marxist phrase – has a very precise meaning: quite different from its usual one. Here, it means the overall 'dominance' or 'hegemony' of a particular social class's interests – which can exist within either a democratic or an undemocratic political system. Thus, for Marxists, the 'dictatorship of the bourgeoisie' – capitalism – can operate within either a parliamentary democracy (such as Britain) or an authoritarian one-party state (such as Nazi Germany).

For the Bolsheviks, whilst Britain was a *political* democracy, with a parliament and universal suffrage, the *economic* interests of the capitalist (bourgeois) class always predominated because of their much greater wealth and power – reflected by laws and the dominant values. Consequently, there was no conflict between Trotsky's call for the 'dictatorship of the proletariat' *and* for socialist democracy.

Secret Police

During the period covered by this book, Russia's secret police underwent several name changes. From 1881, under the Tsars, it was known as the *Okhrana* (The Guard Department). After the November Revolution in 1917, such work was taken over by the *Cheka* (Extraordinary Commission) until 1922, when it became the GPU (State Political Administration) which, in 1923, became the OGPU (United State Political Administration). In 1934, the NKVD (People's Commissariat for Internal Affairs) took over the secret police.

TROTSKY'S 'FATAL' FAMILY TREE

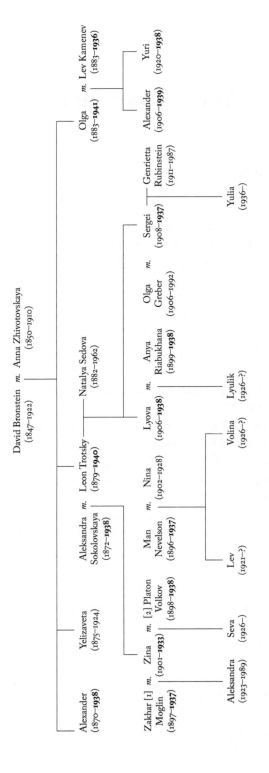

David Bronstein *m.* Anna Zhivotovskaya
(1847–1922)   (1850–1910)

Alexander
(1870–**1938**)

Yelizaveta
(1875–1924)

Aleksandra *m.* Leon Trotsky ——— Natalya Sedova
Sokolovskaya   (1879–**1940**)   (1882–1962)
(1872–**1938**)

Olga *m.* Lev Kamenev
(1883–**1941**)   (1883–**1936**)

Alexander   Yuri
(1906–**1939**)   (1920–**1938**)

Zakhar [1] *m.* Zina *m.* [2] Platon
Moglin   (1901–**1933**)   Volkov
(1897–**1937**)   (1898–**1938**)

Man *m.* Nina
Nevelson   (1902–1928)
(1896–**1937**)

Lyova *m.* Anya
(1906–**1938**)   Riabukhana
                  (1899–**1938**)

Olga *m.* Sergei
Greber   (1908–**1937**)
(1906–1992)

Genrietta
Rubinstein
(1911–1987)

Aleksandra   Seva
(1923–1989)   (1926–)

Lev   Volina   Lyulik
(1921–?)   (1926–?)   (1926–?)

Yulia
(1936–)

Notes

Dates in **bold** font = shot/assassinated/mysterious circumstances/suicide.
? = fate unknown.

ix

Main Characters

Trotsky's Family

David Bronstein (1874–1922) – father
Anna Bronstein (1850–1910) – mother
Alexander Bronstein (1870–**1938**) – older brother
Yelizaveta Bronstein (1875–1924) – older sister
Olga Bronstein (1883–**1941**) – younger sister; an Oppositionist
Aleksandra Sokolovskaya (1872–**1938**) – Marxist revolutionary; Trotsky's
    (first) wife; an Oppositionist
Zina Trotsky (1901–33) – elder daughter; an Oppositionist
Nina Trotsky (1902–28) – younger daughter; an Oppositionist
Natalya Sedova (1882–1962) – Trotsky's (common-law) wife; an Oppositionist
Lyova Sedov (1906–**38**) – elder son; an Oppositionist
Sergei Sedov (1908–**37**) – younger son
Zakhar Moglin (1897–**1937**) – Zina's first husband; an Oppositionist
Platon Volkov (1898–**1938**) – Zina's second husband; an Oppositionist
Man Nevelson (1896–**1937**) – Nina's husband; an Oppositionist
Anya Riabukhana (1899–**1938**) – Lyova's wife
Seva (Esteban) Volkov (1926–) – grandson
Aleksandra Moglin (1923–89) – granddaughter (she met Seva – her half-
    brother – who travelled from Mexico to Russia just before she died; but
    they couldn't communicate, as she had no Spanish or English, and he
    had forgotten Russian)
Lev Nevelson (1921–?) – grandson; fate unknown
Volina Nevelson (1926–?) – granddaughter; fate unknown
Lyulik Sedov (1926–?) – grandson; fate unknown
Yulia Sedov-Rubinstein (1936–) – granddaughter

Trotsky's Main Supporters

Vladimir Antonov-Ovseenko (1883–**1938**)
Jan Frankel (1906–84)

Joseph Hansen (1910–79)
Jean van Heijenoort (1912–86)
Adolfe Joffe (1883–**1927**)
Rudolf Klement (1908–**38**)
Nikolai Krestinsky (1883–**1938**)
Anatoly Lunacharsky (1875–1933)
Raymond Molinier (1904–94)
Nikolai Muralov (1877–**1937**)
Alexander Parvus (1867–1924)
Yevgeni Preobrazhensky (1886–**1937**)
Georgei Pyatakov (1880–**1937**)
Karl Radek (1885–**1939**)
Christian Rakovsky (1873–**1941**)
Ignaz Reiss(1899–**1937**)
Alfred Rosmer (1877–1964)
David Ryazanov (1870–**1938**)
Max Schachtman (1904–72)
Ephraim Skylansky (1892–**1925**)
Ivan Smirnov (1881–**1936**)
Vladimir Smirnov (1887–**1937**)
Grigori Sokolnikov (1888–**1939**)
Moisei Uritsky (1873–1918) – Chekist; assassinated
Erwin Wolf (1902–**37**)

Other Leading Russian Marxists

Paul Axelrod (1850–1928) – leading member of the RSDWP; later a Menshevik
Nikolai Bukharin (1888–**1938**) – leading member of the RSDWP; later a Bolshevik; later an Oppositionist
Felix Dzershinsky (1877–1926) – Bolshevik; head of the Cheka, the GPU & then the OGPU
Lev Kamenev (1883–**1936**) – leading member of the RSDWP; later a Bolshevik; one of the anti-Trotsky triumvirate; later an Oppositionist (also Trotsky's son-in-law)
Nadezhda Krupskaya (1869–1939) – leading Bolshevik; Lenin's wife
Mikhail Lashevich (1884–**1928**) – initially a Bolshevik; later an Oppositionist
Vladimir I. Lenin (1870–1924) – early Russian Marxist; leading member of the RSDWP; later head of the Bolsheviks

Julius Martov (1873–1923) – leading member of the RSDWP; later Menshevik, Internationalist Menshevik

Georgi Plekhanov (1856–1918) – early Russian Marxist; leader of the RSDWP

Alexander Potresov (1869–1934) – leading member of the RSDWP; later a Menshevik

Joseph Stalin (1878–1953) – Bolshevik, and one of the anti-Trotsky triumvirate

Vera Zasulich (1851–1919) – leading member of the RSDWP; later a Menshevik

Gregorii Zinoviev (1883–**1936**) – leading member of the RSDWP; later a Bolshevik; one of the anti-Trotsky triumvirate; later an Oppositionist

Introduction

Against the Stream

'I don't want them to undress me...I want you to do it.'[1]

Those were the last words ever spoken by Leon Trotsky who, over a period of almost forty years, wrote and spoke extensively and passionately. Those poignant words are probably not what some would expect from a man who rose from obscurity to play such important roles in both the 1905 and the November 1917 Revolutions in Russia, to found and lead the Red Army during the dramatic years of the Russian Civil War, and to spend the last sixteen years of his life standing up – unflinchingly – to the increasingly murderous rule of Joseph Stalin in the Soviet Union.

In particular, those words contrast sharply with the style of speaking most associated with him, and which so often thrilled the crowds. His style was theatrical and heroic, and, as Deutscher stated: 'He spoke an intense and dramatic language not from affectation or craving for stage effect, but because this was his most natural language, best suited to express his dramatic thought and intense emotion.' This was even true of how he spoke in private with family and friends: often using 'the same rhythmical cadences which he used on the platform and in his writings.' In many ways, he appeared as an 'heroic character in historic action.' Though, when the heroic and revolutionary phase of history ended, he seemed increasingly unsuited to the new reactionary times.[2]

Trotsky 'in the Round'

Nonetheless, it seems appropriate to begin with those words, whispered to his life companion, Natalya Sedova, in Mexico City's hospital on 20 August 1940. They were uttered as nurses began to cut away his clothes in preparation for an operation, following what proved to be a fatal assassination attempt. Fittingly for someone who had lived such a dramatic life, played out on the world's stage, Trotsky's end was equally dramatic – coming as a result of a head wound, inflicted by an ice axe, wielded by one of Stalin's agents.

Shortly after saying those words, and having responded to Sedova's kisses, he lost consciousness. He died the next day, 21 August, without regaining consciousness.

Yet what those last words do is provide at least a hint that he was much more than just the famous – or infamous – revolutionary who, for over twenty years, inspired either love or hate in so many people and, indeed, in historians. Surprisingly, for those who only focus on the deeds of 'great men' in history, Trotsky was much more than just a revolutionary political activist. To begin with, he was passionate about writing in general. Amongst other things, he was an accomplished journalist, essayist and war correspondent, and a lively and influential art and literary critic. His prose was elegant and closely crafted:

> 'Writing…often took precedence with him over speaking and organizing…He simply loved to be seated at a desk, fountain pen in hand, scribbling out his latest opus.'

Although writing soon took second place to working for revolution, it remained immensely important to him. So much so that, after having helped bring about the desired revolution in 1917, he hoped to return to that love: 'After the seizure of power, I tried to stay out of the government, and offered to undertake the direction of the press.' Though had he been allowed to do so, the Bolsheviks wouldn't have won the Civil War.[3]

In addition, as a youth, he developed a passion for opera – and this 'future scourge of the bourgeoisie' was also a 'passionate croquet player for much of his life.' He was passionate, too, about hunting and fishing – activities he continued to the end of his life. While, in Mexico, he developed a new passion: collecting cacti.[4]

Perhaps most unexpected of all, though, Trotsky was also reputed to be something of a 'ladies' man'. Issac Deutscher, his first academic – and sympathetic – biographer, described his behaviour towards women as a kind of 'articulate gallantry, not free from male vanity and sensitiveness to female admiration', which led him to 'dashing displays of seductive verve and wit.' Deutscher saw such 'flirtations' – which were very different from his usual high-minded seriousness – as essentially 'old-fashioned chivalry.'[5]

However, he is known to have had a short but passionate affair in 1937, with Frida Kahlo, the fiery Mexican artist who, at the time, was almost thirty years his junior. In addition, it is rumoured he also had brief romantic liaisons with two other strong, independent – and, again, younger – women: Larisa Reissner (a Russian journalist and revolutionary activist) and

Clare Sheridan (the accomplished English sculptor). Certainly *Trotsky* – the eight-part Russian TV mini-series, first broadcast in 2017, to coincide with the centenary of the 1917 November Revolution – makes much of this allegedly amorous side of his nature.

Myths of Trotsky

It says something of Trotsky's nature, and his political campaigns and writings, that he is still being written about eighty years after his death. Because he was at the centre of some of the most dramatic episodes of twentieth-century History – as a passionate revolutionary theorist and practitioner; and then as a factional leader exiled and finally assassinated by Stalin – a large number of books have been written about him. His passionate espousal of revolution, and his prominent roles in the Russian Revolution and its aftermath, have aroused strong passions. Even today, 'Trotskyism' and 'Trotskyist' are still often used – by left and right alike – as terms of political abuse.

Consequently, many of the History books about him have tended to be one-sided: portraying him either as a Marxist hero, far-sighted political analyst and prophet, and a global icon of revolutionary change – or as someone whose ideas and actions helped pave the way for Stalin's dictatorship. Yet Stalin described Trotskyists and their leader as 'a barefaced gang of wreckers, spies and murderers' and, until the late 1980s, subsequent Soviet governments 'continued to heap odium on him [Trotsky] as on no one else.'[6]

After Lenin, Trotsky has often been portrayed as 'the best Bolshevik' and, from 1922 onwards, he worked with Lenin in what proved to be an unsuccessful attempt to replace Stalin and to reverse the bureaucratic degeneration that was undermining the ideals of the November Revolution. In addition, Trotsky is credited with developing the internationalist theories of 'Permanent Revolution' and world revolution, which he consistently upheld after his fall from power. Although Deutscher described Trotsky as 'one of the most outstanding revolutionary leaders of all times, outstanding as a fighter, thinker, and martyr', he strenuously denied his biography was an attempt to 'indulge in any cult of Trotsky.' On the contrary, his intention was to avoid glorifying him as 'a man without blemish.'[7]

However, since Deutscher wrote his three-volume biography of Trotsky, several historians have challenged aspects of those views as being part of 'the Trotsky myth'. Between them, such historians have questioned Trotsky's significance in the November Revolution and in the Russian Civil War: Richard Pipes – an established 'Cold War Warrior' historian – managed to write an account of the Russian Civil War, with only one mention of Trotsky: despite, during it, Trotsky having been the Commissar for War, and the founder and leader of the Red Army!

The most recent of such historians is Robert Service, describing Deutscher as Trotsky's apologist who 'worshipped at Trotsky's shrine'. On 22 October 2009, the *Evening Standard* reported that, at the press launch of his new biography of Trotsky, Service declared: 'if the ice pick didn't quite do its job of killing him off, I hope I've managed it!' One review described Service's book as the 'second assassination' of Trotsky. Though even Service accepts that Trotsky was such a colossal character that he cannot 'be cut down to a regular size and shown to be just like the rest of us.'[8]

While 'all too often the political passions of the biographer determine the nature of the biography', other historians have been more balanced about Trotsky's historical significance:

> 'For good or ill, the Bolsheviks would not have come to power without Trotsky, and they would have lost power in less than a year if he had not been put in charge of the Red Army. It is equally certain that if Trotsky had remained in the leadership of the 1920s, the Soviet Union would have been a more technocratic and less terrorised society.'[9]

As well as history books, Trotsky has inspired, or part-inspired, several fiction books. Most notably, Anthony Burgess' 1983 novel, *The End of the World News*; and Barbara Kingsolver's 2009 novel, *The Lacuna*, which touches on Trotsky's final exile in Mexico. While, more recently, Dan La Botz's 2020 counter-factual historical novel, *Trotsky in Tijuana* – published on the eightieth anniversary of Trotsky's assassination – imagines Trotsky surviving the assassination and moving to Tijuana, to carry on his political work. Trotsky's dramatic life – and death – as well as inspiring the 2017 Russian TV series, can also be seen in full-length feature films, such as Joseph Losey's 1972 film, *The Assassination of Trotsky*, starring Richard Burton (available on YouTube); and Julie Taymor's 2002 film, *Frida*, in which Geoffrey Rush plays Trotsky.[10]

To get some idea of the man – as opposed to the myth – it is useful to contrast those final words of his, aged 60 and spoken on his death bed, with what he wrote in early 1901, when aged just 21, in his short essay *On Optimism and Pessimism*:

'Dum spiro spero [While there's life, there's hope]…If I were one of the celestial bodies, I would look with complete detachment upon this miserable ball of dust and dirt…But I am a **man**. World history which to you…book-keeper of eternity, seems only a negligible moment in the balance of time, is to me everything! **As long as I breathe, I shall fight for the future**, that radiant future in which man, strong and beautiful, will become master of the drifting stream of his history and will direct it towards the boundless vision of beauty, joy and happiness!…

'It seems as if the new century…were bent at the very moment of its appearance on driving the optimist into absolute pessimism…"Death to Utopia!…Death to love! Death to hope!" thunders the twentieth century in salvoes of fire and in the rumbling of guns. "Surrender, you pathetic dreamer. Here I am, your long-awaited twentieth century, your future."

'"No", replies the unhumbled optimist. "You – you are only the **present**."'[11]

The indomitable spirit of the man, so evident in this early essay, stayed with him until the very end of his life – despite living through what was a decidedly Learesque 'hell-black night' for the last decade of his life. As this book will attempt to show, from being a very young man, he held to this optimistic refusal to give in or stop struggling for the better world he wanted to see. This was despite many political setbacks and disappointments, isolation, and personal losses.

Rather like the words of Bob Dylan's 'Forever Young', Trotsky was always courageous, standing upright and strong – even through the darkest moments in history and in his life. This was because he had a strong foundation: both his Marxism, and an unshakeable belief – whether true or not – that he was nearly always right. As we shall see, he certainly withstood the buffeting that came his way when the 'winds of change' shifted. There is a saying, attributed to W. C. Fields, that: 'It takes a live fish to swim against the stream.' Only a 'live fish' can swim against the currents of History – and Trotsky proved that whatever else he was, he certainly was very much a 'live fish'.

But, to be such as 'live fish' requires a certain amount of self-belief – especially during difficult times. As both friends and foes have commented, Trotsky had plenty of that – which some called egotism, and some saw as arrogance. Akesandra Sokolovskaya, his (first) wife, whilst acknowledging he could be both very tender and sympathetic, stated he could also be assertive and arrogant. Though, as she conceded: 'In all my experience I have never met any person so completely consecrated [to the revolutionary cause].' As Grigorii Ziv, a one-time friend and comrade from his early days, commented: '[Trotsky's] Ego dominated his whole behaviour, but the revolution dominated his Ego.' That he devoted everything to revolution is indicated by Trotsky himself: 'From my youth on, or, to be more precise, from my childhood on, I had dreamed of being a writer. Later I subordinated my literary work, as I did everything else, to the revolution.'[12]

Ultimately, he never lost hope – even when he suffered defeats. Although it's possible to see his life as a Shakespearean tragedy, he did not view it as such. As he wrote in 1930, whilst exiled in Turkey:

> 'I do not measure the historical process by the yardstick of one's personal fate.
>
> '…I know no **personal** tragedy…In prison, with a book or a pen in hand, I experienced the same sense of deep satisfaction that I did at the mass meetings of the revolution.'[13]

Chapter 1

The Young Trotsky, 1879–1896

'For several months I was mutely in love with the coloratura soprano bearing the mysterious name of Giuseppina Uget, who seemed to me to have descended from heaven to the stage-boards of the Odessa theatre.'[1]

Trotsky was born on 7 November 1879; thirty-eight years later, to the very day, he would lead the Bolshevik Revolution in Petrograd. The seeds of that dramatic and world-shattering political role were sown in the first seventeen years of his life.

Trotsky's family

Trotsky's parents were David and Anna Bronstein. In all, his parents had eight children – but only four survived into adulthood. Trotsky's siblings were Alexander, Yelizaveta and Olga. As a child, Trotsky had most to do with Olga, his younger sister – as he was four years older, he often tended to take the lead.

In the summer of 1879, his parents had moved into Yanovka, an isolated farm near the small town of Bobrinetz, in the province of Kherson, on the steppes of southern Ukraine. This was to be Trotsky's home for his entire childhood. It was a remote rural setting, around fifteen miles from the nearest post office, and twenty-three miles away from the nearest railway station. His parents were Jewish, but Yanovka was too far from the nearest synagogue for regular worship.

As well as buying this 250-acre farm, Trotsky's father had also leased a further 400 acres. It was unusual for Jewish people to take up farming – but, at that time, there were about twenty Jewish faming colonies on the Kherson steppe. They were there to escape the poverty of the crowded ghettoes of 'The Pale of Settlement': the towns in the western provinces annexed by Tsarist Russia at the end of the eighteenth century, when Poland was partitioned.

Ordinarily, Jews were not allowed to live in Russia outside 'The Pale'. However, the fertile land on the southern steppe near the Black Sea was only thinly populated. In order to encourage its colonisation, successive Tsars allowed Jews – as well as foreign immigrants – to settle there. For Jewish settlers, the big advantage was they no longer faced the threat of expulsion or pogrom. Generally, these Jewish settlers came from the lower classes, compared to the majority of Jewish people who remained in the towns of 'The Pale'. David Bronstein was typical of such Jewish settlers: he was illiterate; spoke a mixture of Russian and Ukrainian instead of Yiddish; and was not really interested in religion.

Trotsky's mother, Anna, had had an urban middle class upbringing and, unlike her husband, was educated enough to read, though with some difficulty. Unusually, compared to the vast majority of Russian Jewish women, she subscribed to a lending library and read Russian novels, thus helping to give her children – Trotsky included – an early love of knowledge and culture, despite living in rural Russia. Also unlike her husband, she did observe several Jewish rites. Trotsky seems to have had a distinct preference for his father over his mother, seeing him as her 'superior' in both 'intellect and character', and saying he was 'quieter' and more gentle as a parent than his mother. But this relationship with his father became increasingly strained as Trotsky became political.[2]

To Trotsky's growing embarrassment, his father was unusually ambitious as well as hard-working, and drove both himself and his labourers hard, in order to develop his farm into a prosperous estate. The family was prosperous enough to have a maid and a cook. David Bronstein was soon in a position to buy even more land; but, in 1881, the Tsar ruled that Jews could no longer buy land – even in the steppe. So Trotsky's father could only rent more land – doing so on a large scale, eventually extending to thousands of acres. Because of his parents' industriousness, their wealth grew, and they developed a strong self-confidence. Trotsky later developed a similar self-confidence and commitment to hard work – though not with the object of acquiring wealth.

Trotsky's early years

Trotsky's first nine years were spent at Yanovka. Although his first home was a thatched cottage, built of clay, it had five rooms – most peasant families at that time lived in mud huts of just one or two rooms. Some of those rooms were small and dark, and had ceilings which leaked during heavier rain, but these were improved as his parents' wealth increased. In time, the Bronsteins were able to build a more spacious house.

Though his parents put a great deal of effort into becoming prosperous, they also did their best to give their children a good start in life. By the time Trotsky was born, his elder brother and sister were at school in town, and he had a nursemaid. Later on, his parents paid for a music teacher, and planned for the boys to go university. As Trotsky himself noted, as the son of a prosperous landowner, he belonged to the privileged classes, not to the oppressed.

However, Trotsky later wrote that his parents were usually too preoccupied in their work to give their youngest children much tenderness: 'My childhood was not one of hunger and cold...We knew no need, but neither did we know the generosities of life, its caresses...Mine was a greyish childhood of a lower-middle-class family.' His father seems to have been gruff and his mother demanding: they expected a lot from all their children, often becoming angry if expectations were not met. But Trotsky usually earned praise because of his brightness, and he received loving attention from his two sisters, and from his nanny, Masha. As he grew up, his intelligence and good nature delighted his parents, his siblings and the farm's servants and labourers.[3]

He was generally a healthy child, though he suffered occasional blackouts at intense moments – something inherited from his mother. This tendency continued to plague him into adulthood. In his early years, Trotsky was particularly interested in the farm's workshop – and in the skills displayed by their chief mechanic, Ivan Greben. As well as teaching Trotsky about tools and materials, he also made him a bike and taught him how to ride it, and made him croquet balls – thus starting a long-lasting passion. In his autobiography, Trotsky later claimed Greben was the main influence in his early childhood. And what he wrote of him shows a respect for working people that was 'among the earliest social attitudes developed by Trotsky' and which 'explains his lifelong appreciation of technical experts.'[4]

However, in those early years, Trotsky also first became aware of the existence of economic inequalities and social injustices: 'He stared at scenes of poverty, cruelty, and helpless rebellion; and he watched the strikes of half-starved labourers in the middle of the harvest.' One particular instance of his father's harshness to a labourer caused Trotsky to burst into tears and bury his face in the pillows of the dining room's sofa. Actually, the Bronsteins treated their labourers no worse than did most other employers. Interestingly – given that many children witness far worse, without later becoming revolutionaries – such scenes began Trotsky's move towards revolution.[5]

His first school

In 1886, just before his seventh birthday, his parents sent him to stay with an aunt and uncle in the village of Gromokla, so he could attend a private Jewish school there during the week. As Gromokla – a Jewish-German colony – was only a couple of miles from Yanovka, it meant Trotsky could return for weekends. The school taught in Yiddish, which Trotsky didn't know. As well as thus struggling to understand his teacher and classmates, he also witnessed examples of violent religious intolerance meted out to those who broke the conventions. Interestingly, he was drawn much more to the neat, tidy cottages of the German settlers than to the poorer abodes of the Jewish settlers.

Because he was so evidently unhappy at that school, his parents brought him back home after only a few months. By then, though, he had learned to read and write Russian, and frequently copied out passages from the few books at home – and even began to write essays and poems. At the age of eight, he managed to persuade one of his elder cousins to join him in producing a handwritten magazine – a very early indication of his later literary and journalistic future. He also began to help his father with his accounts and bookkeeping.

As a result, his proud parents showed off his intelligence to neighbours. At first, Trotsky often ran away in embarrassment: 'I composed verses, feeble lines which perhaps showed my early love for words but certainly forecast no poetic future…They would ask me to read my verses aloud before guests. It was painfully embarrassing.' Later, though, he began to enjoy being the centre of attention – and even to seek it.[6]

In 1888, a year or so after he'd left the school in Gromokla, an elder cousin of Trotsky's came to Yanovka, and stayed there for the summer. This was Moishe Spentzer, one of the urban middle class branches of Anna's family. Spentzer lived in Odessa, but had been debarred from Odessa University because of his radical views and a minor political offence. He had stayed with Trotsky's family before and had taken an early interest in Trotsky's education. Spentzer was a moderate, liberal freelance journalist – and was destined to have a decisive influence on aspects of Trotsky's development over the next few years.

Whilst at Yanovka that summer, he tutored Trotsky who, by now, was clearly very bright, but in real need of being stretched intellectually. At the end of the summer, he suggested Trotsky should stay with his family, as a paying lodger, so he could go to high school in Odessa, over 200 miles away. This was agreed and, in the autumn of 1888, after tearful 'goodbyes' to his mother and sisters, Trotsky left Yanovka with his father. On reaching Nikolaev, the SS Potëmkin took them across the Black Sea to Odessa.

School in Odessa

In 1888, the Black Sea harbour town of Odessa was seen as Russia's Marseille: sunny, multinational, cultured, and – most importantly for Trotsky's later career as a revolutionary – tolerant of new ideas. Trotsky spent the next seven years there – but it was the Spentzer family, not political developments in Odessa, that really influenced Trotsky's initial development. He later stated he had no political views whilst there – and had no desire to acquire them. But he did develop 'an intense hatred of the existing order, of injustice, of tyranny' under the restrictive rule of Alexander III.[7]

Trotsky was too young for St Paul's Realschule, the school the Spentzers had selected for him. However, this was overcome when the registrar back home forged his birth certificate, making him a year older than he really was. But a much bigger obstacle was the 1887 Tsarist *ukase* which restricted the admittance of Jewish children to secondary schools. Potential Jewish entrants had also to pass a competitive entrance examination. Because Trotsky had not attended a primary school for very long, he failed the entrance exam. Consequently, he spent a year in the school's preparatory class, from which Jewish pupils were then admitted to the first form, with priority over outside Jewish applicants. At the end of that year, he gained maximum marks in every subject, and this early academic success continued throughout his school career. Although the school did not teach Greek or Latin, it gave a good grounding in mathematics, science, and German and French. This curriculum appealed to progressive intelligentsia families such as the Spentzers, as it provided children with a rationalistic and practical education.

By the time Trotsky arrived there, this German Lutheran school had been 'Russified', so teaching was in Russian. However, there was a real mixture of nationalities – German, Polish and Swiss, as well as Russian: 'In a sense, St Paul's gave Lyova [Trotsky] his first taste of cosmopolitanism.' Trotsky was to be a pupil there for the next seven years. From the very beginning, he proved a very able model student: in his very first lessons, he gained top marks in both mathematics and German, and quickly became top of his class: 'No one had to take charge of his training, no one had to worry about his lessons. He always did more than was expected of him.' As Service commented: 'Once taught something, he seldom forgot it. His leanings were mainly towards the scientific side and he loved mathematics. In fact no subject in the curriculum foxed him.'[8]

His intelligence and industriousness were quickly noted by his teachers. Like many gifted youths, Trotsky was self-centred, eager to please and determined to be first. Trotsky himself felt he could achieve more than his fellow pupils, and those boys who became his friends acknowledged his superiority. It is perhaps significant that, although he had many followers amongst his schoolmates, none actually became an intimate friend. As Max Eastman – a supporter – commented, such an awareness of superiority is a trait those who are not so gifted often find disagreeable. Strangely, though – given that fishing and hunting later became favourite pastimes – he shunned physical exercise and pursuits. In all the time he was in Odessa, he never went fishing, swimming or rowing. It may be he simply equated city life with study and culture, and felt physical activities were best left for the countryside.[9]

Although he avoided playground activities, his excellence in the classroom gave him increasing self-confidence. His essays were often read aloud to the class by his teacher as a model. During his time there, he even produced a school magazine – the *Realist* – most of which was written by himself: including a poem about a drop of water falling into the sea, meant as an allegory of the magazine being a drop in the 'ocean of enlightenment.' Such magazines were prohibited by the Ministry of Education – when a teacher pointed this out to him, Trotsky conformed and stopped producing it.

In his second form, he was part of a group who booed and hissed a disliked teacher, whom they felt had discriminated against one of their class. The head detained several of the offenders – but Trotsky was not amongst them, as the head assumed such a model student would not have acted in such a way. But some of those detained 'betrayed' Trotsky, whom the insulted teacher then called a 'moral outcast'. As a result, Trotsky was expelled in 1890. He expected to be in serious trouble when he returned home, given that his father put Trotsky's glowing school reports on display, and clearly saw him as even more gifted than his older brother Alexander, who was training to be a doctor. However, the Spentzers were sympathetic and this no doubt helped his father take this quite lightly.

The following year, he was readmitted, after having to pass an examination. In a very short time, he once again became the pride of the school – and, apart from one exception, he made sure to avoid any future trouble. The exception occurred in one of his upper forms, where he joined with some other boys in refusing to write essays for a lazy teacher who never read them or returned them. This time, however, there was no punishment.

A Life of Culture

By then, Trotsky's physical appearance – as well as his emerging character – was becoming formed. He was handsome, of medium height, with a swarthy complexion, and sharp but well-proportioned features. He had lively blue eyes, and a thick crop of brown-black hair. He also took considerable care over his dress: he was always neat and tidy, and often stylishly dressed. In addition, thanks to the Spentzers' efforts to smooth out his rural habits, he was very polite and well-mannered – at this stage in his life, he appeared a typical bourgeois cosmopolitan youth.

The Spentzers were less well-off than Trotsky's parents – their main source of income was provided by Spentzer's wife, Fanni, the head of a state secular school for Jewish girls. Although Spentzer was initially hampered by his expulsion from the University, he later became a successful and eminent liberal publisher in the south of Tsarist Russia. However, the Spentzers were cultured, and their instructions in urbanity and politeness were useful complements to Trotsky's application to academic work and his reliability. They worked on his Russian-Ukrainian mix, to ensure he could speak proper Russian. They also polished his manners. Because he was impressionable, and eager to learn and 'improve', these things stayed with him throughout life.

To ensure he didn't overwork at his studies, they got him to help look after their young daughter, Vera, who was born two years after Trotsky first arrived in Odessa. Fanni later said of him: 'The worst trouble I had with him was that he was so terribly neat…He had to have everything perfect.' However, he did kick over the traces once: stealing several valuable books from them, and selling them for sweets. He felt guilty and so didn't enjoy the fruits of his crime – and the Spentzers forgave him.[10]

Trotsky later described his time in Odessa as the period in which he became 'an urbanite'. In 1923, he wrote a short book, *Problems of Everyday Life*, which made a strong case for overcoming the crude behaviours of Russian popular culture. Culturally, the Spentzers introduced him to classical Russian poets like Pushkin, Lermontov and Nekrasov – the latter known as the 'citizen poet', as his verses protested against the miseries and injustices of Tsardom. They also exposed Trotsky to Tolstoy's writings – and he read his play, *The Power of Darkness*, which had just been banned by Tsarist censorship. He also read works by European 'greats' such as Goethe and Dickens. As he said of the Spentzers in later life: 'It was a good intellectual family. I owe it a lot.'[11]

Trotsky responded to the love his cousins showed him, as well as their obvious admiration of his abilities – and they both spent time helping Trotsky develop his increasingly obvious intellectual abilities, having recognised his great potential. He was particularly excited by their intellectual interests, and appreciated that many of the Spentzers' visitors were editors of local liberal newspapers and other *literati*. As he notes in his autobiography: 'From early years my love for words had now been losing, now gaining in force, but generally putting down ever firmer roots. In my eyes authors, journalists, and artists always stood for a world which was more attractive than any other, one open only to the elect.' He particularly admired the writing of V. M. Doroshevich, a celebrated and courageous local liberal journalist, whose semi-literary/semi-journalistic essays – despite censorship cuts – were highly popular in Odessa's liberal circles. These were just the kind of essays Trotsky himself would come to excel at.[12]

Trotsky arrived to stay just as Spentzer had begun his publishing business. Consequently, his house was always full of books, manuscripts and printers' proofs, which hugely interested Trotsky. He loved the whole process of book-making – and soon began to familiarise himself with different typefaces, printing layouts and bindings, and even helped with proofreading: 'My love for the freshly printed page has its origin in those far-away days as a schoolboy.'

It was also in the Spentzers' house that a local author, who was an expert on Shakespeare, asked him to write an essay comparing one of Pushkin's poems with one by Nekrasov. Despite Trotsky's fears he wouldn't be able to, he was praised for the way in which he'd used words to construct his argument, and the author said to the Spentzers: 'He is a smart fellow, I swear!' Such praise from an established author was immensely pleasing to the young Trotsky and, as will be seen, the pen soon became – and remained – his chief love and political weapon.[13]

Also whilst at the Spentzers, he was introduced to the theatre and opera: *'The magic of the theatre held its spell over me for several years. Later I developed a fondness for Italian opera, which was the pride of Odessa.* The drama, 'passions and conflicts' of the theatre impressed the adolescent Trotsky, and he retained his love of opera, the theatre and literature. In his later political life, he would act a role that was, at times, intensely dramatic and one that, ultimately, bore the marks of 'classical tragedy'. As yet, there was still no sign of the revolutionary he would become in just a couple more years. Instead of politics, he was interested in mathematics, in which his abilities led him to consider a university course in pure mathematics, followed by an academic career.[14]

However, what he had developed by the end of his schooling in Odessa, was a growing appreciation of the greater sophistication, civilisation and freedoms of western Europe, compared to the cultural backwardness of Tsarist Russia. This was to stay with him, and would be one of the reasons why he eventually fell from power. In this, Trotsky was like many members of the liberal intelligentsia, who saw western Europe as the very antithesis of intolerant and unfree Russia. Although he would later see the darker underside of western Europe, he remained very much a cosmopolitan. This would influence the development of his hallmark theory of 'Permanent Revolution', which stated that moving backward Russia towards socialism would depend on successful revolution in the more developed West.

Tensions at Home

Although he returned to his family every summer holiday, as well as usually for Christmas and Easter, he was increasingly embarrassed to see that, at every return, there were more and more signs of his family's increasing prosperity. This growing sense of conflict left Trotsky with mixed feelings: as a boy brought up on the wide and open steppe, he was still enough of a country boy to feel constricted by city life, and to feel himself unwinding on his walks and horse rides. Yet, as he became more cultured, he found his parents' manners and interests coarse and limited. In particular, he was increasingly aware – as he helped with the bookkeeping and wages – how much his family's prosperity was based on the unfavourable, though not utterly ruthless, terms agreed between his father and the peasants and labourers who worked on his lands.

At times, this led to quarrels – made worse because, much to his father's anger, they were sometimes witnessed by the labourers, as Trotsky already displayed tendencies towards a lack of discretion and an inclination to contradict. His father was also angered by the fact that, when Trotsky helped calculate the wages, he was always more generous than his father – something noted by the labourers, who began to sense Trotsky was on their side. He also tended increasingly to mingle with the migrant labourers and domestic servants. His sense of himself and his self-esteem were undermined by the consciousness that he was the son of an increasingly wealthy *kulak*.

As Trotsky commented later: 'Something new had grown up like a wall between myself and the things bound up with my childhood.' Such tensions were heightened by Trotsky's growing sense of intellectual and cultural superiority as regards rural life, which often ignored his very rational approach to life. However, the emerging rebelliousness in Trotsky was also engendered by a growing awareness of the brutality and cruelty of rural life and officialdom in general. He was already showing signs of a vague sympathy for the downtrodden, coupled with a growing sense of unease about his increasingly privileged position.[15]

9

Eventually, in the summer of 1895, his time with the Spentzers in Odessa came to an end, because St Paul's – unlike most other similar schools – only had six forms, not the usual seven. Thus, his father arranged for his transfer to the Realschule school in Nikolaev, so he could complete his high school education and then go on to university.

Political Developments in Russia

By 1895, opposition to Tsarism came from middle class intellectuals, in two forms: either liberalism or populism. Liberals believed in using peaceful methods to persuade the Tsar to democratise Russian politics – but there were very few freedoms, and no parliament. Populists – usually known as *Narodniks*, from the Russian for 'people' – had begun to emerge in the 1860s, basing themselves on the peasantry, who formed the overwhelming majority of Russia's population. However, from the 1870s, they had increasingly resorted to terrorism in order to force change.

Trotsky, though, was still not attracted to any political philosophy – he hadn't even heard of Karl Marx! This was not particularly surprising as, following the assassination of Alexander II in 1881 by *Narodnaya Volya* (People's Will), the new Tsar, Alexander III, had clamped down hard on any signs of unrest and opposition. As a result, the *Narodnik* movement had initially fizzled out and, in the decade that followed, many populists – who were not already in prison or exile – turned to the political retreatism and peaceful opposition preached by Leo Tolstoy.

However, some ex-*Narodniks* – like Georgi Plekhanov – had begun turning towards Marxism as an alternative political option for achieving change. In 1883, he – and other political refugees – had formed the Emancipation of Labour Group in Switzerland. This inspired some early Russian Marxists to begin expounding this new political programme and method of action, and several groups of social democratic students and workers rapidly sprang up. By 1895, there was even such a group active in Odessa itself – despite the repressive activities of the ever-present police. But the young Trotsky wasn't aware of its existence and there doesn't seem to have been a socialist circle within his school.

Then, in the autumn of 1895 – just as Trotsky moved to Nikolaev – the Union of Struggle for the Emancipation of the Working Class was founded by Lenin in St Petersburg. This was a Marxist group initially focussed on the fight for civil liberties, and getting workers to fight for economic improvements. By the late 1890s, Marxism was becoming increasingly dominant amongst the revolutionary intelligentsia in Tsarist Russia – although Nikolaev, as a relative backwater, was somewhat lagging behind the times.

However, because Marxists saw the industrial working class as the 'revolutionary agency' for change, and rejected terrorism as a political method, the *Narodniks* mainly avoided it. Then, from the end of 1895, students had to swear an oath of loyalty to the new Tsar, Nicholas II. In St. Petersburg, Moscow and Kiev, most students refused. Later, in May 1896, over 30,000 workers in St Petersburg went on strike, in part as a result of Marxist agitation: Russia's first strike on such a scale.

From Conformity to Rebellion

It was in this political context that, in the autumn of 1895, Trotsky – not quite sixteen – arrived in Nikolaev, which lay 50 miles to the north of the Black Sea. As well as arranging for his transfer to the Realschule school in Nikolaev, his father had also arranged lodgings for him with a respectable family. What his father hadn't known was that, because Nikolaev was not an important city, the political police thought it a safe place for settling political revolutionaries – including veterans of the People's Will struggles of the 1880s – once they'd served their sentences of exile in Siberia. It was in Nikolaev that Trotsky, for the first time, took a serious interest in politics. Within months of arriving as a 'swell bourgeois', wearing 'a nicely pressed tan suit and stylish hat', Trotsky swapped such clothes for those worn by workers. He himself later described his move there as 'the turning point of my youth'. [16]

Initially, though, Trotsky fully intended to continue his exemplary application to his studies and fulfil his academic potential. However, the sons of the family he lodged with were attracted by socialist ideas and the groups associated with them. They tried to get Trotsky interested but, at first, he actively resisted their attempts – vigorously opposing their arguments, and dismissing such ideals as mere 'Socialist Utopia'. Their mother, worried by her sons' dangerous views, was impressed by Trotsky's 'good sense' and rejection of their philosophy, and so tried hard – but unsuccessfully – to get her sons to adopt his example.

Trotsky was still essentially a conventional young bourgeois, with a humanitarian sympathy for the downtrodden. However, this emotional mood was not accompanied by any clear idea of the actions needed to bring about positive change. Nonetheless, these political arguments during his first few months with this family began to stir Trotsky's interest in politics. Though, as Trotsky himself later commented, he was slow to develop a serious political awareness of the differences between 'Populism' and Marxism: 'The conflict of these trends engrossed me...Restlessly I cast about me.'[17]

Although he continued to reject socialism, the constant talk of social injustices, and the need to change the many negative features of Tsarist Russia, reminded him of his earlier emotional unease about the poverty and exploitation he'd witnessed during his childhood in rural Russia. He also came to respect the two sons for their high-minded idealism. Initially, though, he continued to resist their ideas and, instead, remained a cultured, liberal but essentially apolitical middle class youth. In part, this was down to a deep-seated contrariness that grew out of his desire to excel and triumph in argument.

Yet, like many teenagers, Trotsky soon underwent a rapid and dramatic shift of direction and, after only a few months, he began to yield. This was another characteristic that continued into later life:

> 'He is confronted with a new idea to which up to a point he is conditioned to respond; yet he resists at first with stubborn haughtiness: his resistance grows with attraction; and he subdues incipient doubt and hesitation. Then his inner defences crumble, his self-confidence begins to vanish; but he is still too proud or not convinced enough to give any sign of yielding.' [18]

It was in this frame of mind, in early 1896, that, through one of his co-lodgers, he first met Franz Shvigovsky. Shvigovsky, in his late twenties, was a Czech gardener, and a largely self-educated intellectual, who had rented an orchard on the outskirts of the town. There, in his hut, he had formed a small discussion club for radical students and working men. He spoke several languages; was well-versed in both Russian and German literature; subscribed to many foreign newspapers and journals; and, most important of all, had many banned books and pamphlets, which he lent out to the members of his group. He and his brother held revolutionary views which were essentially *Narodnik* – but had a tolerant attitude to Marxism, even though they criticised it as being too narrow a theory.

When Trotsky joined the group, he found himself in the middle of an intense and fierce political debate concerning the various political trends of populism, socialism and liberalism. However, these theories were 'not easily demarcated, and anyone new to opposition politics would be open to many possible influences.' By 1895, the two main currents in Russia were the *Narodniks* and the socialists: Trotsky saw these two 'cross-movements' as giving rise to 'whirlpools of theory'. Political developments connected to socialism, however, had had little impact in Nikolaev.[19]

Thus, as a newcomer, Trotsky's political choices were, at least in part, dependent on accident and location; by what literature was – despite Tsarist censorship – available; and what people were around.

Shvigovsky's group mainly consisted of those who espoused different strands of *Narodnik* politics – in particular, those associated with Chernyshevsky, the radical peasant social populist of the 1860s. Some of the older *Narodniks* in Nikolaev sometimes attended these discussions, imparting their romantic revolutionary outlook and past to the younger members of Shvigovsky's group. When Trotsky joined the group, he was the youngest member.

Pressed to take sides, Trotsky quickly declared himself a *Narodnik*, and affirmed his opposition to Marxism. According to Grigorii Ziv – a medical student in Kiev, who joined the group in the winter of 1896, and was himself moving towards Marxism – Trotsky was extremely sharp in his criticisms of Marxist theories. Yet, in fact, he had little real knowledge of Marxist ideas – and not much more of the *Narodnik* philosophy he so warmly espoused! Unlike Lenin, who calmly weighed up all the pros and cons before firmly adopting Marxism, the teenaged Trotsky proved to be too passionate for such an approach.[20]

Shvigovsky's discussion group didn't plan revolutionary actions – most of those who came did so simply because it was possible to discuss the problems of Russia and a better future in a truly free way. As well as studying illegal political pamphlets, they also studied more orthodox political texts – and, in addition, read Russian and European literature. Nonetheless, the group came to the attention of the police, who sent in spies, disguised as labourers working in the gardens. Their reports merely noted essentially 'cranky' but harmless discussions, held over cups of tea and the eating of apples.

When Trotsky joined the group's discussions, the focus of this small revolutionary *Narodnik* group was on the student protests and workers' strikes that broke out in 1896, collecting information and discussing it. They had very little knowledge of Lenin's group or of the political differences between the Marxists and the *Narodniks*. Increasingly, the model student began to neglect his studies: 'More and more frequently I played truant.' In part, he was able to do this – and still remain a 'star pupil' – as he felt his new school was less academic than his previous one, thus allowing him to rely on knowledge already gained.[21]

Trotsky had made what was essentially a rushed political choice – even though he didn't seem to be particularly attracted by either: 'There was an odour of putrefaction emanating from populism. Marxism repelled by its so-called "narrowness".' Trotsky's father – on his frequent business trips to Nikolaev – increasingly became aware of Trotsky's political activities. On several occasions, he tracked him down to the orchard and, once, argued with his now-wayward son in front of the group.[22]

The young Trotsky, however, now identified much more with the poor, educated and revolutionary youngsters than he did with his increasingly prosperous middle class father – even though he was living on his allowances. After one argument, David Bronstein cut off Trotsky's allowance for a time, which led to him leaving his respectable lodgings and instead living with other would-be revolutionaries in a commune in Shvigovsky's grounds.

This was a huge disappointment for his father. Another disappointment was soon to come, when Olga, Trotsky's sister, followed him down the path of revolutionary politics.

Nonetheless, Trotsky soon made peace with his father, and was thus not usually short of funds. This enabled him, like the others, to make contributions to keep the group going. They also appealed to wealthier citizens who were critical of the Tsarist system to donate funds to enable them to get things done. They then formed a society, which they called *Rassadnik* ('Seed-Plot').

In the summer of 1896, despite having neglected his studies, he managed to graduate from school with first-class honours. He then returned to Yanovka for the summer holidays, and attempted to patch up relations with his father. In the autumn of 1896, he enrolled to study mathematics at the New Russia University in Odessa, staying with another of his mother's brothers, who was an engineer and the owner of a small factory. This pleased his father and, while there, Trotsky showed a real gift for the subject: 'Trotsky loved mathematics, whose abstract world fascinated him with its mystery, its logic and its inexhaustible possibilities. He…might have become a scientist…' However, after attending only a few lectures, he dropped out and returned to Nikolaev, to rejoin Shvigovsky's revolutionary group.[23]

Aleksandra Sokolovskaya

Shvigovsky's group did, however, have one Marxist amongst its members: Aleksandra Sokolovskaya. Born in 1872, and thus almost eight years older than Trotsky, she came from a poor family and had been brought up by her *Narodnik* father. Initially adopting their generalised rebel mood and philosophy, she began to move to a more active revolutionary position after reading the account of the trial of Vera Zasulich who, in 1878, had shot the head of St Petersburg's police. Whilst attending a midwifery course at Odessa University, Sokolovskaya met students who worked with Zasulich – then in exile in Geneva – in smuggling illegal Marxist literature into Russia, and she quickly become a firm Marxist.

After successfully completing her course, she had been involved in revolutionary activity in the Ukraine, before returning to Shvigovsky's group in the summer of 1896. Having read several Marxist publications by then – including Marx and Engels' *The Communist Manifesto* – she tried to persuade the other members of the group to embrace Marxism as the best, most scientific, way to achieve revolution. She had been told by several of its members that they'd got a new member who would defeat her in argument: 'Expecting some momentous and whiskered professor, who would "inform her of the errors underlying the economic system of Karl Marx", she was utterly amazed when this smooth young child appeared with the close-cropped black hair and the pale-blue eyes.'[24]

To the young Trotsky, Marxism seemed to be too: '…narrow and dry as dust – an offence to the dignity of man, whom it portrayed as the prisoner of economic and social circumstances, the plaything of anonymous productive forces.' He thus quickly became Sokolovskaya's most bitter opponent in debate – accusing her of being an 'obdurate' Marxist, in thrall to its grinding economic determinism. Trotsky and nearly all of the others believed Nikolai Mikhailovsky – one of the most influential *Narodnik* theoreticians – was absolutely right in saying that revolutionaries should be rounded characters, but Marxists allegedly only focussed on one aspect of human personality. Trotsky's attacks on Marxist theory were essentially 'youthful outbursts against a dry theory of which he knew nothing.' In fact, as an older and more informed revolutionary, Sokolovskaya was clearly by far the more politically experienced of the two, especially given that Trotsky was still essentially a high school pupil![25]

Yet Trotsky – despite his youth – was, because of his 'eminent gifts and talents', already being seen as the group's most able debater, and he quickly became the most audacious and determined controversialist, speaking with 'pitiless sarcasm' about Sokolovskaya's Marxist beliefs. On one occasion, Trotsky attempted to provoke her:

> '"You still think you are a Marxist?...How on earth can a young girl so full of life stand that dry, narrow, impractical stuff!" "How on earth", Sokolovskaya would answer, "can a person who thinks he is logical be contented with a headful of vague idealistic emotions?"'[26]

Despite this, Sokolovskaya – confident in the soundness of her beliefs, and absolutely not a woman prepared to follow the conventions of the time by bowing to the 'greater wisdom' of men – though at times provoked into sharp retaliation, usually remained calm, patiently explaining the essence of Marxism, even when her young opponent made jokes at her expense. Yet, imperceptibly, her logical arguments were beginning to undermine Trotsky's confidence in his own, hastily-declared *Narodnik* beliefs. This internal confusion made his criticisms even sharper, and his jibes more boorish.

Nonetheless, despite these sharp intellectual clashes, the two became attracted to each other: 'Into their relationship there crept an ambivalent emotion almost inevitable between two young and close political opponents of different sex, meeting regularly in a tiny group, attracted and repelled by each other and incapable of escaping from each other.' In fact, most of the men were 'a little infatuated' with her; and she inspired some of the group to write her love poems. Some of their group later claimed they had soon noticed a growing 'explosive' sexual chemistry between these two political opponents.[27]

Trotsky was so determined to 'win' these debates against Sokolovskaya that he even read Schopenhauer's *The Art of Controversy* to improve his debating skills: such as using ridicule as one way of trying to push an opponent into anger, to make the logic of their argument fall apart. As Service comments, Trotsky acted like 'an intellectual bully' and ridiculed any sentimentality. Yet their apparently antagonistic relationship, seemingly thriving on insulting repartee, soon revealed a growing mutual and intense attraction.[28]

However, on New Year's Eve, 31 December 1896, Trotsky seemed to have well and truly burned his bridges with Sokolovskaya, as a result of a particularly cruel juvenile 'joke'. The group met to celebrate the arrival of 1897, as well as to continue their political discussions. When Trotsky arrived – to the surprise of his *Narodnik* friends, and to Sokolovskaya's delight – he declared her arguments and explanations had finally won him over to Marxism. She was delighted, and the group began to drink toasts to the imminent downfall of Tsarist tyranny and the emancipation of the working classes.

But, when it came to Trotsky's turn to make a toast, he turned towards her, and burst out with a totally unexpected attack: "'A curse upon all Marxists, and those who want to bring dryness and hardness into all the relations of life!'" Embarrassed in front of the group, Sokolovskaya stormed out, swearing she would never again shake the hand of that 'little boy'. She then temporarily left Nikolaev. Nonetheless, this was by no means the end of their relationship.[29]

Chapter 2

Revolution, Love and Exile, 1897–1902

> "'Shurochka…I'm sitting so close to you now that I can almost feel your presence. Next time you go downstairs for exercise, say something, as I'm bound to hear you. Try Sashenka! I'm finding it hard…I want to hear your voice and I want to see you….'"[1]

The years 1897 to 1902 proved momentous for the young Trotsky. By 1897, 'He needed a cause to serve, a cause exacting sacrifice; and when he found it, his youthful and passionate temperament came into the open.' Marxism proved to be that cause and, during those years, he completed his relatively rapid progress towards an eventual life-long commitment to it. He also began his literary career as a journalist, critic and revolutionary propagandist. He became increasingly involved in clandestine revolutionary activity that, very quickly, led to his first arrest and exile. In addition, when he was not yet 18, he began his first serious romantic liaison – contributing to his alleged reputation for having several affairs.[2]

Coming to Marx

As 1897 began, Trotsky was still criticising Marxism. Early in the New Year, he wrote a superficial polemical article for a *Narodnik* journal, pointing out the many 'errors' of Marxist theories. However, it was never published; though as Trotsky eventually commented, this was fortunate for his later reputation as a powerful writer! Around the same time, he began working on a play with Sokolovskaya's elder brother, Ilya, dealing with the *Narodnik*–Marxist political controversy. Although the intention was that the play would show the superiority of *Narodnik* ideas, it soon became apparent that the Marxist characters were getting all the best lines. What is more, the older male *Narodnik* character was starting to fall in love with the young Marxist girl – who seemed to have many of Sokolovskaya's best features, such as 'courage, youth and hope'! Thus the play was abandoned.[3]

As regards the romance between Trotsky and Sokolovskaya, which developed shortly after, the unkind schoolboy 'joke' which he had played on her, on New Year's Eve, may well have had more than a little to do with him having been teased by Shvigovsky that, like many of the other young men in their group, he had been falling under her spell, and that was why he was beginning to question his earlier opposition to Marxism. In fact, a sexual chemistry between them – initially expressing itself in rivalry – had already been noted by some of their group. They were thus not too surprised to learn – within only a few weeks of her having stormed out of that New Year's Eve gathering – Trotsky (then aged seventeen) and Sokolovskaya (aged around twenty-five) had become lovers.

However, apart from mutual physical attraction, what also brought them close together was joint revolutionary activity. After abandoning their attempt at a play, the group decided on a 'revolutionary' action against the board of Nikolaev's public library, which had announced its intention of increasing the annual subscriptions for readers. By encouraging a large number of new subscribers to join, they overthrew the board at the library's AGM – and thus stopped the increase in fees.

The South Russian Workers' Union

In February 1897, Sokolovskaya's other brother, Grigory, made contact with a worker. Trotsky, Sokolovskaya and her elder brother then quickly established a revolutionary workers' cell which, despite only existing in the small town of Nikolaev, they called the South Russian Workers' Union (SRWU)! Initially, this group – soon joined by Ziv – mainly consisted of student activist intellectuals.

About 6,000 workers were then employed in Nikolaev's factories, and a further 4,000 in the shipyards and docks. They were mostly skilled, well-paid workers who – having won an eight-hour day – had enough leisure time to read pamphlets and books. They were increasingly critical of Tsarist Russia's oppression and injustice, but did not have a trade union. Trotsky and his co-revolutionaries quickly began producing and circulating revolutionary – and thus illegal – literature. Within a short while, the SRWU had attracted around 20–25 workers as regular members who came to their secret discussion meetings. Trotsky and the others transformed these into a university: Trotsky lectured in sociology. Around this time, he adopted what would be the first of several aliases – 'Lvov'.

Initially, the SRWU included *Narodniks,* along with Social Democrats who espoused Marxism. However, these political differences didn't prevent common work, as their main aims were to help the workers gain higher wages and a shorter working week. Significantly, they avoided references to the ongoing political controversies, which continued to be discussed amongst the members of Shvigovsky's 'orchard' circle. It was during this period that Trotsky began to have increasing doubts about the *Narodnik* position. For a brief time, he seriously considered the possibility of becoming a Social Democrat without necessarily embracing Marxism.

The spring of 1897 proved to be a politically turbulent one across Tsarist Russia. In March, a student by the surname of Vetrova, who had been imprisoned in the Peter and Paul Fortress for her protests, committed suicide. This provoked a wave of protests and demonstrations in the universities. In reprisal, the authorities deported large numbers of undergraduates – but this just led to even more unrest. These even spread to Odessa; while students from Kiev brought news of the latest developments, sparking real excitement amongst the members of the SRWU. Because of this unrest, an increasing number of workers flocked to them. By the end of the year, the SRWU had around 200 members, organised in small cells of no more than 25 members each. The cells met twice a week, to discuss current events, read clandestine publications, and review their work and activities.

Given the constant problem of police spies, Trotsky and the rest of the core group deliberately avoided having an overall controlling central committee. This was to prevent the damage that would follow if the police infiltrated just one group. Yet their attempts at secrecy were amateurish, and their group was easily penetrated by agents of the *Okhrana*. The SRWU became particularly involved in revolutionary activities in Odessa, which was the main point of entry for smuggled revolutionary literature. Sokolovskaya's Marxist contacts there became increasingly influential and, in April 1897, the SRWU declared itself to be Social Democratic, decisively rejecting the populist ideas of the *Narodniks*.

The Russian Lassalle?

At this time, Trotsky became especially interested in Ferdinand Lassalle (1825–64), the early German socialist and founder of the first ever modern Labour party, who'd later had some significant political differences with Marx himself. Trotsky had several things in common with Lassalle: like himself, Lassalle was the son of a wealthy Jewish family, and had turned his back on his class in favour of revolutionary politics and the emancipation of the working class. Lassalle had been one of the most colourful and romantic figures of his age – he was killed fighting a duel! It seems Trotsky wished to become the 'Russian Lassalle'. Trotsky was certainly not the most modest of people – although he was aware his first attempts at public speaking were inadequate.

An Apprenticeship in Revolution

Trotsky then established the first of many revolutionary newspapers: *Our Cause (Nashe Delo)*, which became the main organ of the group. This paper, and their leaflets – printed in purple ink, so as not to strain readers' eyes – exposed the abuses of employers and officials, and commented on working conditions. When those who'd been criticised refuted the allegations, the SRWU rapidly produced more leaflets attacking those 'defences' – much to the amusement of the workers.

Trotsky saw this as the beginning of his literary work, and the paper was very much his creation: he acted as editor, wrote most of the articles, and even drew the cartoons! It was also almost entirely produced and distributed by him. Typically, he was very proud of his achievements: 'But what a satisfied feeling I had when I received the information from mills and workshops that the workers read voraciously the mysterious sheets printed in purple ink, passing them about from hand to hand as they discussed them!' Though, by the time of his arrest, he had only managed to produce three issues of his newspaper.[4]

As well as circulating the newspaper and his leaflets in Nikolaev, Trotsky also travelled regularly to Odessa and Yekaterinoslav, to spread the message there. Trotsky's workload increased in August when, much to his anger, Ziv temporarily left to complete his medical degree. Nonetheless, Trotsky described this as an extremely happy time, giving him important practical experience in revolutionary activity. As well as writing political pamphlets, he collected dues, distributed money to various strike funds, organised mutual self-help schemes, built up workers' 'libraries' of revolutionary literature, and conducted educational circles. All this gave him valuable insights on how a revolutionary organisation could function in the repressive Tsarist police state.

Within a year, Trotsky had undergone a startling transformation: from being the son of a prosperous farmer, who seemed more interested in literature and opera; to a student who identified as a *Narodnik* and who bitterly attacked Marxist ideas; to being one of the main founders of an illegal clandestine revolutionary group that had embraced social democracy, if not quite declaring explicitly for Marxism. The young Trotsky had clearly been overflowing with: '...an inborn exuberant energy and with an ardour and imagination for which conventional pursuits provided little or no outlet...Both his friends and his enemies agree that he was the moving spirit, the mouthpiece, the organizer, and also the most energetic and devoted worker of the Union.' This explanation of what, from an early age, drove him, is an assessment shared by many who knew him, and is referred to by several of his biographers, both sympathetic and unsympathetic.[5]

Although the SRWU was just a small organisation, its activities nonetheless came to the attention of similar groups in other towns and cities, who were more political, and who were planning a congress for what was to become the Russian Social Democratic Workers' Party (RSDWP). There were even tentative suggestions of Trotsky attending this congress, as the delegate of the SRWU – though some had concerns about his youth. However, before that could be settled, Trotsky and his group had been rounded up by the police, and were in prison awaiting trial.

The Gathering Storm

It wasn't just social democratic groups in the bigger cities that had become aware of the activities of the SRWU. The *Okhrana* had been able to infiltrate some of their cells almost from the beginning. Although aware for some time about the growing political agitation in the factories and docks of Nikolaev, the *Okhrana* were slow to realise that the centre of this unrest was the unlikely small, mainly adolescent, group which met in Shvigovsky's hut! So, initially, they searched for a more significant group of revolutionaries. Eventually, though, they renewed their interest in the SRWU, and observed its members' movements much more closely.

Towards the end of 1897, the leaders of the SRWU themselves began to fear that, because of their successes, repression was not far away. So they decided to disperse for a while, and to resume their activities after a short interval. However, before they separated, they agreed that – in the event of the police arresting any workers – they would return, so the authorities couldn't tell the workers their student leaders had run away and left them to the mercy of the authorities.

Arrest and Imprisonment

Trotsky was one of a small group who left Nikolaev – the others stayed in the town, or nearby – travelling to an estate where Shvigovsky had begun a new job. On 28 January 1898, the police pounced in Nikolaev, eventually arresting over 200 would-be revolutionaries and workers. Trotsky – despite having been warned by Sokolovskaya's younger sister about the arrests – stayed where he was. He was arrested and taken to Nikolaev prison.

The high number of those arrested was an indication of the amount of unrest amongst Russian workers, especially the skilled shipbuilders – and of the success Trotsky and his collaborators had had in such a short space of time. It was mainly as a result of Trotsky's revolutionary literary efforts, that the authorities and the workers in Nikolaev had initially believed the Union was much bigger than it really was. For Trotsky, this was his first proof of the 'power of the written word'. This belief was to remain with him until his death. In every situation – including the most dire, politically and personally – he would always resort to his 'pen'.[6]

Although the conditions in Nikolaev prison were poor, Trotsky was pleased to be reunited with Sokolovskaya, Ziv and the others. They remained there for three weeks, and were questioned about their activities. It was during his first few days in prison that Trotsky finally decided to embrace Marxism. Whilst there, he didn't waste a single day, using the time to improve his mind and deepen his understanding of the main political debates.

The police quickly came to the conclusion that Trotsky was the main ringleader, so he was transferred to a prison in Kherson, where he was kept in solitary confinement for almost three months. He was kept in very poor conditions, during what was a bitterly cold winter. As bad as these conditions were, it was worse for a small number of the others: they experienced physical torture, leading to some becoming informers, while others had mental breakdowns or even committed suicide. Eventually, towards the end of his confinement, Trotsky's mother was able to bribe some of the guards into allowing him to receive food parcels and 'luxuries' such as soap and fresh clothes.

It was whilst in the Kherson prison, that Trotsky first suggested he and Sokolovskaya should get married. As he was only twenty at the time, he needed his father's permission. The latter refused to do so, not just because she was significantly older than his son, but mainly because he was convinced it was because of her that Trotsky had become so deeply involved in revolutionary activity. In addition, Trotsky's parents feared their hard-won prosperity would end up in the hands of Sokolovskaya's poorer family. All this widened the rift between father and son.

Trotsky later claimed the reason they got married was simply in order to avoid separation, so they could continue their joint revolutionary activities. It was in fact common for political deportees to arrange fictitious marriages, as married revolutionaries were allowed to be deported to the same place of exile, and thus would not be totally isolated. However, although Trotsky implied the marriage was a sham, the way he got so angry over his father's refusal to sanction it suggests this was much more than a marriage of convenience – as does the quotation, from one of his prison letters, that began this chapter.

In May 1898, he was transferred to Odessa prison, where one of the guards happened to have the surname 'Trotsky'. It was there he was reunited with Sokolovskaya, her two brothers, Shvigovsky, Ziv and other co-revolutionaries. Although he continued in solitary confinement for much of the time, he was nonetheless able to communicate secretly with his fellow revolutionaries. It was also while in Odessa prison that Trotsky and the others first heard about the founding Congress of the RSDWP in Minsk. On 1 March 1898, before being arrested, nine members of the RSDWP had agreed the party's constitution.

In between interrogations, Trotsky – like the other prisoners – read avidly in order to deepen his understanding of Marxism. Initially, he was restricted to what was in the prison library, but he was soon able to get books smuggled in from the outside. He also brushed up his reading knowledge of German, French, English and Italian. More importantly for his political evolution, the works smuggled in included Darwin's works which, amongst other things, confirmed him as an atheist. Especially relevant for his commitment to Marxism, was a French edition of the philosophical essays of the young Italian, Arturo Labriola (1873–1959), who subscribed to a form of Marxism. Labriola's undogmatic, lucid and stylistic writing impressed him, as well as his actual ideas which, however, at this time he only half-understood.[7]

As a result of such books, he made his first public statement as a Marxist to his co-revolutionaries, sometime in late May 1898. His long resistance to Marxism had finally collapsed. As he wrote in his autobiography: 'I resisted the theory of historical materialism [Marxism] for quite a long time…At that time I was still comparatively ignorant of the basic literature of the Marxists...But I groped my way to them, and somewhat independently.' At the same time, the prison authorities eventually turned a blind eye to his age, and gave permission for he and Sokolovskaya to marry.[8]

Sentenced Without Trial

In November 1899, after almost two years in prison since their arrest, the prisoners received their punishment for their revolutionary activities. Instead of the expected trial, they were dealt with by an administrative tribunal, which handed down verdicts of deportation and exile. Trotsky and three of his fellow revolutionaries were to be exiled, for four years, to Yakutia, a region in eastern Siberia just below the Arctic Circle. Others were exiled for shorter terms; and some were released. Not only had they been refused a proper trial, but their time in prison was not taken into account as regards the length of their exile.

They were then moved to the Butyrsky transfer prison in Moscow: whilst there, Trotsky met older and more experienced revolutionaries who were also awaiting deportation. Once again, he used this time to deepen his understanding of Marxism – and, for the first time, read one of Lenin's important works, *The Development of Capitalism in Russia*: 'I used the interim for intensive studies in theory. Then for the first time I heard of Lenin, and studied his book on the development of Russian capitalism, which had just appeared, from cover to cover.' [9]

Whilst in the transfer prison, he also encountered books and arguments relating to developments in west European socialism – in particular, Edouard Bernstein's attempts to move the German Social Democratic Party from revolutionary Marxism to a more evolutionary, reformist path. This heated debate between 'Orthodox Marxism' and 'Revisionism' did not cause dissention amongst the Russian revolutionaries in the Moscow prison: they were all for the revolutionary path to socialism. Trotsky also used that time to write, and smuggle out, a pamphlet describing the activities of their Nikolayev group and developments in the local labour movement. This was quickly published in Geneva in 1900.

Throughout, he showed real tenderness to Sokolovskaya – and to the other women who came to visit their menfolk. Unusual for such patriarchal times, he refused to allow women to take away his linen for washing and repair. As well as seeing to his own, he chided those who placed this burden on their women for being conventionally 'bourgeois'.

Even those who later became his opponents remembered his many kindnesses, and were surprised at the ruthlessness he exhibited, at times, during the Civil War.

Marriage and Exile

Despite having been sentenced to exile at the end of 1899, they remained in the transfer prison in Moscow for over six months. It was there, in the spring of 1900, that Trotsky and Sokolovskaya were finally married – just before the start of their summer journey into exile. The service was conducted in a cell by a Jewish chaplain, with the wedding ring borrowed from one of the prison guards.

In his autobiography, first published in 1930, Trotsky dealt with their marriage in a dismissive way. After describing their journey to the initial place of exile – Ust-Kut, on the western loop of the Lena River – he wrote: 'Alexandra Lvovna had one of the most important positions in the South Russian Workers' Union. Her utter loyalty to socialism and her complete lack of any personal ambition gave her an unquestioned moral authority. The work that we were doing bound us closely together, and so, to avoid being separated, we had been married in the transfer prison in Moscow.' This extract is somewhat economical with the truth as, by then, they had been lovers for three years before they married, and Sokolovskaya was now pregnant with their first child! Several historians have suggested this later off-hand comment was made out of consideration of the feelings of his second 'wife' – though they were both to maintain good relations with Sokolovskaya throughout.[10]

In fact, Trotsky's personal correspondence makes it clear he married Sokolovskaya for love, not convenience. In addition, at least one of those who was in the Moscow transfer prison with them, and then later accompanied them for much of the journey into exile, attested to the genuine warmth and affection Trotsky showed Sokolovskaya – even to the extent of neglecting his other friends and co-revolutionaries. His true feelings are shown by this letter, written whilst they were still in Odessa prison: 'What if they won't let us get married? It's impossible! There have been times (hours, days, months) when suicide seemed the most decent way out. But I hadn't got the nerve.'[11]

Even after Trotsky and Sokolovskaya had begun their journey, they still had spells in other prisons, with their group of deportees eventually arriving, via the Trans-Siberian Railway, in Irkutsk. After that, deportees were dropped off at different points. Trotsky and Sokolovskaya then travelled, for three weeks, by barge down the Lena, finally being deposited in Ust-Kut. So it wasn't until late autumn in 1900 that Trotsky finally reached his first place of exile.

By the time Trotsky and his new wife had arrived, there were around one hundred peasant huts, but most were dirty and infested with vermin; whilst, in the summer, mosquitoes were a constant problem. Ust-Kut was within the East Siberian forest, between the Yenisei and Lena rivers, and just below the tundra. The area has an extreme subarctic climate, with long, cold winters and short, but very hot, summers: with temperatures ranging from −62°C in winter, to 40°C in summer. Trotsky gives a colourful picture of the conditions during their time there: 'Life was dark and repressed, utterly remote from the rest of the world. At night the cockroaches filled the house with their rustlings as they crawled over table and bed, and even over our faces. From time to time we had to move out of the hut for a day or so and keep the door wide open, at a temperature of thirty-five degrees (Fahrenheit) below zero.' [12]

Despite such conditions, Trotsky continued studying Marxism: for instance, reading Marx's *Das Kapital* – occasionally having to brush cockroaches off the pages! Though, before he got down to studying and writing – mostly working through the night – he remained true to his principles concerning equality between the sexes, doing his fair share of housework and childcare. His indomitable spirit at this time can be seen from his essay, *Optimism and Pessimism*, written in early 1901 (see the **Introduction**).

Eventually, Trotsky and Sokolovskaya successfully requested a transfer to Ilimsk, further to the east, on the Ilim river, where they had friends, and where he worked as a clerk and bookkeeper for an illiterate millionaire peasant-turned-merchant. The money he earned from this, and from his writings, were a useful supplement to the monthly state grant. Then, after only two months, he made a serious accounting error and was unceremoniously sacked – somewhat ironic for someone so gifted in mathematics. Thus they had to travel back to Ust-Kut, by sledge, in the middle of the severe winter of 1901–02. With them was their first daughter – Zinadia (Zina) – who'd been born, ten months before, at the end of March 1901. At various stops on the journey, they had to unwrap Zina, to make sure that in protecting her from the bitter cold, they hadn't suffocated her. After a brief stay, they moved further south, to a small house in Verkholensk, halfway on the road to Irkutsk, up in the mountains above Lake Baikal. Verkholensk had a large colony of deportees and, more importantly for those keen to keep up with revolutionary developments, a good postal connection with Irkutsk.

Becoming 'The Pen'

Despite the authorities' best attempts, the deportees were able to communicate between their various places of exile – and even with exiles abroad – by letters sent on the barges that frequently brought in new deportees and carried away those who had served their terms. They were also able to move about relatively easily, and thus engage in lively political discussions. In general, neither imprisonment nor exile was as restrictive or terrible as it was to become under Stalin. For these reasons, despite the surveillance, it was relatively easy for exiles to escape, obtain forged papers and thus get across the frontiers of Tsarist Russia.

Trotsky was quickly engaged as a paid correspondent for an Irkutsk paper, the *Eastern Review (Vostochnoye Obozreniye)*. This was a mainly liberal 'progressive' paper, started by exiled Populists, and read by exiles and local people. Unlike many of his fellow deportees, Trotsky relished the idea of writing for a wider readership, beyond that offered by revolutionary journals alone. It was then he dropped his first revolutionary alias for 'Antid Oto', which he used for many years. Trotsky said he decided on it simply by opening an Italian dictionary and seeing the first word, *'antidoto'* – Italian for 'antidote': 'Later he would jestingly explain to friends that he wanted to inject a Marxist antidote into the legal press.'[13]

It was certainly a good fit for his revolutionary writing. His style of writing in Siberia – despite some excessive flourishes at times – became increasingly succinct, unembellished, well-polished, often ironic and, sometimes, sarcastic. Over the coming years, his style changed very little – even though he was then only twenty-one. Although the censorship in Siberia wasn't too strict, Trotsky didn't write many overtly revolutionary political articles. He mostly concentrated on social reportage on rural life and, increasingly, on literary criticism, reflecting his earlier interest in literature and art.

From the beginning of what would be a long career of literary criticism, Trotsky's writing – although clearly from a Marxist perspective – was not marked by the narrow political outlook that was often the approach of much so-called 'Marxist criticism'. In particular, he didn't claim political class interests lay behind every single poem, novel or play; nor, although he was not impressed by the idea of 'art for art's sake', did he favour narrow realism. Even his more political writing recognised the strengths of other sections of the revolutionary movement, even when he disagreed with their conclusions.

Unusually for a man in his early twenties, who had only recently embraced Marxism, he was free of the sectarian impulses that ruled out artistic appreciation of individuals or works that didn't reflect his political and cultural values. In particular, he didn't hesitate to show how socialist and non-socialist writers and their beliefs might actually have some common ground; or that there could be at least a grain of truth in any viewpoint which, overall, he rejected. In the course of his exile in Siberia, both his reading and his writing reflected a wide interest in literature – European as well as Russian. Although by no means did he reject Russian culture in favour of the 'westernising' arguments that were common at that time. Amongst those who became topics for his essays, were: Gogol, Gorky, Tolstoy, Zola, Ibsen, Ruskin, Maupassant and Nietzsche.

His approach was based on seeing the relationship between art on the one hand, and economic and social progress on the other. In his literary work, he examined the social developments, and the political and cultural contexts, that the writers were attempting to express – and the impact of those works on those features. For instance, whilst seeing positive elements in Ibsen, and recognising him as a 'cultural giant' for his exposure of the hypocrisies and restrictions of bourgeois life, he nonetheless criticised Ibsen for being too timid a critic, and for retreating into a sterile individualism instead of creating characters prepared to tackle social conditions.

Trotsky also argued that artists shouldn't be concerned that industrialisation was making the novels of pre-industrial society redundant. Rather, he wrote, novelists should adapt to the new conditions, even if these changes seemed to favour the short story. Ultimately, he argued that revolutionary socialism was the consummation, not the repudiation, of great cultural traditions – it repudiated, instead, the conservative and conventional conception of such traditions. However, as even his largely sympathetic biographer, Deutscher said, some of his writing at this stage was over-elaborate and often designed to impress – even though his judgements were much more mature.[14]

His articles and essays soon became popular with the exile communities in Siberia, and knowledge of the writings of 'Antid Oto' was spread by returning deportees. As a result, the literary talents of the unknown 'Antid Oto' reached the attention of revolutionary circles in Kiev and St Petersburg – and even émigré groups in exile in western Europe. Deutscher relates an anecdote from his own experiences as a Trotskyist militant, which shows the impact Trotsky's writings were having: 'The author knew personally old ex-deportees, who, in the 1920s and 1930s would in conversation still refer to Trotsky as Antid Oto and ask, for instance, "What does Antid Oto say about the situation?"' These essays – and his more overtly political writings – soon earned him the nickname 'The Pen': Krzhizhanovsky, Lenin's agent in Samara, was the first to give him that nickname.[15]

The 'Centralisation Question'

Like other exiles, Trotsky was particularly interested by reports of growing protests against the Tsar during the spring of 1901. There were demonstrations by university students and strikes by factory workers. Consequently, a new bunch of deportees began to arrive in Siberia, with news of the latest developments. Although excited by this, Trotsky was not hopeful of a good outcome, as he sensed there was too little national coordination and direction amongst the various groups. Thus, in 1901, he wrote what became known as his 'Siberian Essay', arguing for a party organisation based on central discipline – very similar to how the Bolshevik Party would eventually be organised.

It was widely circulated and debated within the exile communities in Siberia. Reactions were very mixed – with many making the same points Trotsky himself would make from 1903 onwards: that revolution should be based on a mass movement of workers, so there was no need for a small group of leaders to have strong powers over the membership. Some even said his approach smacked of a return to the *Narodnik* idea of small conspiratorial groups. Yet, as several historians have argued, some centralisation was necessary, given the lack of democracy in Tsarist Russia: 'Yet, it was true that at this time the revolutionary movement in Russia could not advance a single step without national integration and discipline and that a national leadership was sometimes bound to impose its discipline sternly on reluctant groups.'[16]

However, it can be argued that the seeds of Stalin's later dictatorship can be found in this essay – whereby, via purge, expulsion and excommunication, the party substituted itself for the workers, then the party leaders substituted for the party, and then one man for the party leaders. This would prove doubly ironic for Trotsky as not only did he repudiate such an organisation in 1903 – but it was precisely that type of centralised organisation, in the hands of Stalin, which ensured Trotsky was eventually cut off from any meaningful role in revolutionary politics in the Soviet Union and within the wider world Communist movement.

Despite this controversy, Trotsky continued his Marxist studies, and soon became involved in the political disputes between those still espousing *Narodnik* populism or anarchism, and those who argued for socialism and Marxism. He rapidly obtained a reputation as an increasingly influential Marxist lecturer. Particularly exciting for Trotsky was news that a Social Democratic Siberian Union (SDSU) had just begun, and was busily recruiting members – not just amongst deportees but also amongst workers then extending the Trans-Siberian Railway. The leaders of the SDSU asked him to write leaflets and, within a short time, recognised him as their main leader and spokesperson.

At this stage, Trotsky continued to argue for a party with a strong central control and discipline. Although the SDSU was initially 'Economist' in outlook, he was able to persuade them both to recognise that revolutionary politics outweighed economic issues, and to join the organisation based around The Spark (*Iskra*), a new social democratic paper launched by Lenin, Martov and other RSDWP revolutionaries in exile abroad. A year later, in 1903, he would represent this SDSU at the historically significant RSDWP Congress (held in Brussels and then London) which saw the party split into Bolshevik and Menshevik factions. Yet, at that Congress, Trotsky would side with the Mensheviks – who argued *against* tight central control; later, the SDSU did the same.

Time to Escape

By early 1902, after four and a half years of imprisonment and exile, Trotsky began to yearn for a bigger stage. By then, because of a rise in protests in Russia in 1902 – and especially the 'great upsurge' of the labour movement – many exiles were eager to get back to their revolutionary struggles. As early as 20 February, he obtained permission to travel to Irkutsk for a day – there he informed friends he was planning to escape. In the summer of 1902, this desire was further excited by his receiving, via the underground postal service, a copy of Lenin's *What Is To Be Done?* – along with some back-issues of *Iskra*. These were printed on very thin paper, skilfully hidden within the bindings of other books.

Trotsky was gratified after reading Lenin – who was also advocating the need for a centralised organisation of committed revolutionaries, bound together by the iron rule of action – to realise he had come to similar conclusions independently, despite being confined to the political backwaters of Siberia. Equally pleasing was the discovery that a couple of his articles had been printed in *Iskra*. He thus became increasingly bored by the political discussions within the Siberian colonies of exiles – even his literary successes with the *Eastern Review* were no longer sufficient compensation. He longed to move from Verkholensk to Petersburg or Moscow – and maybe even the capitals of Europe, where Russian émigrés had established revolutionary centres. Significantly, Trotsky felt that was where he was needed.

It appears that, by 1902, Sokolovskaya herself saw that Trotsky was someone destined for greatness within the revolutionary movement to which they both belonged. According to Trotsky, it was Sokolovskaya who first suggested he ought to try to escape – even though it was clear that she herself would not be able to accompany him as, just four months previously, she had given birth to their second daughter, Nina. Although no doubt hoping that, once she had been able to escape, they would be reunited, there was no certainty this would happen. Yet, despite these real hardships and risks, they nonetheless agreed on his escape. Plans reached completion towards the end of August – given some urgency by the impending approach of autumn, which would bring conditions that would make the roads increasingly impassable, and thus any escape more arduous and even risky.

Trotsky recognised that, on top of the very real hardships of life in Siberia, he would be leaving his wife to cope with the sole care of two young children alone: what he himself referred to as the 'double burden' he was placing on her shoulders. In 1929, over twenty years after his escape, as he was writing his autobiography whilst exiled in Turkey, he retained a warm appreciation of their five-year relationship and her sacrifice. Referring to his doubts about leaving her behind, he wrote: '...she met this objection with the two words: "You must." Duty to the revolution overshadowed everything else for her, personal considerations especially...From abroad I could hardly keep up a correspondence with her. Then she was exiled for a second time; after this, we met only occasionally. Life separated us, but nothing could destroy our friendship and our intellectual kinship.'[17]

Their continuing bond was shown by the fact that even when writing to him after their separation, she ended her letters with warm endearments. Of course, neither of them was to know just how high a price she – and their children – would eventually pay for their personal and political attachments to him. Volkogonov has dismissed Trotsky's version of a joint decision that he should escape on his own as 'unadorned pragmatism, an urge to free himself from a burden in order to move on to higher things.' Service goes even further in his criticisms of Trotsky's decision to escape without the rest of his family, arguing he treated Sokolovskaya (and, later, his other female companions) with callousness and neglect. Swain, however, accepts Trotsky was essentially right to say: 'life separated us'. [18]

However, such negative interpretations tend to overlook the sense of duty and sacrifice that animated so many of those who joined in the revolutionary struggle against Tsarist absolutism. Not only were they prepared to abandon promising careers, thus risking imprisonment and exile, but even the very real prospect of death was no deterrent.

Work for the revolution was the prime concern of the lives of such committed revolutionaries. In fact, such a decision was in keeping with the revolutionary code of conduct, within which all revolutionaries saw the 'cause' as of overriding importance: outweighing personal feelings and family commitments. Service noted that: 'Alexandra fitted the stereotype of the Russian revolutionary: dedicated, determined, altruistic.' Despite challenging Trotsky's claim it was she who first raised the issue of escape, Volkogonov nonetheless states: 'She did not object, although one can imagine what it must have cost her...But in her eyes Lev [Trotsky] was a genius, and was destined to become famous. She thought she was being true to the revolutionary cause by sacrificing him in the name of her ideals.' Overall, the evidence suggests Sokolovskaya was convinced she was doing her duty as the partner of a revolutionary – hence the apparent lack of melodrama concerning the decision that Trotsky should escape.[19]

Until 1935, when Sokolovskaya disappeared into Stalin's gulags, Trotsky attempted to retain links with her and their children. Over the years, letters were exchanged, and sometimes money sent. Trotsky also frequently talked of his concerns about Sokolovskaya and their children with his second family; and Trotsky's diary shows that Sedova (his second 'wife') also worried about the fate of his first family. While it is true that, in the coming years, Sokolovskaya ended up losing her husband, both their daughters, their sons-in-law and their grandchildren, she and Trotsky always maintained friendly relations. According to Sedova: '... the deep affection and intellectual bond between him and Aleksandra were to last to the end of their lives.' This even remained true when, two years after his escape, they met again, only for Sokolovskaya to be told that, in the meantime, he had found love with another woman. Although, sadly, her continuing attachments to Trotsky – personal and political – would cost her life, her last words to Trotsky, before he began his escape, proved to be very prophetic: 'Go, a great future awaits you.'[20]

Chapter 3

Escape, Splits and Revolution, 1902–06

'Even now she [Sedova] still walks beautifully, without fatigue, and her gait is quite youthful, like her whole figure... [one night in Paris in 1903] we ran home from the Paris Opera to the rue Gassendi, 46, au pas gymnastique, holding hands... our combined age was 46.'[1]

During this period, Trotsky moved from the obscurity of exile in Siberia on to a much bigger political stage – first, to the centre of the fraught politics of Russian émigré groups in Europe, and then into the maelstrom of the 1905 Russian Revolution. While, in Paris – shortly after his escape – he also met Natalya Sedova, who would be his companion for the rest of his life: the extract above is from his diary entry for 27 March 1935. Many of his actions and writings during this period would shape his later political fortunes.

Becoming Trotsky

Escapees from Siberian exile risked drowning in rivers or freezing to death in the forests – but many tried: '...there was an epidemic of escapes. We had to arrange a system of rotation.' Trotsky's own escape – and his journey to fame – began on the evening of 3 September 1902 when, along with 'E.G.' (a female escapee), he lay in a peasant's cart, hidden under a load of hay: 'The driver sped on in the Siberian fashion...I counted all the bumps with my back, to the accompaniment of the groans of my companion.'[2]

Meanwhile, Sokolovskaya hid Trotsky's absence from the police by placing a straw dummy in his bed. When the police inspector came to make the routine check, she claimed Trotsky was ill. But two days later, his escape was discovered, and, on 14 September, he was placed on the *Okhrana*'s 'Wanted List', as No. 5530. After he arrived in Irkutsk, Sokolovskaya's brother Ilya provided him with new clothing – and a false passport, in the name of 'Leon Trotsky': the name by which the world would know him.[3]

From Irkutsk, Trotsky travelled on the Trans-Siberian Railway, quietly reading 'Homer's hexameters in a Russian translation' on his journey west. He got off at Samara, on the R. Volga, where the headquarters of Russian branch of *Iskra* were situated. Lenin's agent there, Gleb Krzhizhanovsky-Clair – who had sent a glowing report on Trotsky's writing to *Iskra's* foreign HQ in London – informed him his articles and essays had earned him a literary reputation: and the nickname of 'The Pen' (*Piero*). Trotsky was then sent to Kharkov, Poltava and Kiev, to inspect the socialist groups there; and to negotiate with those producing the *Southern Worker*, another Social Democrat newspaper. He returned to Samara, reporting that most refused to cooperate with each other – with the *Southern Worker* group even prepared to cooperate with the Liberals. He also was given a message from Lenin, asking 'The Pen' to report immediately to *Iskra's* headquarters.[4]

From Samara, he travelled with increasing excitement, surreptitiously crossing frontiers. On reaching Vienna, he found he had insufficient funds to complete his journey. So he roused Victor Adler – the founder of the Austrian Socialist Party – from his Sunday rest, asking for help and money to get him to his next destination. Arriving in Zurich in the middle of the night, he then knocked on the door of Paul Axelrod, the veteran Russian Marxist, requesting additional help for completing his journey, via Geneva and Paris, to London.

Lenin and *Iskra*

Finally, in the early hours of an October day in 1902, in a lower middle class area not far from King's Cross, he knocked loudly (three times, as instructed) on the door of 10 Holford Square – whilst his cabman waited to collect his fare, as Trotsky had run out of money again. As Deutscher puts it: 'He was indeed "knocking at the door of history."' The house was rented by a 'Mr and Mrs Richter': better known to history as Vladimir Ilyich Lenin and Nadezhda Krupskaya. When the latter answered the door, she immediately exclaimed to Lenin – who was still in bed – 'The Pen has arrived!' Over the following days, Trotsky reported on political trends amongst the Siberian exiles; on the reluctance of local socialist groups to be part of an integrated national organisation; and on various aspects associated with clandestine work. Lenin was particularly impressed by Trotsky's precise and organised information. Even more, he was delighted that this young man – nine years

34

younger than him – supported the idea of a centralised party. They thus talked of how to weld the disconnected groups into a coherent movement.[5]

Lenin had found Trotsky a room in a nearby house, where two other editors of *Iskra* – Martov and Vera Zasulich – were living. Almost immediately, Trotsky wrote his first article for the paper, which appeared in the 1 November 1902 edition. *Iskra*'s editorial board then comprised six people: Plekhanov, Zasulich and Axelrod (the three émigré pioneers of Russian social democracy); and the much younger Lenin, Martov and Potresov. While Plekhanov and Axelrod lived in Switzerland, the rest lived in the St Pancras area. Trotsky was now in the company of the leading lights of Russian socialism. As he lived with Zasulich and Martov, the young Trotsky – still in his formative years – became closer to them than he did to Lenin, whom he saw only intermittently. Initially, Trotsky thought Lenin dry and prosaic – only years later did he come to see Lenin's strengths. Unlike Lenin, both Zasulich and Martov 'belonged to the romantic breed of rebels, guided less by theoretical principle than by moral indignation at social injustice.' They thus 'struck a deeper chord' in Trotsky.[6]

Not long after he'd arrived in London, Trotsky also met Plekhanov who, like Zasulich, had been a legendary figure to him, having been one of the founding fathers of Russian socialism, and someone who had worked alongside Engels for a time. However, from the very first meeting, Plekhanov showed a dislike of the young and enthusiastic revolutionary: possibly because of jealousy – when Trotsky's first, unsigned, articles began to appear in *Iskra*, many had assumed they were Plekhanov's. Apparently, when Zasulich once praised Trotsky's talents in Plekhanov's presence, saying 'The lad is undoubtedly a genius', the latter 'sulked, turned aside and said: "I shall never forgive him this."' Not for the last time in his political career, Trotsky's brilliance earned him the enmity of others less gifted.[7]

With only six members, the editorial board was equally divided, and disagreements often resulted in deadlock. To remedy this, in March 1903, Lenin proposed that Trotsky become the seventh member. All except Plekhanov agreed – with Lenin commenting on his 'rare abilities', and Martov saying: '"His [Trotsky's] literary works reveal indubitable talent… and already he wields great influence here thanks to his uncommon oratorical gifts. He speaks magnificently."' But Plekhanov used his veto to block Trotsky's addition, objecting that Trotsky's style was too florid; certainly, Trotsky's 'early contributions' were marked by 'the passionate character of his revolutionary invocations'. However, Plekhanov also opposed Trotsky joining the board because Lenin supported it – there was increasing tension between these two. In the end, Trotsky became an advisor to the board.[8]

Finding Natalya

Whilst in London, Trotsky took part in public lectures, to defend Marxism from its *Narodnik* and anarchist critics amongst the Russian émigrés. Although inexperienced, his early speeches revealed a real talent – their exuberant vitality, and the intensity of thought and emotion, amazed and delighted his audiences. Shortly after what he describes as his 'test' public appearance in Whitechapel, he was sent on a lecture tour to Paris. He arrived there in November 1902, to promote Marxism amongst the Russian émigrés there, and to counter the growing influence of the recently-formed Social Revolutionary Party (SRs).

It was during his first major speech there, in late 1902, that his path first crossed that of Natalya Sedova. A contemporary described Trotsky's appearance thus: '[a] lean, tallish man, with large fierce eyes and a large, sensual, irregular mouth, perched on the platform like a "bird of prey."' Sedova – almost ten years younger than Sokolovskaya – was already a seasoned revolutionary. The daughter of well-off parents, she had been expelled from a ladies' grammar school in Kharkov, for taking part in Russia's revolutionary movement. After briefly attending Moscow University, she went to study science and botany in Geneva, where she joined Plekhanov's émigré group. After making a trip to Russia, smuggling illegal literature, she moved to Paris to study art history at the Sorbonne, and there began working closely with the *Iskra* group.[9]

Trotsky's comrades had found him a room to rent – in the same house where Sedova lived. Unlike her, Trotsky was not initially impressed by what Paris had to offer, being more interested in revolutionary politics. She, however, was determined to open him up to Paris's cultural delights – and they quickly discovered a shared interest in literature. As with his earlier opposition to Marxism, he at first resisted her efforts: 'At first, I "denied" Paris, and even tried to ignore it.' However, visits to the Louvre and Baudelaire's tomb led to a growing attachment. At the time, Sedova was in a relationship, but soon became fond of 'his attentiveness, graciousness and difference from the others.' Before long, they'd become lovers, and began living together in early 1903. It is not clear whether Trotsky and Sedova married; what is certain is that their sons bore her surname, not his. Amongst revolutionaries, who rarely followed the legal niceties of 'bourgeois convention', common-law marriages were not unusual. They remained lifelong companions and, together, faced all the political vicissitudes and personal heartaches to come.[10]

Despite his new love, Trotsky kept in intermittent touch with Sokolovskaya – still in exile in Siberia – telling her about his lectures and writings, and encouraging her to read copies of *Iskra*. In 1904, she left Siberia and, leaving their daughters with her parents, joined the Social Democrats in Geneva. In the autumn of that year, she visited Trotsky in Paris on her way back to St Petersburg. They agreed that their younger daughter, Nina, would stay with her, whilst Zina would stay with Trotsky's elder sister, Yelizaveta. Despite practical communication problems over the coming years, Trotsky, Sedova and Sokolovskaya maintained a respectful friendship. His parents also visited him in Paris; his father, seemingly reconciled to his son's political 'career', even intermittently sent him funds. After a brief recall to London, Trotsky returned to Paris. Then, travelling as 'Samokliev' – with a false Bulgarian passport – he went on lecture tours to several Belgian, German and Swiss cities, to persuade Russian émigré circles to support the *Iskra* group.

Controversies and Splits

On 30 July 1903, Trotsky – at only 23 – attended the Second Congress of the RSDWP, as the delegate of the Social Democratic Siberian Union (SDSU). This Congress – in effect, also its foundation Congress – witnessed the party split into two factions which, eventually, became two separate parties. The Congress opened in Brussels; however, because of the operations of the Belgian and Russian secret police, it was forced to move to London.

The Congress was intended to bring together the various clandestine social democratic groups in Russia, to form a united centralised party, with an elected leadership. The assumption was that the *Iskra* team would form the core of the new leadership. Initially, that team – including Lenin and Trotsky – were united on the need for the RSDWP to be a centralised, disciplined and clandestine party. The only slight disagreement amongst them – just before the Congress opened – was over how the leading bodies of the party should be organised. At first, all the *Iskra* members remained united; but this unity proved short-lived. The initial cause for the split was Lenin's suggestion to reduce the number of *Iskra*'s editors from six to three: Plekhanov, Martov and himself. Lenin saw this as another way to break the deadlock on the editorial board. Although the other three had contributed far less in terms of writing and organisation, and although Plekhanov had no problem with this, Trotsky reacted emotionally against what he saw as Lenin's callousness in proposing that the services of

Axelrod and Zasulich – two of *Iskra*'s founder members – should be dispensed with.

This issue then became bound up with more serious organisational issues, which seemed designed to ensure the *Iskra* group retained overall control of the proposed Central Committee (to operate clandestinely in Russia) and Council. The final rift came over the terms of party membership. Given the repression in Tsarist Russia, Lenin argued that a member had to be someone who not only accepted the party programme and supported the party materially, but also 'personally participates in one of its organizations'. This 'hard' interpretation was opposed by Martov's alternative 'soft' draft, which was the same as Lenin's – except that his stated a member need only 'co-operate personally and regularly under the guidance of one of the organizations.' Initially, there had been little disagreement over these two versions. However, the personal feelings aroused by Lenin's proposals for the editorial board eventually led to an open clash between Lenin's and Martov's versions.[11]

Trotsky – much to Lenin's surprise – supported Martov's version, making vitriolic claims that Lenin's ideas would lead to the creation of a small, closed organisation of conspirators instead of a wider party of the working class. Lenin argued that, because Tsarist Russia was a police state, and the working class was so varied in political awareness, the RSDWP should concentrate on the vanguard of the working class: those with the greatest political awareness and understanding. Lenin tried hard to persuade Trotsky to support him, but to no avail. When it came to the vote, the Congress sided with Martov's draft by 28 votes to 23. However, this majority included delegates of defeated minority groups which then left the party. Lenin then presented his proposals concerning the editorial board – and won by two votes. The same majority then backed his candidates for the Central Committee. Hence Lenin's supporters became known as the *Bolsheviki* (the Majority), whilst his opponents became known as the *Mensheviki* (the Minority). Though, in the party as a whole, the Mensheviks constituted the majority.

On 23 August, the Congress broke up in uproar: the Mensheviks boycotted the newly-elected Central Committee, Martov resigned from *Iskra*'s board, while Trotsky stopped contributing articles. Lenin – who believed that, however narrow a winning margin, all should abide by majority decisions until the next Congress – was angered by those actions. For several years to come, Lenin and Trotsky remained politically separate – although Trotsky was a radical revolutionary, he initially ended up siding with what soon became clear was the reformist wing of the party.

Trotsky and the Mensheviks

Trotsky's support for the Mensheviks was based mainly on his warm affection for Martov, Axelrod and Zasulich, and his instinctive dislike of what he saw as Lenin's ruthlessness. For Trotsky, the split was unnecessary and would only weaken the party. Yet his choice in 1903 would, just twenty years later, play a part in his eventual fall from power. What he failed to see – which Lenin had already grasped – was that the Mensheviks were reformists rather than committed revolutionaries: as confirmed by their actions in the 1905 and 1917 Revolutions. Yet, typical of Trotsky's rashness, he almost immediately wrote his *Report of the Siberian Delegation*, in which he attacked Lenin in the strongest of terms, calling him 'the party's disorganizer', and accusing him of imposing his own 'self-centredness' rather than working for genuine centralism.[12]

However, when the Mensheviks met in conference in Geneva in September 1903, to decide what to do next, Trotsky opposed calls for a new party. Instead, he argued for maintaining pressure on Lenin, to get him to reinstate the veterans and so reunite the party. Trotsky, along with Martov, drafted a resolution along those lines, which was adopted. Trotsky then became part of a 'shadow' bureau, formed to end the split. Plekhanov, who had initially supported Lenin, then tried to persuade him to restore the old editorial board. Lenin refused, arguing it was unconstitutional to reverse a democratic decision taken by their national congress. Nonetheless, Plekhanov invited the dismissed editors back, giving the Mensheviks control of *Iskra* – though he still refused to give Trotsky a prominent role.

Plekhanov's attitude towards Trotsky hardened in March 1904, after Trotsky's article, *Wise Birds*, on the Russo-Japanese War – which had broken out the previous month – criticised the RSDWP's propaganda as crude and mistaken, and attacked both factions. Trotsky also castigated Russian liberalism's cowardice and rotten compromises; instead, he urged Russia's working classes to: '…undertake its own political campaigns…with its own slogans, under its own banner of social democracy...' Plekhanov – now favouring cooperation with the Liberals – demanded that *Iskra* refuse to publish anything else from Trotsky. Although Martov and the others agreed with Trotsky, they caved in when Plekhanov threatened to resign if Trotsky were not dismissed. By then, some of Trotsky's colleagues saw how his sharp writing and speeches, and his sometimes arrogant and insensitive demeanour, were tending to set him apart – as did his general appearance: 'the exaggerated care over his external appearance, dress and gestures: all this had the effect of alienating people and even thrusting them away from him.'[13]

In April 1904, Trotsky moved to Munich, staying with Alexander Parvus, a Russian exile, on the far left of the German Social Democratic Party. Like both Trotsky and Lenin, Parvus agreed on the need for independent working class leadership of the revolution, and tried to act as a peacemaker between the Mensheviks and the Bolsheviks. However, political differences began developing between Trotsky and the Mensheviks: in particular, when some leading Mensheviks advocated an alliance between socialism and liberalism. Although Martov was opposed, he was unable to stem this drift to compromise.

Ironically, given the fierceness of his attack on Lenin on this issue, Trotsky was now closer politically to the Bolsheviks than to the Mensheviks and, for several months, he avoided all Menshevik circles. Yet, nonetheless, he continued to attack Lenin over organisation and centralism, advocating instead Axelrod's idea of a more open party, along the lines of European social democracy.

On 6 September 1904, Trotsky's pamphlet, *Our Political Tasks* – dedicated to Axelrod – appeared in Geneva. This was such a personally vindictive diatribe against Lenin – whom he accused of 'bullying the revolutionary intelligentsia into a Marxist orthodoxy' – that it seemed to rule out any reconciliation. In particular, Trotsky argued Lenin's insistence on central control would lead the leadership to substitute itself for the working classes: 'Lenin's methods lead to this: the party organization [the caucus] at first substitutes itself for the party as a whole; then the Central Committee substitutes itself for the organization; and finally a single "dictator" substitutes himself for the Central Committee.' Exactly what Stalin would later do.[14]

Yet all Lenin had done was insist on the validity of the mandate the Congress had given him, and warn the Mensheviks that, if they persisted in obstructing congress decisions and boycotting its institutions and leadership, then action would have to be taken. The Mensheviks, who'd taken control of the party, then proceeded to warn the Bolsheviks that they faced expulsion if they didn't accept the new leadership – even though this was not what the Congress had decided. For Trotsky, this meant both the Bolsheviks and the Mensheviks were led by extremists. He thus became the spokesperson for those Russian Marxists who wanted unity, calling on both factions to wind up their separate organisations. The Mensheviks opposed any idea of reconciliation, seeing Trotsky as a traitor who was moving towards the Bolsheviks. By the autumn of 1904, Trotsky was at loggerheads with both factions. As Service notes: 'He liked to burst the bindings of party discipline…He treasured his personal independence.'[15]

Trotsky then formally notified the Mensheviks of his resignation in an *Open Letter to Comrades*, intended for publication in *Iskra*; he also privately informed Martov and Zasulich that he hoped soon to reach an agreement with the Bolsheviks. But the Mensheviks decided not to publish it, as they didn't want Russian revolutionary émigrés to know that the strongest anti-Bolshevik was now also criticising them. They kept Trotsky quiet by promising to disband their separate organisation – though they failed to do so. They also allowed him to write a political notebook for *Iskra*. One eventually appeared on the back page of an issue in October 1904. Thus, to the Bolsheviks, Trotsky remained a Menshevik. Much to Trotsky's relief, Sedova returned that month from a clandestine mission in Russia: amongst his first words when he met her off the train in Berlin were that they: 'must not be parted ever again.' They then rejoined Parvus in Munich.[16]

Trotsky's disagreements with the Mensheviks were widened by developments in Russia. As the war with Japan became disastrous, the Tsar allowed a Liberal-dominated national convention to meet in November 1904, followed by political banquets in many Russian towns. Many Russian socialists – the Mensheviks included – began to argue for joint Socialist–Liberal cooperation. Trotsky rejected this – as did the Bolsheviks – and he wrote a pamphlet attacking this, arguing the Liberals were more afraid of revolution than even the Tsar. Unsurprisingly, the Mensheviks refused to publish it.

As well as castigating the Liberals, Trotsky also argued revolution was now on the agenda in Russia – and that it would probably come via a general strike, which would 'eventually transform' protest into revolution. This was a new idea, borne out by what actually happened the following year and, later, in 1917. It arose from Trotsky's romantic revolutionary imagination and, given he was still so young and inexperienced, showed a surprisingly realistic grasp of the mechanics of revolution.[17]

In late January 1905, news of revolutionary developments in Russia reached the émigrés. Trotsky was in Geneva at the time, having arrived there from a lecture tour. His predictions seeming to have come true, he rushed back to Munich. Parvus finally persuaded the Mensheviks to publish Trotsky's pamphlet, adding his own preface in which he stated that Russia would end up with a revolutionary government with a socialist RSDWP majority – even though the immediate tasks would be to carry out a bourgeois–democratic, not a proletarian, revolution. When Trotsky's brochure appeared, the conclusions of Parvus' preface were opposed by both Mensheviks and Bolsheviks. The former argued that as the revolution was against autocracy and feudalism, it would be the Liberal middle classes alone who would form the government. The Bolsheviks argued that the socialists should enter the new government, in order to strengthen the resolve of the middle classes to bring about a bourgeois/capitalist revolution – but would only be a minority in such a coalition, as the proletariat was still too small.

Trotsky then wrote a series of essays, which appeared later as *After the Petersburg Insurrection*. In these, he continued his attacks on the Liberals, calling for a: 'ruthless struggle against liberalism for influence on the masses, for the leading role of the proletariat...'

He also called on the workers to arm themselves in preparation for a countrywide revolution, and to persuade the army to come over to the side of the people. Once again, his calls were very close to what actually happened later in 1905 and in 1917. After finishing another exhausting lecture tour, he and Sedova then moved to Geneva.[18]

Trotsky was now eager to return to Russia, despite the risk that if caught – as a fugitive from Siberia – he would automatically be deported for hard labour. Sedova went ahead of him, to prepare secret lodgings in Kiev; by February 1905, he was on his way back. He stopped in Vienna to call on Victor Adler, where he shaved off his moustache and beard to make it more difficult for the police to identify him. Of all the émigré leaders, it was only Trotsky who initially returned.

Trotsky in the 1905 Revolution

Trotsky arrived in Kiev – the hub of the underground organisation – assuming the identity of 'Corporal Arbuzov'. He hid for several weeks, in various secret lodgings. Whilst there, he met Leonid Krasin, a member of the Central Committee, who was in charge of the underground party, and second only to Lenin in the Bolshevik hierarchy. Krasin, although a Bolshevik, was a 'conciliator' and thus prepared to cooperate with Trotsky who, at that time, was the only prominent socialist in Russia. With things moving fast in Russia, Krasin and the underground movement came to rely on Trotsky, rather than waiting for instructions from abroad. Trotsky became increasingly influential because, unlike the leaders of the two factions, he reflected the mood of most RSDWP members and supporters, who wanted unity. But while he – like them – failed to see logic was leading to two separate parties, he also understood the dynamics of the 1905 Revolution better than either Lenin or Martov. Consequently, he was much better equipped – as well as better placed – to play a leading role in the revolution.

In the spring, Krasin took Trotsky and Sedova to Petersburg, where Trotsky assumed the name of 'Peter Petrovich' and, as revolutionary unrest died down, spent his time motivating the Russian organisation, and writing essays, articles, pamphlets and leaflets, as well as letters to *Iskra*. In *Iskra* No. 93 (17 March), he concluded that only the RSDWP was in a position to organise a nationwide armed insurrection, because: 'Neither the peasantry, nor the middle class, nor the intelligentsia can play an independent revolutionary role in any way equivalent to the role of the proletariat.'[19]

Abroad, Lenin, too, advocated armed insurrection, saying the workers shouldn't cooperate with the liberals. This was adopted by the Bosheviks' separate Congress in London, in April–May 1905. The Mensheviks, however, argued an armed insurrection could not be organised, but could only happen 'spontaneously'. This was based on their belief that the leadership of revolution in Russia belonged to middle class liberalism, not to socialism. Even Martov argued it was the historical mission of the middle classes to bring a radical democracy to Russia. Trotsky countered this, arguing that although the middle classes were constrained by autocracy and wanted a more liberal regime in order to allow capitalism to develop, they feared revolution too much to back genuine democracy.

On one of the May Day protests in Petersburg, Sedova was arrested: she was sentenced to six months imprisonment, but was released early and sent to live under police supervision at Tver. As a police spy within the organisation was beginning to track him down, Trotsky hurriedly left for Finland which, though part of Tsarist Russia, enjoyed greater freedoms. He stayed in Hotel *Rauha* (Peace), writing, and maintaining contact with Krasin.

On 19 August, the Tsar issued a Manifesto, promising a consultative *Duma,* to be elected by a property-based franchise which excluded most of the working classes. Miliukov and the Liberals welcomed this – but Trotsky, in an *Open Letter to Miliukov*, sharply ridiculed him and, instead, called for a boycott of the elections. Trotsky's call for a boycott was echoed by the Bolsheviks, but not by the Mensheviks. However, unlike Lenin, Trotsky saw the value in countering the Liberals' arguments, in order to win over the undecided amongst the intelligentsia and the advanced workers. Consequently, over the coming months, Trotsky wrote extensively for these different audiences.

Then, on 25 October, a general strike broke out in St Petersburg – Trotsky, even though he knew the police were on his trail, rushed back. It took the leaders of the socialist underground by surprise – as did the emergence, on 26 October, of the first *Soviet* (Council) of Workers' Deputies. The

Soviet was the first elected body to represent the disenfranchised working classes in undemocratic Tsarist Russia – around 200,000 people had voted, comprising almost 50% of the city's workers. Meeting in the Polytechnical Institute, it thus acquired a genuinely revolutionary character from the very beginning, and soon had from 400 to 560 deputies; it also published its own newspaper, *Izvestya* (*Tidings*).

The Mensheviks and the SRs supported it, but the Bolshevik leaders in Petersburg initially viewed it with suspicion. It was only towards the end of November that Lenin sent a letter from Stockholm to the Petersburg Bolsheviks' paper *Novaya Zhizn* (*New Life*), urging his supporters to cooperate with the Soviet – but the paper failed to publish it. Trotsky – representing the Mensheviks – first spoke at the Soviet on 28 October, under the name of 'Yanovsky' ('the man of Yanovka'). Although his articles were signed 'Trotsky', he was only know as 'Yanovsky' by members of the Soviet. He remained so immaculately dressed that some of his socialist friends were shocked by his bourgeois appearance – Lunacharsky referred to his 'unusually elegant' appearance, commenting that, as well as being 'very handsome', he often spoke in a 'condescending manner'.[20]

Krasin invited Trotsky to address the Bolshevik Central Committee: he urged them to join without prior conditions, arguing the Soviet should be a broad representative body, made up of all political groups supported by the working classes – as the only way to get a united front for the general strike, and for revolution. This argument was still going on when, on 30 October, the Tsar issued the *October Manifesto*, promising a constitution, civil liberties and universal suffrage. Sedova returned and, for a time, they lived in the house of a financier.

While crowds celebrated in the streets, General Trepov, the new Minister of the Interior, prepared to stamp out the protests. Later that day, Trotsky moved with a huge celebratory crowd towards the Soviet's meeting place – although mounted police rode into them, the crowd continued in good humour, decorating buildings with red flags.

However, when they reached the Technological Institute, they were halted by a barrier of police. Rather than provoke violence, the crowd moved instead to St Petersburg University. From a balcony, Trotsky then tore up the *Manifesto*, telling the crowd it had only been issued because of the Tsar's fear of the general strike, thus much more had to change before they really tasted freedom. He then called on the workers to struggle for revolution. It was the first time that Russia's capital heard from Trotsky, who became the great orator of revolution.

That evening, the Soviet elected an Executive – with advisory votes for three Mensheviks, three Bolsheviks and three SRs. Trotsky – even though he had resigned from them – was the chief Menshevik representative. By then, he had persuaded the Petersburg Mensheviks to turn against their émigré leaders, and had persuaded the Menshevik and Bolshevik committees in the city to form a Federal Council to work together in the Soviet, and to work towards reunification of the party. The Soviet's decisions were mostly influenced by the Social Democrats; and the records show Trotsky was an important 'moving spirit', often speaking at critical points for both the Social Democratic groups. He wrote most of the Soviet's manifestoes and resolutions, and edited *Izvestya*. With the help of Parvus, who had come to St Petersburg, he obtained control of a radical Liberal daily, *Russkaya Gazeta* (*The Russian Gazette*), which he proceeded to turn into a popular organ of militant socialism. Trotsky's reputation grew: unlike the other leaders, he refused to hide away, braved the dangers and, instead, challenged the government.

On 1 November, Trotsky persuaded the Soviet to call off its general strike, to avoid further bloodshed; the strike ended two days later. The Soviet then announced a funeral on 6 November, for those workers who had been killed. However, the day before the planned funeral, they learned that Trepov intended to suppress the funeral. So Trotsky successfully urged the cancellation of the funeral, proposing this motion: 'The Soviet declares: the proletariat of Petersburg will give the Tsarist government the last battle not on a day chosen by Trepov, but when it suits the armed and organized proletariat.'[21]

However, the Soviet also voted to form fighting squads – though, like the squad that guarded the Soviet, they only had sticks and iron bars, and a few revolvers. Its political activities continued, including taking advantage of the *October Manifesto*'s promise of freedom of the press – but the old censorship continued. So the Soviet declared print workers would refuse to produce anything that had been presented to the censors. The government gave in, and thus, for the first time, Russia had a taste of a free press. On 13 November, in alliance with Parvus and Martov, Trotsky began writing for *Nachalo* (*The Beginning*) – which rapidly became very popular because of his articles which, as Zinoviev once remarked, had 'quite a Bolshevik character'. Like the other papers he wrote for, this paper was much more popular than the Bolsheviks', because his writing was much more vivid and exciting. It was in the pages of *Nachalo* that Trotsky began to advocate his idea of 'permanent revolution'.[22]

The Soviet then began to enact the longed-for eight-hour day – 'by revolutionary means', with workers simply going home after eight hours' work. When the government declared a state of siege in Poland, the Soviet declared its support of Poland's right to secede from the Tsarist Empire, received a Polish delegation, and called a new general strike to support the Poles. When the government announced that 1,200 Kronstadt sailors who'd taken part in the October strike would be court martialled – thus facing possible execution – the Soviet added the campaign for their release to their demands. The government capitulated. On 18 November – with workers in some of the provinces growing weary – Trotsky, on behalf of the Executive, successfully called for the general strike to end on 20 November, urging workers to start preparing for armed insurrection.

By the middle of November, all the leaders of the various groups – including Lenin – had returned. The events of 1905 brought about a reconciliation between Trotsky and Lenin, although some differences remained. According to Lunacharsky, when Lenin was told that Trotsky, acting as a 'free agent' who was neither Menshevik nor Bolshevik, was the 'strong man' in the Soviet, he – despite Trotsky's recent attacks on him – said: 'Well, Trotsky has earned that with his fine and tireless work.'[23]

Another reason for Lenin's conciliatory attitude was that both he and Martov accepted that their differences were now largely irrelevant, as these had been about what was needed for underground work. Now, the RSDWP was able to operate above ground. In addition, the Mensheviks had seen that middle class liberalism – even that of the newly-formed Constitutional Democratic Party (Kadets) – was not progressive, whilst their followers in Petersburg supported Trotsky's radicalism. Thus, by the end of the year, the two factions continued the process of reunification, as advocated by Trotsky. While Trotsky's writings directed at the peasantry probably never reached them, by late 1905, his influence even reached the liberal middle classes. As early as 1906, Miliukov, the founder and leader of the Kadets, spoke about the popularity of 'Trotskyism' amongst middle class professionals and enlightened business people who constituted the 'democratic public'.[24]

However, the government finally decided to act against the Soviet. First, press censorship was reimposed; then, on 9 December, the Chair and some other leaders of the Soviet were arrested. The SRs pressed for terroristic reprisals, others called for another general strike. The Social Democrats were against both, and Trotsky pleaded for cool-headedness – instead, he proposed a motion to elect a new Chair and to continue preparing for an armed insurrection. The Soviet elected him as Chair of a three-member Presidium.

A police detachment was posted outside the Free Economic Society buildings, where the Soviet was then meeting. In response, the Soviet proclaimed a financial boycott, calling on people to stop paying taxes; to accept only gold coins, not banknotes; and to withdraw deposits from the banks. This *Manifesto on the Finances of the Empire* – mainly written by Parvus and Trotsky – also warned foreign countries that the Russian people, after a victorious revolution, would not pay what they saw as the Tsar's illegitimate debts. This, it argued, given the lack of preparedness for an armed insurrection, was the only way to overthrow Tsarist autocracy. On 15 December, nine liberal newspapers published this *Manifesto* – and were promptly closed down by the Tsar.[25]

On 16 December, Trotsky presided over a meeting of the Soviet Executive, reporting on government steps to repress opposition – including reintroducing the ban on socialist parties. Both the Bolsheviks and the Mensheviks proposed another general strike. News then reached them that the building was surrounded by soldiers and police, and that a raid was imminent. Whilst sending some members away to continue the Soviet's activities, they resolved to continue the session, but to offer no armed resistance. Trotsky ordered delegates to break the locks of any revolvers before handing them to the police. A detachment of soldiers and police entered whilst the meeting was taking place, and the police officer in charge began reading the arrest warrant. Trotsky interrupted, saying a trade union delegate was already speaking and that: 'If you wish to take the floor, you must give your name and I shall ask the meeting whether it wishes to listen to you.'[26]

Once the speaker had finished, Trotsky asked the Executive if they wished to hear the warrant 'for the sake of information'. Once the officer had read it out, the meeting continued. When the officer began to protest, Trotsky told him not to interrupt and, when the meeting shouted they didn't want to listen to the officer anymore, Trotsky ordered him to leave. In great embarrassment, the officer left. Before he returned with troops, Trotsky called on the Executive to destroy all documents and not to reveal their names to the police. When the officer returned with troops, a member of the Executive addressed the soldiers, saying they were being used by a Tsar who was already breaking the promises of the October Manifesto. The officer, afraid of the impact of those words, led the troops out – but the speaker just raised his voice, his words still reaching them. Eventually, a large detachment of police entered, and Trotsky declared the Executive meeting closed – he, and fifty-one other members of the Soviet were then arrested. After an existence of fifty days, the first Soviet in history came to an end – neither with a bang nor a whimper but, because of Trotsky, with peaceful defiance and humour.

Although the first Soviet had ended, its ideas had not. Both Trotsky and Lenin saw the 1905 Revolution, in many ways, as '… a dress rehearsal for the revolution of 1917.' Whilst no real gains had been made, the important thing was that the Soviet's actions – and Trotsky's words – had won the workers for the *ideas* of an eight-hour day, and of a general strike growing over into a revolutionary insurrection. This was reflected in the immediate reaction to the arrests of the Soviet leaders: strikes in Petersburg, and a general strike and ten days of fighting on the barricades in Moscow, that began on 23 December. Throughout December and into January 1906, revolts flared up across Tsarist Russia, and were harshly repressed.[27]

Permanent Revolution

After their arrest, Trotsky and the others spent almost the whole of 1906 in prison, awaiting trial. Though they were meant to be kept in solitary confinement, their doors were left open, and they were accorded political prisoner rights – including receiving books and visitors, and continuing their political activities. Trotsky was allowed conjugal visits from Sedova, which resulted in her becoming pregnant with their first child, Lyova. Trotsky also wrote to Sokolovskaya, asking for a recent photo of their daughters; later, his daughters visited him in prison.

Typically, Trotsky didn't waste this time – spending it reading and writing, and passing his books and papers to other prisoners to help continue their political education. Much of what he wrote then appeared in the party's publications. Part of his reading included reading the classics of European literature – especially French novels. He also read more modern novels – by then he was fluent in both German and French, preferring German for politics and economics, and French for literature. As ever, even in prison, he maintained his neat appearance.

However, his most important work was undoubtedly *Results and Prospects*, written as a concluding chapter to *Nasha Revolutsia (Our Revolution)*, a collection of essays about the 1905 Revolution. It turned out to be one of his most controversial works, setting out what became and has remained the essence of 'Trotskyism': the theory of 'permanent revolution'. Though there were later refinements, his core arguments never really changed.

When he wrote it, virtually all Marxists saw 1905 as a bourgeois revolution, to end Tsarist autocracy and Russia's semi-feudal economy, allowing Russia to be modernised by capitalist development. According to orthodox Marxism, only after capitalism had increased the size and cultural development of the proletariat would revolutionary socialism be on the agenda. The main point of contention between the Mensheviks and the Bolsheviks was whether it would be the middle classes or the working classes which would play the leading role in this bourgeois stage of revolution.

Trotsky agreed with the Bolsheviks that, because the Russian middle classes were too weak – and feared a socialist revolution too much – the workers would have to lead that bourgeois revolution. He also stated that the workers should form an alliance with the peasantry who – unlike the Bolsheviks – he believed incapable of playing an independent role. More significantly, Trotsky argued that, once in power, the working class would have to push ahead with socialist revolution – even before the victory of socialism in the more developed countries of western Europe. Trotsky's theory owed something to Marx, but he developed it way beyond what Marx had written. Lenin, too, had written about an 'uninterrupted revolution' following on from a democratic revolution. But, crucially, Lenin felt Trotsky was wrong to think this could happen *before* the workers were the majority of the population.[28]

Trotsky's theory of permanent revolution also had international aspects: he argued that, once it had obtained land, the peasantry would begin to oppose moves towards collectivism and internationalism. Thus, in order to build socialism, Russia's workers' state would have to rely on revolution in more developed states, in order to overcome its economic backwardness and peasant conservatism: 'Without the direct state support of the European proletariat, the working class of Russia will not be able to remain in power and transform its temporary rule into a stable and prolonged socialist dictatorship...' He couldn't envisage the Russian Revolution, isolated in such a backward country, surviving for decades without things moving backwards to an authoritarian non-socialist state.[29]

Initially, there was little interest in Trotsky's book as, by the time it came out, the revolution was coming to an end, and the police confiscated most of the copies that had been printed. Nonetheless, by then, Trotsky had definitely established himself as an important social democratic leader, and someone with a proven track record for taking revolutionary action.

Trial and Deportation

The date for their trial, originally set for June 1906, was frequently postponed, giving the prisoners plenty of time to prepare their defence. The Mensheviks wanted to deny the prosecution's claim that the Soviet had planned armed insurrection, and instead claim the Soviet had merely tried to achieve the *October Manifesto*'s promises of freedom of assembly. Trotsky sharply rejected this, pointing out this was a 'Liberal' defence, and that: 'The programme of the *October Manifesto* has never been the programme of the Soviet.' Instead, he argued they should deny they had made any *technical* preparations for armed insurrection, but accept responsibility for *political* preparation.[30]

Trotsky's stance was to use the trial as a political platform to expound their socialist principles, rather than just defend themselves. This was supported by the Bolsheviks, leading him to tell Martov: 'as a social-democratic politician I feel myself closer to the [Bolsheviks].' Ziv, from the Nikolaev days – who was also imprisoned – wrote: '...his [Trotsky's] words were full of warm sympathy for the Bolsheviks, to whom he was spiritually akin, and of a hardly suppressed antipathy to the Mensheviks...' Khrustalev-Nosar, the Soviet's first Chair, was persuaded to go along with Trotsky's suggestions. Trotsky then assigned the main defendants various roles – he himself would deal with the most serious charge: that of armed insurrection.[31]

The trial – which lasted several weeks – finally began on 2 October, in an open court that could impose long sentences of hard labour. The court was surrounded by Cossacks and police, as tens of thousands of workers had sent in resolutions protesting against the trial. Consequently, only one hundred people were allowed into the court itself – including Trotsky's parents. Those on trial now numbered fifty-one, not fifty-two, as one of them had been executed in the interval. During the trial, members of the public regularly gave the defendants letters, newspapers and flowers. The judge felt unable to object and, in the end, police officers often carried flowers from the public galleries to the dock. When the defendants rose to pay homage to their executed comrade, even the police rose to their feet.

From the beginning, the defendants made it clear they were only taking part in the trial to tell the truth about the Soviet's activities. On 17 October, Trotsky rose to speak about armed insurrection. On several occasions during his speech, his mother cried; and, at one point, Trotsky suffered one of his blackouts. He referred to the violence used by the state, and to how the general strike had paralysed the authorities – thus making the Soviet a *de facto* power. After saying how a rising of the masses results from social and political conditions, he went to say:

> 'To prepare for the inevitable uprising – and, gentlemen of the court, we never **prepared an insurrection**...; we prepared **for** an insurrection – meant to us, first and foremost, enlightening

the people, explaining to them that open conflict was inevitable…that only might can defend right…That is what preparing for an insurrection meant to us.'[32]

On 15 November 1906, the verdict – 'Not Guilty' of insurrection – was delivered before an empty courtroom. But Trotsky – and fourteen others – were found guilty of subversion and sentenced to deportation to Siberia for life, with the loss of all civil rights; any attempt at escape would carry the additional punishment of hard labour. They were then put together in a large hall in the Moscow Transit Prison, while it was decided where to send them – much to Trotsky's annoyance, as this made writing difficult. Whilst there, his and Sedova's son, Lyova, was born on 7 December 1906.

However – as with his first sentence of deportation – Trotsky had no intention of remaining in Siberia for long. Even before he was moved from St Petersburg, he made sure he kept his boots because, hidden in the sole of one, was a passport – and, in the heel, were some gold coins provided by his father.

Chapter 4

The Vienna Years, 1907–13

'I clench my teeth and yearn for electric street-lamps, the noise of trams and the best thing in the world – the smell of fresh newsprint... But when I was... travelling in a comfortable carriage on the Perm railway I knew that I had won... the train... was carrying me forward, forward, always forward.'[1]

Those words describe Trotsky's feelings as he began his second journey into exile, and then his second escape from Siberia in 1907. The seven years following that escape were described by Deutscher as 'The Doldrums'. Certainly – unlike what happened after his first escape in 1902 – this escape did not carry him forwards to anything like the 1905 Revolution.

Stalin – soon to become Trotsky's inveterate enemy – shrewdly observed that Trotsky's strength was revealed during revolutionary periods, but that his weakness became apparent when revolution was in retreat. Nonetheless, Trotsky was far from idle, though his main activity during this period would have a serious impact on his long-term political future.[2]

Escaping Again

On 16 January 1907, Trotsky and the other prisoners were moved to the transit prison. Two days later, without any warning, they were woken before dawn and told their journey into exile was about to begin. Nonetheless, before leaving, they were able to smuggle out a 'Farewell Message' to the workers of St Petersburg, thanking them for their solidarity during their trial. Significantly, the authorities decided it necessary to bring a large escort detachment from Moscow, as the Petersburg soldiers were considered politically 'unreliable'.

Their journey into exile began by train, though as yet they were not informed of their ultimate destination. From Petersburg, they travelled across the Urals – at every station they stopped at en route, their carriage was surrounded by a dense cordon of police, to prevent any attempts at rescue. Many of the soldiers openly showed their sympathy – and were clearly relieved they weren't escorting the prisoners to their execution. Trotsky made use of this sympathy to get letters smuggled out to Sedova, describing his journey.

At Tiumen, they left the train and, for over three weeks, travelled on horse-drawn sleighs to Tobolsk. To prevent escape attempts, travelling ended well before dusk each day. This stretch of the journey passed several deportee settlements, so the prisoners were often greeted by lines of political exiles singing revolutionary songs and waving red flags.

On 11 February, they reached Tobolsk, and were housed in the local prison; it was there they were told that their final destination was Obdorsk, on the River Ob. Obdorsk lies in the mountains, just above the Arctic Circle and, in 1907, was 1,000 miles away from the nearest railway station. Trotsky suspected his high profile made an escape attempt too risky, and so still expected Sedova, and their newly-born son, Lyova, to join him in exile. From Tobolsk, the convoy continued its journey and, as they moved further into the sparsely-populated taiga, the horses had to be replaced by reindeer. On 25 February, they reached Berezov – around 300 miles from Obdorsk – where, once again, they were lodged in the local prison.

As this was the blizzard season, the police assumed no one would attempt to escape, so the prisoners were allowed out of their cells during the day. However, a chance meeting with a deportee doctor led Trotsky to decide to escape, before he had travelled even further into the Siberian wilderness. As he knew, it was not too difficult to escape from Siberia, as the police struggled to maintain effective surveillance. When he asked a Menshevik friend and fellow deportee about the possibility of an escape, he was advised that, although it was possible, no one had tried to do it during the storm season! However, this didn't put him off, and he started to plan a route.

As advised by the doctor, he complained of sciatica, and was thus left behind in the local hospital, with a small guard, until he was well enough to continue the journey. With the help of a sympathetic peasant, he found a guide called Nikifor who, in return for keeping the reindeer and furs that Trotsky paid for, agreed to take him west, across the white desert of the roadless tundra, along the River Sosva, to the gold-mining settlement of Bogolovsk in the Urals, almost 500 miles away. Bogolovsk had a small single-line railway that would take him to the Perm–Viatka line; from there, he could get to Petersburg and then Finland.

On the agreed escape day, 3 March, Trotsky told the police chief he was feeling better, and that he could continue the journey the following day.

Consequently, he was released from hospital. That evening, he attended an amateur production of a Chekhov play. He left the play early, shaved off his beard (which his 1905 police photos showed him having) at his friend's house, and picked up a large package of food for the trip. By midnight, his escape had begun.

The journey, across largely-uncharted tundra, took a week, mostly travelling by night, as well as by day. Trotsky calculated, because this route was so reckless, the authorities would assume he'd taken a safer one. On the very first night, Trotsky discovered his guide was a drunkard; thus, Trotsky – often with very little food, and only melted snow to drink – frequently had to stay awake, to make sure the sleigh didn't run into deep snowdrifts: 'I woke him up several times… "Nikifor!" I screamed, pulling the hood off his drunken head and laying it bare to the frosty air…' Yet, despite all the hardships, he managed to take notes on the landscape, the wildlife, and the backwardness, drunkenness, and supernatural superstitions of the people in the occasional isolated settlements where they stopped to renew supplies or the reindeer.[3]

A day after arriving at Bogolovsk, he caught a train to Perm and, from there, travelled westwards towards Petersburg. Despite being known to every police agent there, he sent a telegram to Sedova, asking her to meet him en route. She – along with Lyova – was then living in Terioki, a Finnish village near Petersburg. The telegram was a huge surprise, as the newspapers were still reporting the journey of the convicted Soviet leaders to the Polar Circle! In fact, she described sending the telegram as an 'act of madness', as the police were watching her house.

Although Trotsky's telegram didn't mention which station, Sedova travelled to Petersburg and, using common sense, went to Samino, the most likely junction station. Sedova later described her frantic search for him on arrival: 'I ran through one car after another, and he was not there. Suddenly I recognized L. D.'s fur coat in a compartment…But where was he? I leaped out of the car, and immediately ran into L. D., who was rushing out of the station looking for me.' Nearly forty years after, she described how she was 'trembling with joy at his escape', when they met, describing him thus: '… He was only twenty-eight, well-built, with thick and unmanageable brown hair and a small moustache. He had bold features, a rather bony face and extremely lively blue eyes…'[4]

After a few days staying in Petersburg with friends – and before the police got on their trail – they crossed back into Finland. On arrival, Trotsky was briefly reunited with Lenin and Martov, who were staying in neighbouring villages. They congratulated him on his defence during the trial – though

Lenin also chided him for not joining the Bolsheviks, given that their ideas were so close. With Lenin's help, they settled in Oglbu, a small village near Helsingfors. While there, Trotsky quickly wrote an account of his escape, *There and Back*: the advance royalties bringing in much-needed money. In what was their first holiday together, they walked in the woods and had snowball fights. Sedova and Lyova then returned briefly to Russia, while Trotsky went, via Stockholm, firstly to attend the Fifth Congress of the RSDWP in London, and then to start the search for a more permanent base.

The 'Conciliator'

Trotsky went to that Congress hoping to achieve the reunification of the RSDWP. However, while he and the other leaders had languished in prison after the defeat of the Soviet, much had happened. Beginning in 1906, the Tsar and his new chief minister, Stolypin, had launched a vindictive revenge against all those organisations which, for over a year, had shaken the foundations of Tsarist autocracy. Across Russia, thousands of socialists and anarchists were executed, following courts-martial or summary trials: the hangman's noose soon became known as 'Stolypin's necktie'. Others were simply massacred by the ultra-nationalist 'Black Hundred' militias. This brutal repression demoralised many revolutionaries; whilst, amongst the émigrés, the retreat of revolution unleashed a new wave of internal bickering. Not surprisingly, these 'years of reaction' led many to consider it too risky to continue illegal underground work.

Both factions had taken part in the Fourth Congress of the RSDWP – known as the 'Unity Congress' – which had met in Stockholm from 23 April–8 May 1906. The Mensheviks had slightly outnumbered the Bolsheviks, because many of the latter's groups had been broken up by repression and so were unable to send delegates. Thus the newly-elected Central Committee comprised seven Mensheviks and only three Bolsheviks, while the editorial board of the party's new journal, *Social Democrat,* was entirely Menshevik. There had been many sharp disagreements over policy, and this was a 'Unity Congress' in name only: this didn't bode well for Trotsky's campaign to bring about unity.

The Fifth Congress, which Trotsky attended, opened on 13 May 1907, with around 350 delegates – almost ten times as many as in 1903. In addition to the Bolsheviks and Mensheviks, there were also delegates from the Polish, Latvian and Lithuanian social democratic parties which had joined the RSDWP in 1906. This time, the Bolsheviks won most of the votes on policy, but the Polish and Latvian delegates – who deplored factionalism – ensured that neither faction had a majority on either the new Central Committee or the editorial board.

Trotsky felt both factions were important for the party, and was prepared to work with both – provided they had what he saw as the right ideas! An important reason for his separateness from both factions was because he felt both were wrong: rejecting his theory of permanent revolution, they believed the coming Russian revolution would for some time be merely a bourgeois democratic one. Essentially, he was pro-Menshevik when it came to party organisation, but pro-Bolshevik on tactics and policies. Ultimately, he was convinced another revolutionary upsurge would see the two factions cooperating, as had happened in 1905. However, he was also determined to remain 'his own man' and got the Congress Minutes to record that he belonged to neither faction.

He addressed the Congress several times, speaking with self-assurance: contemporaries testified how he could hold the attention of very different audiences with equal effect, as a result of his 'amazing ability' to 'enter the minds of his audience': 'Whether friendly or hostile, no one could long remain neutral towards Trotsky. He was universally regarded as an extraordinary, larger-than-life figure.' In his speeches – not usually written down – he expounded his theory of permanent revolution, getting support from Rosa Luxemburg (of the Polish Social Democratic Party), whom he had met before. During one speech, he attacked the 'revolutionary pessimism' of those Mensheviks who, because of repression, now wanted to work with the liberal Kadets.[5]

Though differing with Lenin on permanent revolution, and still arguing that the peasantry would not play an independent political role, he nonetheless argued for a bloc of workers and peasants against the liberals. This was similar to the Bolshevik position, and thus gained him Lenin's support, who said, in the final debate: 'We have solidarity of views here as regards the fundamentals of our attitude towards the bourgeois parties.' However, Lenin failed to win Trotsky over to the Bolsheviks. Whilst Trotsky's political spirit and beliefs were much closer to the Bolsheviks, he still had strong ties of friendship to Mensheviks such as Martov. Thus he remained separate from both factions, believing this was the best way of achieving party unity. Instead, he argued for 'unity in diversity' and 'unity in action'. One consequence of his aloofness from both factions was that he failed to get elected to the new Central Committee.[6]

The most significant division between the two factions was over whether to continue with underground activities. Trotsky – like the Bolsheviks, but unlike the Mensheviks – had argued for a boycott of the elections to the First Duma, because they were so democratically flawed. However, because of the increased political interest and turmoil in Russia following the 1905 Revolution, he had argued for participation in the March 1907 elections for the Second Duma – though he had continued to oppose the RSDWP forming platforms with other parties, so that the socialist message was not diluted.

Although Martov and Plekhanov argued for clandestine activity to continue, the majority of Mensheviks felt the underground networks should be disbanded. Instead, they argued that – like socialist parties in western Europe – the party should only operate in whatever legal channels the Tsar allowed. Thus this group became known as the 'Liquidators'. However, the Bolsheviks were also split, with a large section opposed to participation in any of the political activities allowed by Tsarism. They became known as the 'Boycotters'. Trotsky – like Lenin – favoured a combination of both political activities. There was, however, a difference between them even on this: Trotsky wanted the party to be more 'Europeanised' in the sense of being less centralised, whereas Lenin argued that underground political life – dictated by the conditions of the Tsarist police state – meant there had to be tighter control from the émigré centre than existed in west European parties that operated in more democratic societies. Consequently, Trotsky opposed Lenin's calls for the expulsion of the Liquidators and Boycotters.

Another aspect which separated Trotsky from Lenin was the question of bank robberies – known as 'expropriations' – carried out by some Bolshevik fighting squads. He joined Martov in denouncing these at the Congress as a hangover from *Narodnik* terrorism. Lenin's attitude was ambivalent, seeing the money gained as useful in helping the party carry out its underground activities. Despite generally having majority support at this Congress, the Bolsheviks were outvoted on this, and the decision was taken to ban them.[7]

While, politically, this Congress – which ended on 1 June – was a disappointment for Trotsky, he spent part of the time between sessions going about London with Maxim Gorky, the famous Russian writer. Gorky had introduced himself – and the renowned Russian actress, Maria Andreyeva, his common-law wife – to Trotsky at the beginning of the Congress. Both Gorky and Andreyeva were members of the RSDWP, and this connection with Gorky later proved useful to Trotsky. Shortly after the Congress ended, on 16 June, the Second Duma was dissolved. Then, in what became known as 'Stolypin's Coup', its sixty-five Social Democratic members were arrested and deported to Siberia, and the revolutionary parties' clubs and newspapers were suppressed. The government also closed down many of the legal trade unions, and imprisoned or exiled many trade unionists. This harsh repression greatly reduced membership of revolutionary groups: in 1905, there had been roughly 100,000 – by 1910, this had dropped to about 10,000.

After the dismissal of the Second Duma, the franchise for elections to the Third Duma was drastically changed, to disenfranchise the majority of working class and peasant voters. This increased the dominance of wealthy rural landowners and businessmen, ensuring a majority for the right wing Octobrist Party. Yet, at the beginning of August, the Third Conference of the RSDWP – despite strong objections from the Boycotters – voted to participate in those elections, due in October 1907. These developments only deepened the factional divisions; consequently, the Fifth Congress was the last congress in which both factions participated. Ultimately, unlike both Lenin and Martov, Trotsky failed to realise that the fundamental difference between the respective Bolshevik and Menshevik positions was that between committed revolutionaries and radical reformists.

Exile in Vienna

After the Congress, Trotsky went to Berlin, meeting up with Sedova, who had travelled there from Petersburg. He was warmly welcomed by Kautsky and other leaders of the German SPD, who supported his attempts to end the RSDWP's factional divisions. Kautsky's home became his main base in Berlin – and it was through Kautsky he was able to get his articles regularly published in the German SPD's journal and daily newspaper. As well as explaining permanent revolution, he also wrote about the RSDWP's factional disputes, continuing to call for unity. Strangely, he initially had little contact with Karl Liebknecht and Rosa Luxemburg – the leaders of the radical left wing of the German SPD – even though they didn't support Lenin, and had very similar ideas to Trotsky's, which was why Luxemburg (posthumously denounced by Stalin in 1932 as a 'Trotskyist') had supported some of his interventions in the 1907 Congress.[8]

Trotsky and Sedova then travelled to Dresden, to meet up with Parvus, newly-escaped from Siberia. They went on a long summer walking holiday with him in Switzerland and Bohemia, during which Trotsky nonetheless managed to write some articles – and even a couple of books – which Parvus got printed. In August, Trotsky went on a lecture tour of Russian Marxist groups in southern Germany, delivering two lectures, both of which expounded, in different ways, his theory of permanent revolution. He then left for the Second International's Congress at Stuttgart – where Luxemburg once again supported his ideas of permanent revolution – whilst Sedova went back to Russia to collect Lyova.

Initially, Trotsky intended Berlin as their permanent exile home, as the German SPD was the biggest and most influential of the social democratic parties in Europe – and it was away from the main bickering factions, based mostly in Switzerland and Paris. But, because of the diplomatic closeness between Germany and Russia, the German police made things difficult for him. So, in October 1907, they moved to Vienna. Because of the tensions between the Habsburg Empire and Tsarist Russia, opponents of the Tsar were more welcome in Vienna than in Berlin. The city had the added attraction of allowing him to maintain close contacts with German political developments. Consequently, he often made trips to Berlin where, in the Rheingold Restaurant or various cafés, he participated in meetings of the left wing caucus of the German SPD.

For the next seven years, Vienna was Trotsky and Sedova's base. After living in various houses, they moved to a small house in Hütteldorf, then a working class suburb. It was there, in March 1908, that their second son, Sergei, was born. They were a close family: on Sundays, they often went for walks in the countryside around Vienna; and Trotsky frequently played football and handball with his sons. No one could remember Trotsky ever raising his voice to them; and, although both he and Sedova were atheists, they had a fir tree at Christmas, which Trotsky helped decorate. He also continued to share household tasks: 'Anxious to…enable her to pursue her artistic interests and to follow the political life of the Russian colony, he lent a hand in domestic chores and in the upbringing of the children.'[9]

They, and their children, soon became close friends with an old Russian émigré, Semyon Klyachko, and his family. The Klyachkos often helped them through the most financially difficult times – at times, Trotsky was forced to sell some of his books. Though, in fact, the Trotsky–Sedova family was better off than many exiles, because of Trotsky's earnings from journalism, which allowed him to devote his time to writing, and travelling to conferences. Although they always lived modestly, he still took care over his appearance.

One regular, and well-paid, commission for Trotsky was as the Vienna correspondent of *Kievskaya Mysl* (*Kievan Thought*), a widely-read non-partisan liberal newspaper. However, Trotsky's articles – under his old pen name, 'Antid Oto' – soon turned it into a popular radical paper, with a distinct Marxist leaning. He was also a frequent contributor to various Russian, German and Belgian papers – including *Odesskie Novosti (Odessa News)*, writing both on politics and cultural matters. In addition, he occasionally received money from his parents, who visited his new family on several occasions. They had previously met up in Paris and Berlin and, in 1907 (and again in 1910), they brought Zina, his oldest daughter, whom he had not seen since 1906, to visit in Vienna. Sokolovskaya also visited Vienna on one occasion, with their younger daughter.

He loved Vienna's intellectual and artistic life, and Sedova continued his artistic education. Trotsky now eagerly accompanied her to Vienna's main art galleries, and on visits to the Vienna Opera. Saturday evenings were frequently spent in the now-famous Café Central, where he met not just leading political radicals, but also artists and intellectuals. All this provided copy for his journalism – and reinforced his view that Russia needed to be 'Europeanised' as regards culture.

The Vienna *Pravda*

In October 1908, Trotsky began editing a new socialist paper, *Pravda* (*The Truth*) – originally an obscure paper set up by a small Ukrainian Menshevik group, who hoped Trotsky's writing abilities would enlarge its readership. By the end of the year, after the first few editions, the Menshevik group wound itself up, leaving Trotsky as main editor. Amongst those also providing copy were two who became and remained close friends: David Ryazanov who, like Trotsky, stood outside both factions; and Adolphe Joffe, who introduced Trotsky to Alfred Adler, under whom he was studying psychiatry. Joffe soon became his main contributor – for both articles and money. Later, on a trip to Russia to organise distribution of *Pravda*, Joffe was arrested in Odessa and exiled to Siberia, where he remained until released under an amnesty following the March Revolution in 1917. Another important contributor was Moisei Uritsky, a former Menshevik, who would – like Joffe – play a big part in the November Revolution in 1917[10]

Lack of money meant editions initially appeared irregularly, so Trotsky appealed to various individuals and groups for funds. Eventually, he set up a system for smuggling it into Russia. Most of his journalistic fees and book royalties went to finance this paper – and he and Sedova often went temporarily into debt to keep it going, until he got occasional grants from the German SPD and other socialist groups, and from individuals such as Gorky. The paper generally evoked a positive response from party militants in Russia and abroad – including from Sokolovskaya, who sent a letter saying how popular it was in Odessa, signing herself 'Your Sasha'.[11]

Impressed by the popular appeal of Trotsky's *Pravda*, Lenin offered him a seat on the editorial board of the Bolsheviks' underground newspaper, *The Proletarian* in 1908 and, in 1909, suggested a merger. By then, the majority of party members and trade unionists in Russia were calling for unity – for a time, even the Bolsheviks in Petersburg reprinted Trotsky's *Pravda*. The Bolsheviks also sent money to help Trotsky out with financial problems, and were prepared to make a regular grant to *Pravda* – but only if Trotsky accepted a Bolshevik coeditor; Trotsky repeatedly refused.

Trotsky aimed his paper at rank and file members rather than the intellectual émigrés, and it increasingly became a vehicle for spreading his ideas on permanent revolution and, in particular, his call for party unity in readiness for the coming Russian revolution which he believed was bound to come. Although the latter call found considerable support amongst ordinary RSDWP members and supporters, his appeals had little impact on the upper layers of the main factions, both of whom disliked and distrusted his stance. However, convinced he was right, Trotsky typically persisted in making such calls. As well as agreeing with Lenin on the need to rebuild the party's clandestine organisation, he also urged the underground activists to 'infiltrate' every open institution, from the *Duma* to the legal trade unions, in order to spread the socialist message. Yet again, this position saw him opposed to both factions.[12]

Reaction and Unity

Trotsky did not succumb to pessimism over the repression in Russia, seeing it as merely an interlude between two revolutions.

While most RSDWP members believed that, under Tsarist repression, an economic upturn was impossible, Trotsky insisted one would come – and that this would strengthen the working class, spark a wave of strikes and thus lead to a revival of the revolutionary movement. As early as 17 December 1909, referring to the general strike of October 1905, he wrote this prophetic message: 'Even today, through the black clouds of the reaction which have surrounded us, we envisage the victorious reflection of the new October.' Initially, however, his optimism was attacked by both factions; and was even ridiculed by the liberal leader, Miliukov. Miliukov claimed Trotsky's ideas about permanent revolution and the dictatorship of the proletariat in Russia were 'purely childish', and that no one in the whole of Europe agreed with him. The Russian Revolution, which would prove him wrong and Trotsky right, was less than eight years away.[13]

The industrial boom Trotsky predicted came in 1910, as a result of increased foreign investment. As wages rose and unemployment fell, strikes began to break out once more – despite the Tsar's ongoing counter-revolution. By 1912, with the brutal suppression of the Lena gold mines strike, protests spread rapidly across Russia. For Trotsky, this evidence of increasing militancy simply made unity even more important. Convinced revolution would soon be back on the political agenda, Trotsky was thus pleased when, in January 1910, the leaders of the two main factions agreed at a Central Committee meeting in Paris to try to patch up their differences. This Paris meeting saw the moderates who wanted reconciliation and unity carry the day – even though leaders like Lenin and Martov wanted to bring things to a head. Both factions agreed to disband their separate organisations and to merge; to suspend their separate publications; and to place their funds into a common pool, to be supervised by three leading members of the German SPD. Both factions also agreed to expel their respective 'extremists': the Menshevik Liquidators and the Bolshevik Boycotters. Finally, they agreed to meet at a joint Sixth Party Conference, to be held within six months.

In recognition of Trotsky's efforts to achieve reunification, the Central Committee decided to support his *Pravda* in several ways, including financial. This deal included having his Bolshevik son-in-law, Kamenev – who supported reunification – on the editorial board as the CC representative. However – much to Trotsky's anger – this agreement broke down within weeks because the Mensheviks refused to disband their faction, or to expel their Liquidators, even though Lenin had already begun to expel the Bolshevik Boycotters. This was partly because the majority of Mensheviks were Liquidators.

Yet Trotsky's criticisms of these Menshevik refusals were mild; and, when Kamenev – who'd moved from Paris to Vienna, bringing Trotsky's younger sister Olga – urged him to take a firmer line in support of the recent votes in the Paris Conference, he refused, seeing it as the Bolsheviks trying to use his paper for factional purposes. Thus, in August 1910, Kamenev resigned from *Pravda* and the CC withdrew funding. As even his sympathetic biographer, Deutscher, points out, Trotsky's attitude at this point was contradictory – and was yet another example which led to him being seen as an anti-Bolshevik Menshevik:

> 'Since, from one angle, this difference could be seen as a conflict between the upholders of discipline and the defenders of the right of dissent, Trotsky took his stand against the

disciplinarians…He, the fighter for unity, connived in the name
of freedom of dissent at the new breach in the party brought
about by the Mensheviks.'[14]

Not surprisingly, the Bolsheviks thought him untrustworthy, whilst the
Mensheviks – although appreciating his skills in attacking the Bolsheviks –
were wary of his views which, in many respects, remained much closer
to the Bolsheviks. Trotsky made matters worse as regards the Bolsheviks
as, whilst attacking them in public via his articles in *Pravda* and other
publications, he made his criticisms of the Mensheviks mainly by private
discussions or letters. This period shows Trotsky's inability to work with
others, and to build up a large team of close supporters. The situation then
worsened as the Bolsheviks, in view of the Mensheviks' refusal to honour
the Paris agreements, began to act as if they were now in control of the party.
Trotsky attacked these moves in the German socialist press, making the
point that the movement in Russia – not the émigré leaders in Europe – were
the true representatives of the party and that the majority wanted unity.[15]

In October 1910, Trotsky went to the Congress of the Second
International in Copenhagen. On the way there, whilst changing trains, he
met up with Lenin, who was travelling from Paris. He angered Lenin when
he informed him about an article he'd written for the Congress – about to be
published in *Vorwaerts* – which attacked the Bolsheviks over the question
of 'expropriations' which, despite the decision of the 1907 Congress
of the RSDWP, hadn't completely stopped. Lenin asked him if he could
cancel publication, but Trotsky informed him it was too late – and anyway
defended it. With hindsight, Trotsky realised the article – based on the
mistaken belief that unity was still possible – was 'not right' as: '…in
reality the party was formed by a merciless war of the Bolsheviks against
the Mensheviks.' Trotsky also upset the Mensheviks at the Congress, via
an article in *Neue Zeit*, which attacked their increasingly reformist ideas.
The factional dispute then saw the Bolsheviks unsuccessfully demanding
the Second International take action against Trotsky for his articles in the
German socialist newspapers, in what Trotsky later described as his sharpest
conflict with Lenin – whose temper was not helped by a raging toothache!
Then each faction squabbled, unsuccessfully, for control of the funds being
held in trust.[16]

During 1911, the two factions held separate meetings – the Bolsheviks in
Paris, and the Mensheviks in Bern: both of them deciding to call the agreed
party conference under their own auspices. In September 1911, Trotsky
went to the Congress of the German SPD, to appeal – on behalf of the

Mensheviks – for release of the funds; even though most of that money had been gained via the Bolshevik bank raids that the Mensheviks opposed. He had also been invited by Liebknecht – who had given much help to Russian escapees – to speak about the political situation in Russia. However, when news of Stolypin's assassination broke (see p.68), the leaders of the SPD asked him not to speak, in case the authorities tried to claim they supported terrorism. Despite Liebknecht's objections, Trotsky agreed not to speak – at that time, he didn't think the SPD leaders were as reformist as the left of the SPD did: time would prove the latter right.

In January 1912, Trotsky's unity project entered its final phase when, at what was, officially, the Sixth All-Russian Conference of the RSDWP in Prague, Lenin proclaimed the Bolsheviks to be the true party. This annoyed a large section of the party and, in opposition to this, the Mensheviks and a few Bolshevik dissenters established an Organisation Committee. Once again, Trotsky attacked Lenin's actions in *Pravda* – his attacks were particularly bitter as the Bolsheviks had, with Lenin's approval, begun producing their own *Pravda* in Petersburg – established and edited by Stalin. The Liquidator Mensheviks also began publishing their own paper there – *Luch (The Torch)* – to which Trotsky contributed occasional articles. Yet Trotsky tried once more for unity in advance of the revolution which he felt was fast approaching. Actually, he was not alone in thinking unity was still possible: the previous year, Rosa Luxemburg had pointed out that socialists on the ground in Russia wanted unity. Trotsky thus pressured the Menshevik Organisation Committee to convene another unity conference in Vienna in August 1912, to which both factions would be invited.[17]

By then, the Bolsheviks were in control of the underground, whilst the Mensheviks were losing ground and were considerably divided.

Consequently, the Bolsheviks refused to attend, and so the bulk of the Mensheviks – and some dissident Bolshevik splinter groups which wanted unity – met in Vienna in what became known as the August Bloc. Trotsky castigated Lenin and the Bolsheviks for refusing to come – and his private correspondence shows he had genuinely wanted all the factions to reunite in one party.

Unlike him, both Lenin and Martov had realised for some time that there were no real grounds for unity. That Lenin was right was confirmed when the August Bloc – dominated by the Liquidators – then voted to alter the party's programme, before the 1912 October elections to the Fourth Duma, to make it more acceptable to liberals. Trotsky was appalled by this reformism – but failed to condemn it in public. He thus continued to be seen as aligned with the Mensheviks, which he later saw as an error 'because in all important matters I disagreed with the Mensheviks.' The private correspondence between leading Mensheviks confirm they were aware he disagreed with them on most issues and, because of his desire for unity, would never fully align with them against the Bolsheviks. One consequence was they increasingly delayed publication of his articles.[18]

Art Critic, War Correspondent

Angered by both factions, the 'theft' of what he saw as his paper, and bitterly disappointed by the failure of the August Bloc, Trotsky stopped publishing the Vienna *Pravda*. In early 1912, he experienced bouts of ill health and signs of stress. This coincided with the death of his mother which, despite their earlier strained relationship, shook him. Because he was an escaped convict, he'd been unable to return for her funeral. Then, beginning what he described as a 'waterfall of relatives', Yelizaveta arrived to stay for a fortnight, followed closely by his father, who brought Zina with him – now aged eleven, it was clear she adored her father.

Disillusioned by factional infighting, Trotsky retreated into literary criticism. Vienna, in the early twentieth century, was an ideal cultural centre, and Trotsky had already contributed many perceptive articles on literature, painting and poetry to *Kievan Thought*. He now focussed on writers such as Tolstoy and Dostoyevsky, the German playwright Wedekind, and sculptors such as Rodin and Meunier. He also praised the work of the Vienna Secessionist movement. His essays on art combined appreciations of the work of individuals, with suggestions for how art ought to develop, and were generally positive about the leading exponents of modern art. However, he also pointed out what he saw as a weakness in many: the failure to go beyond the subjectivity of individualism. For him, what was needed was art to be revolutionised in the way the growth of mass urban centres and industrialism were revolutionising everyday life. Ultimately, he believed art would only really reach new heights after revolution.

In September 1912, the editors of *Kievan Thought* asked him to be their war correspondent in the Balkans, where nationalist tensions were about to spill over into war between the southern Slavs and the Turkish empire. He left Vienna at the beginning of October and, shortly after arriving in Belgrade, the First Balkan War broke out. During his stay in Vienna, he'd already made contact with Balkan socialists, and had written several articles for *Kievan Thought* about instability in the Balkans. As early as 1908, fearing a great power clash in the Balkans, he had observed: '...

Immense and terrible events are taking shape, amid enormous tensions, in the heart of what is called civilized mankind...'[19]

In January 1909, he had prophetically described the area as 'the Pandora's box of Europe' – his solution was a Federal Balkan Republic. In July 1910, he'd gone to Sofia to address a convention of Balkan socialists, where he was greeted enthusiastically. Although having sympathy for the southern Slavs' resentment of Ottoman rule, he feared their grievances would be used by the great powers – in particular, Tsarist Russia – for their own ends, and that this could trigger a wider European war. In the following two years, he had made further visits to Belgrade and Sofia.

During the First Balkan War, he travelled to Serbia, Bulgaria and Romania. His regular reports and articles – which number over seventy, and some of which he wrote as 'L. Yanov' – from the belligerent countries were mainly long essays, with lots of background knowledge and local colour. He frequently interviewed government ministers, civilians, wounded soldiers, and prisoners. He also worked closely with war correspondents from other European papers. Despite military censorship, he was mostly able to say what he wanted. He revelled in gathering information on supply lines, military tactics and training; and criticised the corruption of political leaders, the appalling poverty both in towns and villages, the crude national chauvinism and the atrocities inflicted on Turkish soldiers and civilians by some of the Slavs. As a result, the Bulgarian government banned him from visiting the front. Nonetheless, he saw enough to be deeply shocked by the effects of war, and felt European 'civilisation' was just a thin veneer, easily ripped away to reveal that barbarism was not far below the surface: '... when it comes to deciding how to get several tribes to live together on Europe's abundant peninsular, we are powerless to find any other means than mass mutual destruction.'[20]

Trotsky saw it as his duty – in view of the escalating arms race – to make his readers aware of the brutal reality and waste of resources of modern war; and of the way in which the authorities and press worked to dupe and misinform the public, in order to sway the masses towards war fever. Most of his articles were 'classics of anti-war journalism', at times reminiscent of Tolstoy's 'masterpiece *War and Peace*'. He also noted how important it was for supply lines not to get over-stretched – and how armies having an ideal to fight for, and officers who maintained close contacts with rank and file soldiers, were strong motivational factors, able to overcome the horrors of modern combat. Those lessons later proved invaluable when, as Commissar for War and head of the Red Army in Russia's Civil War, he acted as the 'Sword of the Revolution.'[21]

This journalism was a relief from the factional struggles of the Russian émigré communities. When, in May 1913, the war ended, Trotsky returned to Vienna, where he wrote an article accurately forecasting how the great powers would, as a result of wider issues, line up in 1914 over tensions in the Balkans. However, in one very important respect, his political analysis was spectacularly wrong: he assumed the big socialist parties of France, Germany and Austria would be as one in opposing the barbarism threatened by nationalist chauvinism and, instead, would act together to defend peace and civilisation. In part, this can be explained by his close contacts with so many of these socialist leaders during his 'Vienna Years'.

Once back in Vienna, he soon became embroiled in factional politics – in particular, protesting strongly against the Mensheviks and the Liquidators for delighting in a final split from the Bolsheviks, and for wrecking the August Bloc on which he had set such high hopes for a final reunification. He also resigned from one Menshevik newspaper. However, he continued to express his anger via private letters: largely because, despite the deepening political differences, he still felt personal attachments to many Menshevik leaders – an attachment which he'd never had with Bolshevik leaders.

The First Balkan War had immediately been followed by new tensions between Serbia and Bulgaria. The outbreak of the Second Balkan War at the end of June 1913 meant he left Vienna with some relief to report on this latest conflict. This time, having strongly criticised Bulgaria in the first war, he turned his criticism against Serbia and Greece, because of their plunder and violence, and the way they turned so many civilians into refugees. He also wrote a perceptive study of Romania and its continuing feudal system. His trips to Romania also, unusually for him, triggered homesickness for his family home in Ukraine – Romania's regions close to the Black Sea reminded him of home: 'The road is just...as dusty as our Kherson road... There is a smell of grass and the dust of the road... and it feels as though we're off on our holidays...to Yanovka.'[22]

During his visits to Romania, he made the acquaintance of Christian Rakovksy – a socialist doctor and the new leader of the Romanian Socialist Party – who would play an important role in the Russian Revolution, and who remained one of Trotsky's few close friends for many years. Six years older than Trotsky, he too was cosmopolitan in outlook, speaking several European languages. He was also anti-militarist and, like Trotsky, supported a Balkan federation. When the Second Balkan War ended in August 1913, Trotsky returned to Vienna, where he continued his efforts to get the two factions of the RSDWP to unify. However, in December 1913, even Sedova said she thought he was now wasting his time in working for unity: a trip she'd recently made to Petersburg had convinced her that the emergence of two separate parties was now inevitable.

'Old Mole' Resurfaces

At the end of September 1911, Stolypin – the instigator of the harsh repression that had followed the 1905 Revolution – had been assassinated by an SR member. This had sparked a new wave of strikes and, from early 1912, opposition had spread across Russia. It was clear the years of inaction, in face of repression, were over. Trotsky saw this as an emerging pre-revolutionary situation, which he felt justified his optimism and work throughout the period of Tsarist counter-revolution from 1907–13. He later assessed his work thus: 'During the years of reaction my work consisted chiefly of interpreting the revolution of 1905, and of paving the way for the next revolution by theoretical research.'[23]

By 1913, the signs of that 'next revolution' were clearly visible. To Trotsky, this situation was similar to Marx's description of France after years of repression following the 1848 Revolution, when he had referred to revolution as 'our old friend...old mole, who knows so well how to work underground, suddenly to appear.' Once again, Trotsky made attempts at unity. In early 1914, he launched a new workers' journal, *Bor'ba* (*The Struggle)*, in Petersburg. Though he managed to get the necessary money together, he found it difficult to establish a broad editorial team, as both factions refused to cooperate with him. However, one group within Russia which did support him over unity, was the *Mezhraionka* (Inter-District Organisation – IDO) in Petersburg. The IDO had been formed in November 1913 – partly in response to Trotsky's *Pravda* articles – containing both Bolshevik and Menshevik supporters, with a small base in a few working class districts.[24]

Though the IDO leaders supported Trotsky's new publication, many of its rank and file members were less enthusiastic. Nonetheless, Trotsky got several IDO members, and other very gifted Marxist writers, to contribute articles: including Anatoly Lunacharsky and Karl Radek. Despite police repression, Trotsky managed to get it distributed across Russia, and the journal was only stopped by the outbreak of the First World War. However, it too failed to achieve the reunification he'd worked so hard for. Trotsky's final attempt at getting unity was made in the summer of 1914. Along with

Plekhanov and Martov, he went to Brussels to ask the Second International's International Socialist Bureau to intervene and bring about reunification. Though this, too, was unsuccessful, Trotsky's call for legal activists and underground groups to come together in a reunited party met with some significant rank and file support, and helped the recovery of the labour movement in Russia.

However, while most historians see his attempts at unity as doomed to failure, Swain says unity could have been achieved, had the Second International intervened. Yet Trotsky later commented on his seven-year campaign to achieve party unity as being mistaken: 'I was still hoping that the new revolution would force the Mensheviks – as had that of 1905 – to follow a revolutionary path…This was a mistaken stand…'[25]

In the end, it was the First World War which gave 'Old Mole' another opportunity to break through the surface and erupt, in 1917, into revolution. Like that of 1905, it would sweep Trotsky once more onto history's world stage. In the meantime, he was to play an important political role in organising opposition to the horrors of war – and in preparing for revolution.

Chapter 5

War and Internationalism, 1914–17

'…in the moods of the Viennese crowd…I detected something familiar to me from the October days of 1905…No wonder that in history war has so often been the mother of revolution.'[1]

Trotsky was in Vienna when the First World War began: although the outbreak of war took him somewhat by surprise, he detected a certain revolutionary potential in the mood of the crowds celebrating the start of the conflict. The war brought an abrupt and savage end to the 'golden age' of European liberal capitalism, as well as shattering the reformist socialism that had grown up during the past fifty years. The following three years also triggered an important turning point in Trotsky's political life – ending, initially, with him and his family being expelled from war-torn Europe, and ending up in the USA.

Although the differences between himself and the two factions – and, in particular, between himself and Lenin – continued to spark political conflicts, the seeds were sown that would eventually heal many of those differences.

From Vienna to Zurich

In Vienna, Trotsky witnessed, with growing horror and sadness, crowds of civilians carried away on a tide of war chauvinism and hysteria. The patriotic passions aroused even impacted his younger son, six-year-old Sergei, who arrived home with two black eyes for having shouted 'Long live the Serbs!' in opposition to cries of 'Death to the Serbs!' This was a dangerous time to be, as Trotsky was, an outspoken opponent of the war.

Early on 3 August, Trotsky went to the editorial offices of the Austrian SPD's daily newspaper, where he met Victor Adler, who was distraught that so many of his party's members were supporting the war. Adler feared 'Trotsky's personal security was under threat', believing there was a genuine risk that, as Russians, the Trotskys 'would suffer at the hands of a vengeful mob'.[2]

Together, they visited the chief of the political police, to enquire what was planned for Russian émigrés now war between Austro-Hungary and Russia was about to be declared. Trotsky was told they would be interned, so he said they would leave for Switzerland the next day. He was advised to leave immediately. Within hours, Trotsky and his family – always prepared, as revolutionaries, for quick getaways – were on a train bound for neutral Switzerland. Arriving in Zurich, they settled in a *pension*, and soon met up with Radek and Nikolai Bukharin, and other Russian revolutionaries. By then, Lenin was in an Austrian prison, having been interned before he could leave the country – but he, too, soon arrived in Zurich.

Almost immediately, Trotsky addressed meetings at which he denounced the war – and those socialists who supported it. His speeches met with considerable approval: ' [Trotsky] brought with him the belief…that from the war would arise revolution…With Trotsky these were not merely words but his innermost conviction.' As a result, he was very quickly elected – by rank and file members of the Swiss Socialist Party – as a delegate to their national convention. Though the leaders denied him any voting rights, he spoke passionately about how the only solution to the barbarism of global capitalism and imperialism was social revolution, saying he was certain the war enhanced revolutionary prospects.[3]

Trotsky and the Second International

In 1914, the Second International was still, in theory, based on a political programme of irreconcilable class struggle, socialist revolution, anti-militarism and the international solidarity of the world's working classes. However, during the decades after its foundation in 1889, this ideology had been increasingly undermined, in practice, by moves towards parliamentary reformism and the belief that socialism could replace capitalism by entirely peaceful means.

This was most marked in the German, Austrian and French socialist and social democratic parties, which were the largest in Europe. Increasingly, these parties began to abandon internationalism and, instead, adapted themselves to the 'national interests' of their respective countries. Until 1914, however, these parties had continued to profess adherence to Marxism, anti-militarism and internationalism.

Yet, on the very first day of the war, all these ideals were shattered when almost all the parties of the Second International voted the war taxes demanded by their respective governments. Even more of a betrayal for those socialists who, like Trotsky, remained passionate internationalists, was that so many socialists were urging their respective working classes to join up and fight the workers of other countries. Unsurprisingly, the Congress of the Second International – planned for 15 August to celebrate its twenty-fifth anniversary – was cancelled.

Whilst in Zurich, Trotsky wrote *The War and the International*: this pamphlet turned out to be the first major statement of an anti-war policy by any member of the RSDWP. In particular, it attacked the German SPD for arguing that, because Tsarist Russia was so undemocratic, the German war effort against Russia was therefore 'progressive' and so should be supported. As the German SPD was seen by Trotsky – like many of the RSDWP – as the most important member of the Second International, he was bitter about this betrayal of internationalism. Nonetheless, he took comfort from the fact that, within the German SPD, the left – led by Liebknecht and Luxemburg – had almost defeated the call to support the war, and he was convinced they would soon rally anti-war opposition behind them.

Instead of supporting the war, Trotsky argued socialists should demand a peace that was not about restoring the status quo – or even a new balance of power – but was democratic, with no annexations or indemnities, and which would give the right of self-determination to all nations subject to the rule of imperial powers. To get such a peace, he called for an uprising of all the people in the belligerent countries. Despite the betrayal by so many of the leaders and parties of the Second International, Trotsky remained passionately optimistic that a new revolution was on the horizon.[4]

However, instead of new nation states, Trotsky hoped federations would be formed: as well as the Balkan Federation he had already advocated, he also urged the creation of a republican and socialist United States of Europe. That particular aspect was criticised by both Radek and Lenin: Radek thought it too premature, while Lenin saw it as part of Trotsky's theory of permanent revolution in seeming to suggest the Russian Revolution would only be part of a Europe-wide insurrection.

In November, Trotsky's pamphlet was brought out in a German translation and, with the help of Swiss socialists, was smuggled across the border, where it was distributed by German anti-militarists. Many of these activists were arrested and prosecuted; Trotsky was convicted *in absentia* and sentenced to several months in prison. The German SPD accused him of writing the pamphlet in the interests of Tsarist Russia, while his criticisms of all non-German socialists who supported the war led the latter to claim he was whitewashing the Germans.

When *Kievan Thought* asked him to be their war correspondent in France, Trotsky eagerly accepted and, on 19 November, after only two months in Zurich, he left Switzerland. Sedova remained behind to make arrangements for the family's move to Paris.

Paris Again

As well as being keen to observe the war from France, Trotsky also wanted to meet up with Martov who was in Paris, editing *Golos* (*The Voice*), an anti-war paper. Trotsky still saw Martov as an important émigré leader, though also aware of what he saw as his big weakness: 'The man's... first reaction to events was nearly always revolutionary, but before he could put his ideas on paper his mind would be besieged by doubts from all sides.'[5]

Since July, when they had last met, the outbreak of war had led to significant changes in the political positions of the main leaders of the two factions. Martov was increasingly distancing himself from the bulk of the Mensheviks – dominated by the Liquidators – who opposed the Tsar but supported his war. By the end of 1914, Trotsky, Martov and Lenin were all branding the leaders of the Second International – including Plekhanov – as 'social-chauvinists and traitors'.

Both Trotsky and Lenin were keen to renew the close relationships they'd had with Martov before the RSDWP had split into two factions. This desire for unity was shown by what Lenin wrote at the end of 1914: 'The more often and the more strongly I dissented from Martov, the more categorically must I say that he is now doing exactly what a social democrat ought to do.' Martov, too was keen to build bridges: as a result, he publicly welcomed Lenin's *Social Democrat*, and stated that the old controversies had been made insignificant by the war.[6]

These developments naturally pleased Trotsky, who had worked so hard for restoring party unity. Meanwhile, he divided his time between working with Martov on *The Voice*, and writing reports and reviews for *Kievan Thought*. He worked so hard during this period, that he became ill with a fever that baffled the doctors. Nonetheless, he stuck to his hectic work routine, also sending articles to *Novy Mir* (*Our World*), a socialist Russian émigré paper in New York. In addition, he made contact with anti-militarist groups in the French Socialist Party and trade unions. One of these new contacts was Alfred Rosmer who soon became Trotsky's friend.

Trotsky wrote articles for *The Voice*, arguing there were now only two alternatives: either capitalist barbarism and 'permanent war', or 'proletarian revolution'. He also bitterly attacked the betrayal by socialist reformists who'd become part of the system. As early as 1915, he suggested the Second International was possibly beyond reform, and might need to be replaced by a new 'Third International'. This call seems to have been inspired by Lenin, who'd only very recently made a similar call. Once again, this convinced Trotsky unity was still possible.[7]

However, Martov – and the other émigré Mensheviks who were opposed to the war – were reluctant to dismiss the Second International. Instead, they argued that, despite the huge mistake made by those socialist parties, the creation of a new International would simply split the working class movement. In addition, a significant proportion of Mensheviks – unlike either Trotsky or Lenin – were opposed to the war from a pacifist rather than a revolutionary position. Martov found himself torn between such views, and those propounded – separately – by Trotsky and Lenin.

Increasingly, the old divisions re-emerged, with Lenin arguing only his party had remained true to internationalism. Whilst he recognised Martov and Axelrod as true internationalists, he pointed out that the bulk of the Mensheviks had abandoned that fundamental principle. Given Trotsky's developing views, Martov had an increasingly difficult time preventing him from making the logical conclusion and joining the Bolsheviks. Although Trotsky was not yet ready for that step, he was certainly keen to openly distance himself from the August Bloc and its Organising Committee.

The French censors increasingly restricted what could be printed, with the result that, in mid-January 1915, *The Voice* ceased publication. In its place, came *Nashe Slovo* (*Our Word*); by late January 1915, Trotsky had become coeditor, and the most influential contributor. Censorship – and lack of money – made regular publication difficult. But its editors, writers, and even compositors and printers, were prepared to work for it even when wages were late and bills not paid. Collections often had to be made to keep it going. Later in the year, Sergei found a twenty-franc note on a pavement, and donated it to the paper.

Nonetheless, two hundred and thirteen editions were printed, with Trotsky frequently writing 'until three in the morning' and, later, delivering 'his manuscript to the printers when he took Sergei to school'. Despite censorship, Trotsky was often able to get much of what he wanted to say published – even if, at times, it had to be wrapped up in a way that satisfied the censors.[8]

Trotsky once again attracted an outstanding circle of contributors – making this new venture even more impressive than his Vienna *Pravda*. The glittering array of writers included the Menshevik, Vladimir

Antonov-Ovseenko, who became a firm friend, would play a leading role in the November Revolution, and also be part of the Trotskyist Opposition in the early 1920s. It was Antonov-Ovseenko in particular who did most in securing the existence of *Our Word*. Others involved were Anatoly Lunacharsky, Grigori Sokolnikov, Georgy Chicherin, David Ryazanov, Angelica Balabanova, Alexandra Kollontai, Moisei Uritsky, Radek and Rakovsky.

They – and other Russian internationalists – often met for discussions with French anti-war socialist internationalists in the *Librarie du Travail*, a revolutionary syndicalist bookshop on the Quai de Jemmapes. One increasingly frequent topic was the urgent need for an international alliance of anti-war socialist groups, given that the bulk of the Second International had abandoned internationalism.[9]

The contributors of *Our Word* were united in their opposition to 'social chauvinism' – but, otherwise, coming from different political homes, had varying shades of opinion. This made editorial meetings very lively. Antonov-Ovseenko then invited Martov to be joint editor with Trotsky; initially, Trotsky refused, suspecting this would mean only Menshevik views would be advocated. In the end, however, he agreed and – despite constant battles with Martov – was soon able to push his own views to the fore. One important area of dispute was where, exactly, the dividing line between social-patriots and internationalists should be drawn.

Every day, Trotsky met with the paper's other writers in the Café de La Rotonde, in the Montparnasse Quarter. There, over bad wartime coffee, they read the main newspapers and discussed developments. On 14 February 1915, Trotsky published – for the first time – the many disagreements he'd had in recent years with the Mensheviks. He also stated he would not be representing them at a forthcoming conference of allied socialists, due to be held in London. This was an important step in burning his bridges with them, and making possible his joining the Bolsheviks.[10]

Given his personal liking of Martov and other Mensheviks, this was a difficult time for Trotsky. Feelings of sadness at breaking such ties were made worse when his friend, Parvus, decided to support the position of the German SPD on the war, and became a war-profiteer in the Balkans. So saddened was Trotsky by Parvus's actions that he wrote *An Obituary on a Living Friend* which referred to Parvus as 'a political Falstaff' who was now slandering his former self. Although the article referred, generously, to his earlier greatness, it marked the end of their friendship.

Trotsky was thus especially relieved when, in May 1915, Sedova and their sons finally arrived in the city where, twelve years before, she and

Trotsky had first met. They settled, first in Sèvres, in a villa lent to them by a friend. At the end of the summer, they moved to rue Oudry, near the Place d'Italie, a more densely-populated area.

Next to Lenin's *Social Democrat* – the official RSDWP journal – Trotsky's paper was the most important as regards developing revolutionary ideas. Gradually, it became clear that those involved with *Our Word* were dividing into three distinct groups: Martov, who tried to reconcile his internationalism with the Menshevik social-patriots; the former Bolsheviks who were now moving back to Lenin; and Trotsky, who – as ever – occupied an intermediate position, and tried to check the impulses of the other two groups.

Increasingly, though, as Martov argued that the Menshevik social-patriots shouldn't be condemned as traitors to socialism, Trotsky – still reluctant to split from his old friend – nonetheless moved ever-closer to Lenin and the Bolsheviks. In July 1915, he argued that the Bolsheviks now formed the core of the internationalist part of the RSDWP. He remained, however, concerned about the Bolsheviks dominating the non-Bolshevik internationalists; thus, when invited to join the editorial board of *Communist* (*Kommunist*), a new Bolshevik journal being planned, he refused. At the same time, Martov attacked his latest article and threatened to resign; while Lenin attacked him for still cooperating with Menshevik social-patriots and advocating 'the struggle for peace', which he saw as a 'deliberately vague slogan'.[11]

Trotsky and the Zimmerwald Movement

While these disputes continued, from 5–8 September 1915, an international conference of socialists – the first since the war had begun – took place in Zimmerwald, a small village in the Swiss mountains near Berne. This was on the initiative of the Italian socialists, after they'd tried to get the Second International to call such a conference – at least of socialist parties in neutral countries. Their request had been turned down – so they approached Trotsky and Martov, asking them to convene a conference independently of the International.

On 5 September, thirty-eight delegates, from eleven countries – belligerent and neutral – met together. Others had been prevented by their countries from attending; and those who managed to get there, couldn't assume they'd be allowed back. Furthermore, some – like Liebknecht and Luxemburg – were already in prison because of their opposition to the war. Nonetheless, Germany, France, and Italy were represented, along with delegates form the Balkans, Poland and the Netherlands. Lenin represented the Bolsheviks, while Axelrod was there for the Mensheviks. Trotsky was there for *Our Word* – although Lenin had unsuccessfully tried to get him denied voting rights. As it was a crime for citizens of belligerent countries to have contact with each other, this meeting was a symbolic act, showing 'the solidarity of their hatred for the war'; while: '…the mere fact that well-known labour leaders "shook hands across the barbed wire and bleeding trenches" was an unheard-of challenge to all warring governments.'[12]

However, there were profound differences – especially as most were pacifists, and thus not prepared to support revolutionary opposition to the war. Lenin, with the support of Radek and a small section of the delegates, advocated 'revolutionary defeatism' – calling on workers to agitate for the defeat of their respective nations, and to turn the imperialist war into a class-based civil war. He also called for the creation of a new International. Trotsky, who agreed with most of Lenin's stances, opposed the idea of 'revolutionary defeatism' – even though this, because of its international aspects, was close to Trotsky's idea of permanent revolution. He did so because he wanted an anti-war alliance that was as broad as possible.

Instead, Trotsky called for a position supporting the end of the war without 'victors or vanquished', in order to get a commonly agreed outright condemnation of the war. The Conference unanimously agreed on the idea of a joint statement of principles – and asked Trotsky to draft it. He was assisted by Henrietta Roland-Holst, a Dutch radical socialist. A sign of a new political realignment was that Lenin, Radek and Zinoviev – despite their differences with Trotsky – cooperated with him to help sharpen some of the final draft's aspects. The statement which eventually emerged became known as the *Zimmerwald Manifesto*.

In it, Trotsky condemned capitalism and its governments for causing the war, and those socialist parties that had succumbed to social-patriotism. It also called on the workers to put an end to the slaughter: 'Now the task is to enter the lists for your own cause, for the sacred aims of Socialism…by means of the irreconcilable working-class struggle…

"Workers of all countries unite!"'

However, it didn't call for civil war or a new International, as Trotsky wanted to appeal to people who were against the war, but not necessarily Marxists. For this reason, although the statement was adopted unanimously, Lenin and his group placed on record their reservations, and were soon known as the Zimmerwald Left. [13]

Nonetheless, Trotsky's efforts enhanced his political reputation on the far left – though few had 'warmed to him on the personal level'. The

Conference ended by electing an International Socialist Committee – though neither Trotsky nor any other member of the RSDWP was elected to it. This committee was not in theory opposed to the Second International; however, the nucleus of the Third International would later emerge from it.[14]

Back in France

In order not to alert the combatant governments, the Conference placed an embargo on reporting its decisions until all delegates had managed to return to their respective countries. Trotsky himself almost failed to get back to France as, on the frontier, his baggage – containing all the Zimmerwald documents – was searched by an inspector. However, because the top paper had the inscription 'Vive le Tsar!' on it – which Trotsky had doodled during some of the debates – the inspector didn't bother to look any further.

Not surprisingly, the censors tried to suppress all reports of the Zimmerwald Conference. Nonetheless, Trotsky managed a brief reference to it in *Our Word*, asking why – if it was, as officially described, of no significance – all references to it had to be banned. That edition had more white gaps than it had words! More importantly, as news about the Conference, and details of the *Zimmerwald Manifesto*, spread, anti-war movements in Germany and France gained impetus. As well as continuing to work on his paper, Trotsky also began attending, on a more regular basis – despite close police monitoring – the meetings of Alfred Rosmer and his anti-militarist group of mainly anarcho-syndicalists. In particular, he persuaded them to join the Zimmerwald movement – those in the group would later form the French Communist Party.

Trotsky also continued with his articles for *Kievan Thought* – which was about his only source of income. This presented increasing difficulties for him, as the paper was pro-war – thus forcing him only to comment on those parts of the war and associated political developments that didn't clash too obviously with official Russian policy. His war reporting was more straightforward: his visits to the Channel ports, discussions with wounded soldiers in hospitals or cafés, and interviews with wartime refugees and widows, enabled him to comment on the various moods behind the front lines.

In particular, as with the Balkan Wars, he noted with interest the importance of maintaining the morale of combatants and non-combatants alike. His reports were replete with comments showing a real human empathy for those fighting in the trenches, and an accurate understanding of the psychological damage such conditions would do to people. According to Deutscher, Trotsky's military writings would, under normal circumstances, have given him recognition as a gifted and perceptive writer on military matters. However, the controversy surrounding his political writing and actions meant these writings were largely ignored.

Against all expert opinion, he predicted the war – because of the economic parity of the warring coalitions – would quickly result in prolonged stalemate; and he also attacked the French concept of a war of attrition. He was thus able, from 1914–17, to accurately forecast the course of the main military campaigns. In his reports, he speculated that a technological breakthrough might eventually break the stalemate – and even came close to suggesting the concept of the tank. More importantly, he saw that years of stalemate in the trenches would weaken the old order and pave the way for revolution across Europe.

Losing Friends

By the end of 1915, differences in the Zimmerwald movement – between the Bolsheviks on the one hand and, on the other, the socialist pacifists and those who, like Trotsky, held a middle position – had deepened. Increasingly, governments either arrested the leaders and supporters of Zimmerwald, or sent them to the trenches. In Russia, all the Bolshevik deputies in the Duma had already been sent to Siberia. Chkheidze, the Menshevik leader in the Duma, only half-heartedly supported the *Zimmerwald Manifesto*. Lenin thus denounced him, demanding all Russian members of Zimmerwald should do the same.

The bitterness was increased when both Zasulich and Potresov – like Plekhanov – decided to support the war. This was particularly upsetting for Trotsky as both were his friends, and it was to a large extent because of them that, as a young revolutionary in 1903, he'd sided with these RSDWP veterans against Lenin in the original split. Although he had political differences with them, he had maintained friendly feelings for them. He had also had a reasonable relationship with Chkheidze. This prompted him to begin wondering whether Lenin had been right from the start about the political weaknesses of the RSDWP 'old guard'.

Meanwhile, the pages of *Our Word* showed that the pro-Bolsheviks on the paper's staff were nudging Trotsky towards the realisation that, because of the emerging realignments within Zimmerwald, he needed to change his old loyalties. Yet, as Deutscher notes, Trotsky didn't acknowledge their influence in his autobiography, stating instead that he was moving towards Lenin and Bolshevism as a result of his own political development. While these Bolsheviks were critical of aspects of Lenin's 'national narrow-mindedness', they nonetheless made the point that the Bolsheviks had become the core of the revolutionary movement in Russia. Trotsky was also encouraged by the fact that the IDO – which supported his call for unity and was staunchly anti-war – was becoming increasingly dominant amongst the underground movement in Petrograd (as Petersburg had been renamed a month after the outbreak of the First World War), and was cooperating closely with the Bolsheviks.[15]

Although still hesitating to make a complete *rapprochement* with Lenin, Trotsky nonetheless began to argue for close cooperation with the Leninists, pointing out, on January 1916, that the Bolsheviks in Russia were 'the only active and consistently internationalist force'. His insistence this now become a principle of editorial policy, led to Martov's resignation from *Our Word*, thus ending another of Trotsky's early friendships. However, differences between Trotsky and Lenin emerged in the spring of 1916, when the Second International – alarmed by signs of growing support for the Zimmerwald Movement – called a conference of their International Bureau in The Hague. While Lenin argued for a boycott, Trotsky – whilst stating this might be the best policy – also argued that, for a time, it might be necessary to form a left opposition *within* the Second International.[16]

Towards the end of April 1916, the Zimmerwald Movement held their second conference in Kienthal. Trotsky was prevented from attending by the French authorities – and, this time, the delegates supported Lenin's harder line on relations with the Second International. However, Trotsky – in defiance of ever stricter censorship – then used the pages of *Our Word* to announce his complete support for the Zimmerwald Left's positions which had just been adopted by the Kienthal Conference. While not calling for a definitive break from the Second International, it condemned those leaders who'd betrayed anti-militarism and internationalism by supporting the war, and even joined their national governments to help the war effort.

However, there were still differences between Lenin and Trotsky – especially over Lenin's continued call for 'revolutionary defeatism', and Trotsky's call for a socialist 'United States of Europe'. While both agreed socialists should turn the war into a revolution, Trotsky argued that, instead of calling for defeats, revolutionaries should just focus on preparing the revolution, regardless of military situations. Concerning the idea of a United States of Europe, both had called for this in the recent past – but Lenin feared Trotsky's policy implied revolution in Russia would only come about if revolutions broke out across Europe at the same time. In fact, like Lenin, Trotsky had previously stated revolution could break out in Russia first – and that its example would then inspire revolutions in other European countries. In reality, those differences were mainly those of emphasis but, for the moment, they were enough to prevent complete unity.[17]

Leaving Europe

On 15 September 1916, these continuing political discussions in *Our Word* were brought to an abrupt end when the French police banned the paper. The following day, Trotsky was ordered to leave the country. Technically, there were no grounds for the expulsion, as the paper had only been able to print what the censor had allowed. However, it seems the French acted in response to mounting pressure from their ally, Tsarist Russia, whose government repeatedly asked for him to be extradited. An appropriate 'excuse' was provided by a mutiny which had broken out recently amongst Russian soldiers on the warship *Askold*, which had just docked at Marseille – a Russian secret police spy claimed several of the mutineers had had copies of *Our Word*.

Fearing the French would extradite him to Russia, Trotsky spent six weeks unsuccessfully trying to get permission to enter Switzerland, Italy or a Scandinavian country. On 30 October, having been told Italy would not issue a visa, and that Britain refused him passage, he was arrested and told he was being deported. Trotsky, without Sedova and their sons, travelled by train, in a third-class compartment, to Irún, across the border with Spain, with two police escorts. He could neither speak nor read Spanish, and had no friends there. He spent a day in San Sebastián, and then moved to Madrid, still hoping to get into Italy or Switzerland. Whilst in Madrid – where he found the pace of life 'lazy' – he watched various ceremonies, visited churches and museums, and, on 7 November, spent the day in the Prado. Exactly one year later, he would be leading the Russian Revolution. The fruits of Sedova's artistic education of Trotsky resulted in some very perceptive writings on aspects of Spanish art.

This cultural interlude was interrupted when, two days later, he was arrested, on a tip-off from the French police, as a 'dangerous anarchist'. Again, fearing deportation to Russia, he fired off telegrams and letters of protest – including to the Spanish Minister of Home Affairs. As a result, Spain's socialist and republican press called for his release. After three days in prison – where his fingerprints were forcibly taken – he was moved to

Cádiz. There, under very lax supervision, he was told to await the first ship that could take him away from Spain.

He remained there for six weeks, bombarding the Spanish government with protests, spending much time reading French and German books in the old local library, and trying to learn some Spanish. When a ship arrived, bound for Havana in Cuba, he refused to board it and, after yet more protests, was told he could await a ship bound for the USA – so he then began brushing up on his grasp of English. On 20 December, he was moved, under police escort, to Barcelona, where he was reunited with Sedova and their sons, who'd arrived from Paris, and had been enjoying the sea and fruit. On Christmas Day, they boarded the *Montserrat*, a ramshackle Spanish steamer; because all the second-class cabins were already occupied, they were upgraded to first-class, at no extra charge. On 31 December 1916, as the ship passed the towering cliffs of Gibraltar, the Trotskys stood at the rail, watching Europe slip away.

A Revolutionary in New York

On Sunday, 13 January 1917, after a seventeen-day voyage – often on rough seas – they arrived in New York on a cold and wet night. Once disembarked, the author of the *Zimmerwald Manifesto* was enthusiastically given a hero's welcome by Bukharin and other Russian émigré socialists. He was also surrounded by journalists who wanted to interview the revolutionary leader of the 1905 Petersburg Soviet. His friends then helped them settle into a cheap apartment (for $18 a month) in the Bronx, on 164th Street and Stebbins Avenue. For people who'd lived very modestly in Europe, they were delighted to have such luxuries as a telephone, electric lights, and a gas cooker. The furniture they needed was paid for on hire purchase.

While various writers later claimed Trotsky worked as a tailor, a dishwasher and even a film extra, in fact he quickly settled down to earning an income from his journalism once more. One paper which was keen for his articles was *Forverts* (*Forwards*), a Yiddish language daily publication, regularly selling 200,000 copies – this helped his fame spread. Though, later, as its editor adopted an increasingly interventionist and social-patriotic position about the war, Trotsky stopped submitting articles. In addition, after discussions with Bukharin and Kollontai, who by then were editing *New World,* he soon became one of its main contributors. This was Trotsky's first close collaboration with a Bolshevik-leaning group – helped by the fact that it was essentially a non-sectarian group. Consequently, although not identifying yet as a Bolshevik, he developed increasingly close ties with this group.

Almost immediately, Trotsky also began delivering lectures – in New York and other north-eastern cities – about international socialism and the coming revolution. Reports of his fiery oratory led to increasingly large audiences, even if the listeners didn't agree with what he had to say. Emma Goldman, a leading US anarchist writer and activist, described seeing Trotsky at one such meeting: 'After several dull speakers Trotsky was introduced...His speech, first in Russian and then in German, was powerful and electrifying.' These lectures, as well as making him well-known amongst Russian émigré circles, were also an additional and very welcome source of income.[18]

During what was to prove a brief stay – of only three months – he made contact with Ziv, who was now a Menshevik and successful doctor in New York. Although the latter supported the war, Trotsky – accompanied by his elder son – visited his apartment, and the two men played several games of chess. Trotsky also used his time in the US to accumulate statistical information about the USA's rapid economic growth, and speculated about whether the US would make a great contribution to socialism and Marxism in the near future. He also urged the American Socialist Party to avoid the mistake of European socialist parties of falling into social-patriotism or simple pacifism. In the main, he commented negatively on the leaders of the various socialist sects, condemning them – with the exception of Eugene Debs – for their narrow and timid outlooks.

When, in January 1917, Germany announced unrestricted submarine warfare, causing US interventionists to increase their calls for their government to declare war, he wrote *A Repetition of Things Past*, warning the American people not to repeat the recent mistakes of European governments. He also pointed out that, despite the use of slogans referring to 'freedom' and 'justice', what lay behind such calls was greed for new markets and profits. However, Europe remained his main focus whilst in the US. In particular, he expressed concern that the devastation of the First World War would destroy Europe and, if there were no successful revolutions, the result would be the global domination of the much wealthier USA. [19]

Trotsky and the others involved with *New World* were in the process of establishing a monthly English-language Marxist paper when the first confused reports began to arrive about unrest in Petrograd. Only a few months before, as the *Montserrat* had taken him and his family away from Europe, Trotsky had written to Rosmer: 'This is the last time that I cast a glance on that old canaille Europe.' For someone who often made accurate predictions, he couldn't have been more wrong.[20]

Chapter 6

Revolution and Civil War, 1917–19

'We are witnesses of the beginning of the second Russian revolution. Let us hope that many of us will be its participants.'[1]

Trotsky's hope – appearing in *Our World* on 13 March 1917, two days before the Tsar abdicated – was fully granted in the period 1917–19. In articles in *Our World* and other newspapers, Trotsky wrote: 'The powerful avalanche of the revolution is in full swing, and no human force will stem it.' This ever-changing revolutionary situation would give Trotsky his chance to move centre stage once more.[2]

Petrograd Beckons

When reports of 'disturbances' in Petrograd reached the US, Trotsky's son, Sergei, was ill with diphtheria. Nonetheless, he spoke at numerous meetings: 'At all those meetings, Trotsky's speech was the main event and the natural climax.' As soon as he learned the Tsar had abdicated, Trotsky excitedly telephoned Sedova, and they began preparations for their immediate return to Russia. He was quick to see that any Provisional Government would struggle to meet the mass popular demands for peace and land. While pleased the Petrograd Soviet had been revived, he was angry that the Mensheviks and SRs who dominated it – and even Bolsheviks like Kamenev and Stalin – broadly supported the unelected Provisional Government, despite its determination to keep Russia in the war. Even before he left the US, he urged the Soviet to seize power, take Russia out of the war and solve the issue of land redistribution. He also stressed how this Russian Revolution could inspire similar uprisings in the rest of Europe, which he was convinced was simmering with revolutionary discontent.[3]

On 27 March, a crowd of 300 supporters watched as Trotsky – carried on the shoulders of friends – boarded the *SS Kristianiafjord*, a Norwegian tanker bound for Russia. However, on 3 April, on reaching Halifax, Nova Scotia, Trotsky was arrested by police: refusing to cooperate, he was forcibly carried off to a prisoner-of-war camp. Ever the revolutionary, Trotsky – POW Number 1098 – used his command of German to inform the German POWs of the *Zimmerwald Manifesto*, Liebknecht's anti-war campaign in Germany, and the significance of the Russian revolution. His revolutionary influence on them worried the prison authorities – and the German officers – so he was banned from addressing further meetings. Finally, on 29 April, Trotsky was released; as he left, the German sailors sang the *Internationale*.

They continued their journey on the *Helig Olaf*, a Danish ship, to Finland. A delegation of internationalists – including the Inter-Districter, Uritsky – met him on the Russian frontier, where he boarded a train to Petrograd's Finland Station. Arriving on 17 May, he was greeted by a large crowd waving red banners, and carried shoulder-high from the station. Initially without funds, Trotsky had problems finding somewhere to live. Contact with Sokolovskaya and his daughters was speedily resumed: by then, Zina was sixteen, and Nina fifteen. As Trotsky and Sedova became increasingly involved in the political ferment of revolution, their sons (aged twelve and eleven) often spent time in Sokolovskaya's apartment, becoming particularly fond of Zina. Trotsky also quickly contacted his sister Olga, and Kamenev, his brother-in-law.[4]

Almost immediately, Trotsky went to the Smoly Institute, where the Petrograd Soviet was based. As he'd been its last Chair in 1905, the Bolsheviks moved he be elected to the Executive Committee. However, the Mensheviks and SRs were in the majority, and only admitted him in an advisory capacity. This was enough for Trotsky, who just wanted to speak from the main political platform of the revolution. By then, the March Revolution was ten weeks old, and the Mensheviks and SRs had made various compromises with the Provisional Government. Nonetheless, the revival of the Petrograd Soviet ushered in an eight-month period of 'Dual Power', as it became increasingly obvious this body was the *de facto* power.

The Soviet's very first act had been to pass its famous Order No. 1: establishing committees, elected by soldiers, in all army units; placing all weapons at the Soviet's disposal; and stating that military units would only obey those orders of the new government approved by the Soviet. As the moderate Mensheviks and SRs dominated the Soviet, it initially supported the Provisional Government. However, given its frequent elections, the composition of the Soviet often changed quickly, as revolutionary moods fluctuated.[5]

Shortly before Trotsky's return, the Mensheviks and SRs had agreed to enter a coalition with the liberal Kadets, with the SR Kerensky becoming Minister of War. When this was put to the Soviet for approval, on 18 May, there was a loud roar of approval as Trotsky – unusually nervous – rose to speak for the IDO (which had about 4,000 members by then), arguing against socialist parties forming a coalition with the liberals and, instead, urging the Soviet to rely on its own force. He was backed by the Bolsheviks and Menshevik Internationalists – but they were outvoted. Trotsky's speech was not well-received and, after the vote, 'he left the hall amid far less applause than had greeted his entrance.'[6]

Joining the Bolsheviks

Lenin, who'd been in Petrograd since April, had overcome Kamenev and the Bolshevik right wing, moving them much closer to Trotsky's political positions. Consequently, on 20 May, the IDO and the Bolsheviks held a joint meeting to welcome Trotsky's return. Meeting for the first time since the 1915 Zimmerwald Conference, Trotsky told Lenin he no longer favoured unity with the Mensheviks; while Lenin informed him that he now agreed with Trotsky that the outcome of this Russian revolution would be an immediate 'dictatorship' of the proletariat, and on the real likelihood of revolutions in Europe.

Both Trotsky and Lenin now saw grounds for close cooperation between their groups. In fact, as early as March, the Bolsheviks' CC had called for a merger with the IDO. Following the May meeting, the first tentative discussions began on merger. Lenin urged Trotsky and the IDO to join the Bolsheviks; but Trotsky argued that, as both he and the Bolsheviks had changed positions, the two groups should merge to form a new organisation: 'I cannot describe myself as a Bolshevik. It is undesirable to stick to old labels.' Earlier, Lenin himself had suggested that the RSDWP be renamed the Russian Communist Party (RCP).[7]

However, Lenin's proposal that Trotsky and the IDO have seats on the editorial board of the Bolshevik *Pravda* – and on the Bolshevik CC – was vetoed. While Lenin and Trotsky seemed prepared to forget past feuds, several 'Old Guard' Bolsheviks were not: Kamenev reproached Lenin for having abandoned Bolshevism for Trotskyism and permanent revolution. Over the following months, Trotsky's growing ascendancy continued to pique them – even as late as 17 August, they still refused him a position on the board.

When, later in May, the Mensheviks voted once again to support the Provisional Government, the merger talks resumed. Meanwhile, cooperation between the two groups increased and Trotsky quickly reestablished himself as a prominent revolutionary socialist, making numerous speeches at the Smolny Institute and, in particular, almost every night at public meetings in the Cirque Moderne. There he attracted increasingly large groups of enthusiastic workers and soldiers – his popularity often meant he could only leave 'by being bodily passed over the heads of the crowd'. This, and growing support for his ideas of revolution, led Uritsky to conclude: 'Here's a great revolutionary who's arrived and one gets the feeling that Lenin, however clever he may be, is starting to fade next to the genius of Trotsky.'[8]

Trotsky also spoke frequently at the Kronstadt naval base, where he became very popular – especially when, in early June, he defended them when the Provisional Government indicted them before the Soviet, for their rough refusal to accept commissars associated with Tsarism. In a speech foreshadowing events three months later, Trotsky said: '... should a counter-revolutionary general try to throw a noose around the neck of the revolution... the Kronstadt sailors will come and fight and die with us.'[9]

Trotsky also wrote many articles on the unfolding revolutionary situation. Many of these were published in *Forward (Vperëd)*, the IDO's weekly journal, where he joined Joffe and Lunacharsky on the editorial board. In them, he attacked the Provisional Government for continuing the war, and refusing to end the poverty of workers or address the peasants' desire for land. Ultimately, he argued that, because the parties of the Provisional Government were committed to preserving capitalism, it was a betrayal of the Revolution for socialists to be in coalition with them.

From 16 June to 7 July, the First All-Russian Congress of Workers', Soldiers' and Peasants' Soviets met in Petrograd, and elected a Central Executive Committee (CEC), which would continue to sit between Congresses. During it, relations between the Bolsheviks and IDO became even closer. In particular, Trotsky wrote a statement – which the Bolshevik delegates read out – against the new military offensive being planned by Kerensky. When Trotsky spoke, he took the same line as Lenin. He also insisted that the Soviets – which, in the continuing absence of elections for a Constituent Assembly, represented the bulk of working people – should now assume power and help spread revolution across Europe.

To get a majority for this in the Soviets, Trotsky and other IDO leaders – such as Lunacharsky – tried to expand their base. At the time, Martov and the left wing Mensheviks were working with Gorky on *New Life*, which also criticised the Soviet's decision to support a coalition government. However, these talks failed as the Menshevik Internationalists proved unwilling to support the Soviets taking power or to break with those Mensheviks who continued to support the Provisional Government's war policy.

On 21 June, the Bolsheviks and the IDO announced plans in *Pravda* for a mass demonstration on 23 June – around the slogan 'Down with the ten capitalist ministers!' – to urge the Mensheviks and SRs to form a government on their own. The CEC banned it, and it was cancelled, with the Bolsheviks reading out a statement – again written by Trotsky – explaining their decision to call it off. The CEC then authorised one for 1 July, to show support for the coalition and its new offensive. However, this backfired, as the 500,000-strong demonstration was dominated by Bolshevik and IDO banners and slogans – indicating how the political mood was changing.

On 15 July, at a special conference, Trotsky and Lunacharsky persuaded the IDO to vote in favour of joining the Bolsheviks, with Trotsky then publishing this statement in *Pravda*: 'There are in my opinion at the present time no differences either in principle or tactics between the inter-district and the Bolshevik organisations. Accordingly there are no motives which justify the separate existence of these organisations.' However, before it was finalised, the events known as the 'July Days' intervened. After signs that Kerensky's Offensive was failing, the coalition government fell apart. With no stable government, Trotsky and the Bolsheviks decided to call a demonstration for a purely socialist government – under the slogan 'All Power to the Soviets!' But on 16 July, the CEC – still dominated by the Mensheviks and SRs – tried to win support for another coalition government, ruling that any decision would be binding on all Soviet delegates. Trotsky and his supporters thus walked out in protest. Various left wing and anarchist groups – even more radical than the Bolsheviks – decided to organise their own protest demonstration, demanding the overthrow of the Provisional Government.[10]

This was backed by Petrograd's First Machine Gun Regiment, which – along with 20,000 armed Kronstadt sailors – turned up at Bolshevik HQ, demanding the Bolsheviks seize power. The Bolsheviks hesitated, so the angry protesters marched to the Tauride Palace, where the CEC had its offices. At one point, some of the crowd grabbed Victor Chernov – a former SR Minister – and were about to lynch him. Trotsky, the first to react, rushed to save him, managing to persuade them to release him, and escorting the half-fainting Chernov back to the Soviet. Trotsky's own face was 'of a deadly pallor and covered with cold perspiration.'[11]

Early on 17 July, the IDO and Bolsheviks agreed, rather than not join the demonstrators, they should assume leadership, to stop it trying to overthrow the government. Trotsky then telephoned the Kronstadt sailors, asking them to march without weapons. Over the next few days, large demonstrations of workers, soldiers and sailors adopted the Bolshevik slogan, calling on moderate socialists to form a government on their own. During these stormy days there were several clashes, but Bolshevik and IDO speakers managed to restrain the protesters. Even Trotsky's daughters were involved: 'My daughters were being drawn more actively into political life. They attended the meetings in the Modern Circus and took part in demonstrations. During the July Days they were both shaken up in a mob, one of them lost her glasses, both lost their hats…'[12]

The protesters were about to disperse when, on 18 July, troops loyal to Kerensky arrived from the front – just as news broke of the failure of the offensive. These – and right wing supporters of the Tsar – then began to fire on the crowds. The Bolsheviks were accused of instigating the violence, and Kerensky produced fake documents that claimed the Bolsheviks were German spies. Arrest warrants were then issued for leading Bolsheviks – including Lenin, Zinoviev, Kamenev and Kollantai – and a violent repression of the Bolsheviks began. Lenin and Zinoviev, fearing they'd be shot if arrested, went into hiding in Finland; while Kamenev was one of many arrested. As he was still not formally a Bolshevik, Trotsky was asked by the Bolsheviks to act for them.

On 23 July, Trotsky published an 'Open Letter' in which he declared his and the IDO's total solidarity with the Bolsheviks, saying:

> 'You can have no grounds for exempting me from the action of the decree by virtue of which Lenin, Zinoviev and Kamenev are subjected to arrest…I am as irreconcilably opposed to the general policy of the Provisional government as my above-mentioned comrades.'

He then defended the Bolsheviks in the Petrograd Soviet and in the CEC. Consequently, on 5 August, Trotsky and Lunacharsky were arrested and put in the Kresty Prison with criminal prisoners who were incited to rough them up, and were kept on a near-starvation diet.[13]

Whilst there, Trotsky was visited by Sedova and their sons; like his daughters, they too were getting caught up in the unfolding events, becoming angry when they heard people accuse him of being a German spy. Because of signs of an approaching counter-revolution, they were all aware Trotsky faced the real risk of being shot; so, as their sons looked on, Sedova slipped him a penknife, should he need to defend himself. With the boys clearly upset by their father's predicament, Sedova – along with the

Joffe family – took them to the Finnish resort of Terijoki for a short holiday. Whilst there, they met some Kronstadt sailors who, once realising who they were, promised they would set their father free, 'with bayonets and with music'. On 8 August, whilst he was in prison, the IDO formally joined the Bolsheviks. This was confirmed at the Bolsheviks' Sixth Party Congress, necessarily held in secret. Trotsky, along with Uritsky, was elected to the Central Committee, getting one of the four highest votes – Lenin later said of Trotsky that 'from that time there has been no better Bolshevik'. However, this wasn't the 'merger of equals' Trotsky had wanted – and the fact that he was joining the Bolsheviks late would have serious implications after Lenin's death.[14]

On 10 September, General Kornilov – recently appointed Commander in Chief by Kerensky – attempted a right wing coup against both the Provisional Government and the Soviet. A delegation of Kronstadt sailors visited Trotsky in prison to ask what they should do: defend Kerensky against Kornilov, or get rid of both. Trotsky advised the former, and the Soviet formed Red Guards (mostly Bolshevik) who prepared defences and sent delegates to Kornilov's troops, successfully asking them to desert. On 17 September, Trotsky was released from prison on bail, and went immediately to a meeting of the Committee for Struggle Against Counter-Revolution, which the Petrograd Soviet – with Kerensky's approval – had established. Two days later, he was finally appointed as one of the Bolsheviks' chief editors. Thus – with Lenin still in hiding – Trotsky once again became the public face of Bolshevism.

By then, the Bolsheviks had majorities in the Soviets of Petrograd, Moscow and other industrial centres, and in district and regional *soviets*, and the attempted coup only increased the shift to the left. On 22 September, the Menshevik and SR leaders of the Petrograd Soviet called a vote to test the mood – Trotsky spoke, and the left won the vote. The same happened, even more convincingly, two days later, 'after another display of Trotsky's oratory', leading to the resignation of the Menshevik and SR leadership. Negotiations then began to form a new EC.[15]

In yet another attempt to increase support for the Provisional Government, Kerensky called a 'Democratic Conference' for 27 September, to create a Pre-Parliament until elections to a Constituent Assembly – constantly postponed by him – took place in November. Trotsky urged the Bolsheviks to boycott this, and Lenin agreed, but Bolshevik delegates like Kamenev disagreed and initially voted to take part. Eventually, Trotsky won support for withdrawing from its proceedings as soon as Bolshevik opposition to it had been publicly declared. It was thus at this Conference that, for the first time, Trotsky appeared officially as the Bolsheviks' chief spokesperson: his speech even impressed the Menshevik Sukhanov:

> 'This was undoubtedly one of this amazing orator's most brilliant speeches...

'The audience at the Alexandrinsky theatre was electrified at the very sound of Trotsky's name...' Trotsky then led the Bolshevik delegates out of the theatre. On 6 October, the new Petrograd Soviet's EC was elected: thirteen Bolsheviks, six SRs and three Mensheviks; on 8 October, Trotsky was elected President, with a 'hurricane of applause'. He immediately called for the forthcoming Second All-Russian Congress of Soviets to form a new revolutionary government.[16]

Planning the Revolution

From Finland, Lenin urged the Bolsheviks to seize power. The Bolshevik CC was divided, with Zinoviev and Kamenev in particular against. Although Trotsky supported Lenin, he differed from him in believing it should be the Soviet that overthrew the government, not just the Bolsheviks. For Trotsky, the immediate task was to make sure the moderates didn't delay convening the Second All-Russian Congress, scheduled for the end of October. The majority of leading Bolsheviks supported Trotsky's plan; Zinoviev and Kamenev did so as they thought he, too, was against an insurrection. But Trotsky was only against a purely *Bolshevik* insurrection. He was still puzzling how to do this when, on 22 October, following a Left SR proposal, the Soviet set up a Military Revolutionary Committee (MRC), to organise the defence of Petrograd and its Soviet.

As President of the Soviet, Trotsky became Chair of the MRC, which had delegates from the Bolsheviks, the Mensheviks and the SRs. The following day, the Bolshevik CC – with Lenin present – voted ten to two in favour of a seizure of power. The two against were Zinoviev and Kamenev. Trotsky continued to argue they should wait for the meeting of the Second All-Russian Congress. But Lenin, back in hiding, worried when the Menshevik- and SR-controlled CEC once again delayed the meeting.

Trotsky then worked hard to ensure the revolution would unfold according to his plans – especially to ensure that Petrograd's garrison would only obey MRC-approved orders. His plans for putting together the forces needed for the armed uprising included the important Congress of the Soviets of the Northern Region (CSNR), which met in Petrograd 24–26 October. Lenin wanted the CSNR to launch an offensive on Petrograd to support a Bolshevik seizure of power. However: 'Trotsky ensured that the CSNR evolved according to his policy.'[17]

On 26 October, when the MRC was formally constituted, the Mensheviks and SRs refused to take their seats, in protest at rumours about Bolshevik plans for an insurrection. In the end, only the Left SRs joined the Bolsheviks on this crucial body. To show it wasn't a Bolshevik body, Trotsky insisted a Left SR be the MRC's chairperson. On 29 October, Trotsky got the CSNR – over the heads of the CEC – to issue a call to all *soviets* to send delegates to Petrograd. He also got the Petrograd garrison to agree to distribute 5,000 rifles to the Red Guards. On the same day, an enlarged Bolshevik CC met – once again, Zinoviev and Kamenev called for dropping the idea of insurrection, while Lenin pushed for an immediate uprising. This time, the vote went nineteen to two in Lenin's favour.

Trying to stop an insurrection, Kamenev resigned from the CC and published in Gorky's *New World* why he and Zinoviev were against. By 31 October, the papers were full of the Bolsheviks' plans. When asked about this in the Soviet, Trotsky said – truthfully but disingenuously – it was a lie that the Soviet had decided to overthrow the PG: 'I declare in the name of the Soviet that no armed actions have been settled upon by us...' So all assumed nothing was planned – especially when Kamenev and Zinoviev immediately supported Trotsky's statement. Even Lenin thought Trotsky had changed his mind but, in a secret meeting with him, was reassured when Trotsky reminded him that, at the end of his statement to the Soviet, he had also said: '...if the Soviet in the course of events should be obliged to set the date for a coming-out, the workers and soldiers would come out to the last man at its summons.' Trotsky then told Lenin he was making plans for an insurrection, to begin just before the first meeting of the Second Congress of Soviets.[18]

Meanwhile, Trotsky put into practice what he'd learned as a war correspondent about the importance of ideals and morale. He spoke at a great number of meetings of workers, soldiers and sailors – becoming 'the orator-in-chief of the revolution'. At several of them, his daughters were present in the audience – though often he 'could not exchange more than a look or a smile' with them; in the evenings, after school, his sons also turned up. Trotsky himself later commented on how exhausting this period was: 'Each time it would seem to me as if I could never get through this meeting, but some hidden reserve of nervous energy would come to the surface, and I would speak for an hour, sometimes two...'[19]

On 3 November, Trotsky got the Petrograd garrison to adopt a Soviet resolution he had written, saying it endorsed 'all political decisions of the Petrograd Soviet', had no confidence in the Provisional Government, and would defend the revolution if asked to by the Petrograd Soviet or the All-Russian Congress of Soviets. Sukhanov – a former SR and now a Left-Menshevik member of the Petrograd Soviet, and an historian – described Trotsky's activities during this period thus: '…it seemed that he spoke everywhere simultaneously…His influence on the masses and leaders alike was overwhelming. He was the central figure of those days, and the chief hero of this remarkable chapter of history.' On 5 November, Trotsky made possibly his most important speech to the garrison of the Peter-Paul Fortress – which, in general, supported Kerensky – persuading them to recognise the authority of the MRC over that of the Provisional Government. A year later, Stalin congratulated Trotsky on this achievement. Meanwhile, Trotsky had been preparing a 'detailed plan of operations', designating which key strategic points in Petrograd should be seized, should a signal be given.[20]

On 6 November, Kerensky decreed the closing down of the Bolshevik press, and ordered military units in Estonia – part of the CSNR – to march on Petrograd. He also announced he would prosecute key members of the MRC. This was the provocation Trotsky had been waiting for: the MRC immediately took defensive action, calling on the Estonian Soviets in the CSNR to ensure no troops marched on the capital. In addition, when a young working woman and man rushed to the MRC, saying they would still produce the paper, if they were given a military escort, Trotsky issued orders to break the seal. However, this was still slightly earlier than Trotsky had wanted, because it began before the Second Congress was formally in session.

Lenin again sent a note to the CC, urging it to seize power straight away and, convinced he was being ignored, came out of hiding – in disguise – to chastise his comrades. He arrived at around midnight, anxious – because all was so quiet – the insurrection still wasn't taking place. Trotsky assured him the Bolshevik CC – including Kamenev – was helping carry out an insurrection under his instructions. In all, it is estimated that almost 30,000 people took an active part in this November Revolution, giving it more of the flavour of an armed popular insurrection than a purely Bolshevik *coup d'état*.

At 2.00am, on the morning of 7 November, Trotsky – who'd been staying at the Smolny Institute for most of the past week and working flat out – issued his famous Order No. 1, stating that the Petrograd Soviet was 'in imminent danger' from 'counter-revolutionary conspirators', and that each regiment should await 'further orders'. The commissars of the MRC then led their detachments of Red Guards and regular regiments to capture control of Petrograd's main centres of communication. This was done, speedily and almost noiselessly, in just a few hours.[21]

By then, according to Joffe's daughter, Trotsky was so exhausted 'he could hardly remain on his feet'. Consequently, at this most intense and dramatic of moments, and in front of a much-concerned Kamenev, Trotsky – who hadn't eaten for twenty-four hours – briefly suffered one of his blackouts: 'All is well. It could not have gone better. Now I may leave the telephone. I sit down on the couch. The nervous tension lessens. A dull sensation of fatigue comes over me…suddenly…I faint.' Sedova noted his exhaustion, when she returned to the Smolny Institute the following day: 'Leon Davidovitch's features were drawn; he was pale, exhausted and over-excited.'[22]

By then, however, all was moving smoothly along the lines he'd prepared. By 3.00pm, with virtually no resistance (and far fewer deaths than the March Revolution) Trotsky was able to announce to the Petrograd Soviet – and then, two hours later, to a pre-Congress meeting of delegates to the Second All-Russian Congress of Soviets – that: 'On behalf of the Military Revolutionary Committee, I declare that the Provisional Government is no longer existent…' Technically, this was not quite the case, as the Provisional Government hadn't surrendered. At 9.00pm, the battleship *Aurora* fired blanks and, in the early hours of 8 November, the Winter Palace was taken and ministers who hadn't already fled, were arrested. Kerensky escaped and immediately announced the formation of a new government. The night before, Lenin and Trotsky – resting on the floor of a small room next to the Smolny's great hall, where the Second Congress would meet – had discussed what title should be given to those holding posts in the new government. It was Trotsky who came up with the idea of 'People's Commissars' – used during the great French Revolution of 1789, this seemed most apt for such long-term revolutionaries.[23]

Around twenty million people had voted in the elections to this Second Congress and, when it convened, it had an almost two-thirds Bolshevik majority. Those voting for the Bolsheviks were the majority of the urban working class and very large sections of the armed forces, along with poorer peasants and agricultural labourers. Together with the Left SRs, whose support came from the bulk of the peasantry, and who were about to split from their party, they formed 75% of the delegates. The right wing Mensheviks immediately walked out, and the remaining Menshevik and Right SR delegates condemned the uprising, with Martov calling for a coalition. When the Bolsheviks rejected this, these groups too announced their intention of boycotting the new Congress. Trotsky replied with what has become one of his most famous speeches: 'You are pitiful isolated individuals; you are bankrupts; your role is played out. Go where you belong from now on – into the rubbish-can of history!'[24]

Nonetheless, places for the boycotters, in proportion to their numbers, were left on the new CEC. The Congress then approved the formation of a workers' and peasants' government to be called the Council of People's Commissars (Sovnarkom), to rule until the Constituent Assembly met. It also voted for hastily-drafted decrees for delivering 'Peace, Bread and Land'. The new government would be answerable to the Soviets: by passing a vote of no confidence, they could remove the government. Although the old possessing classes were disenfranchised, they were nonetheless allowed freedom of expression. At this stage, the idea of a one-party dictatorship was not part of anyone's future plans.

Although Lenin preferred an entirely Bolshevik government, many Bolsheviks – including Zinoviev and Kamenev – wanted a coalition with, at the very least, the Left SRs. They proposed this on 8 November, and Lenin agreed to offer them seats in the government. However, the Left SRs initially declined. Thus, on 9 November, the majority of the Bolshevik CC took Lenin's side and supported a purely Bolshevik government; Zinoviev and Kamenev resigned in protest. Trotsky let it be known he, too, favoured a coalition, so talks continued. However, on 16 November, they broke down again, when the Mensheviks demanded the exclusion of both Lenin and Trotsky from any government. A large number of leading Bolshevik 'conciliators' – headed by Kamenev who, as Chair of the CEC, was effectively President of the new Russian Socialist Federated Soviet Republic (RSFSR) – were prepared to accept this. Lenin and Trotsky, however, were opposed and the talks collapsed. For the next seven years, Trotsky and Lenin were in agreement on most issues, and Lenin came increasingly to rely on him. Trotsky, full of confidence and energy, failed to notice – or, if he noticed, to care – that this closeness with Lenin was increasingly resented by other leading Bolsheviks who'd supported Lenin since the 1903 split.

Neither Peace Nor War

The new government initially based itself in offices in the Smolny Institute, with the upper storeys converted into family apartments. This allowed Trotsky, under normal circumstances, to return home for lunch – very often, with Zina and Nina joining him. After lunch, he would relax on a sofa, 'sitting the girls next to him and joking with them,. When he was not there, his daughters played with their young half-brothers.[25]

On 9 November, Lenin proposed Trotsky as Chair of Sovnarkom. Trotsky declined, and also refused the post of Commissar of Home Affairs. Neither he nor Lenin wished to assume governmental posts: while Lenin wanted to deal with party matters, Trotsky wished to devote himself to writing: 'From my youth on…I had dreamed of being a writer. Later, I subordinated my literary work, as I did everything else, to the revolution….'[26]

However, the Bolshevik 'conciliators' insisted they take on government responsibilities. Thus Trotsky's suggestion of taking charge of the press was rejected: reluctantly, he accepted the post of Commissar for Foreign Affairs. He spoke regularly with foreign diplomats and journalists who, though they hated his views, were nonetheless genuinely impressed by his energetic diligence, cultured talk and confidence. Such interviews often took place in his family's modest apartment, which US reporter Louise Bryant described as being like 'a poor artists' attic studio'.[27]

As Commissar for Foreign Affairs, Trotsky flouted conventional diplomacy, seeing Russia's revolution as the first step in ending nationalism, militarism and imperialism. He immediately published all secret treaties and agreements, thus exposing the imperialist nature of the First World War. He then established a Bureau of International Revolutionary Propaganda, which immediately began producing leaflets in various languages. Russian soldiers were encouraged to fraternise with the troops of the Central Powers and distribute those leaflets. Trotsky also began issuing proclamations to the people of Europe, calling on them to rise up in revolution against their governments.

Although Trotsky thought he could then concentrate on writing a history of the revolution, he had to take charge of the peace negotiations – and carry out the Soviet decree for an 'immediate and just' end to the war. Initially wanting a general peace, he invited all combatants to the talks. However, the Allies refused to participate, so the new Russian government sought an armistice with the Central Powers – though one forbidding the transfer of troops from the Eastern to the Western Front. Talks began on 2 December, at the German Army's HQ in Brest-Litovsk, with Joffe, Kamenev and the Left SR Anastasia Bitsenko heading the Russian delegation.

Progress proved difficult as, General Dukhonin, the Russian Commander in Chief, opposed an armistice but refused to resign. After he was killed by his own troops on 4 December, the Bolshevik Krylenko was appointed as the new Commander in Chief, and a truce was finalised on 5 December. Peace talks then began on 21 December – with Russia still keeping the option open for the Entente powers to join. However, the Germans insisted on harsh terms. At the same time, the first signs of civil war emerged, with White Guard generals beginning military offensives. By then, the Left SRs had joined the Bolsheviks in a coalition. Lenin, who believed revolutions were imminent, favoured an immediate peace, but left wing Bolsheviks – led by Bukharin, and backed by the Left SRs – wanted a revolutionary war to aid revolutions elsewhere. Trotsky occupied a middle position – favouring neither peace nor war. Instead, he advocated demobilising the Russian army, but refusing to conclude a rapacious or separate peace, and instead concentrating on spreading revolution. Trotsky's option initially won majority support.

On 9 January 1918, Trotsky – accompanied by Radek – arrived at Brest-Litovsk for the second round of negotiations. He immediately ended social mixing with the German and Austrian negotiators in between discussions. These were bewildered by Trotsky who – although well-dressed and well-groomed, and able to make wide-ranging cultural references and witticisms in excellent German – refused to play the part of a defeated country's representative. Trotsky also oversaw the production of *The Torch*, a newspaper explaining the Bolsheviks' position, which – in front of the outraged representatives of the Central Powers – was distributed in the German and Austrian trenches.[28]

In between negotiations, Trotsky found time to write a pamphlet, *The History of the Russian Revolution to Brest-Litovsk*, which was quickly translated into all major European languages. In the negotiations, Trotsky continued to argue for a peace that was just and allowed self-determination for all nationalities. He also insisted all the countries' bargaining positions should be published in their respective newspapers – thus getting Bolshevik aims across to the German and Austrian peoples. Aware that opposition to the war was growing in Germany and Austria, Trotsky even demanded the right to visit Vienna to have talks with socialist leaders there! Unsurprisingly, this was refused. Meanwhile, the Germans – who wanted Ukraine, Poland and the Baltic states as satellite states – sensed that, despite Trotsky's confidence, Russia was in no position to resist.

When the Germans refused to delay any further, Lenin urged accepting whatever terms were offered. Trotsky – who'd seen the empty Russian trenches on his journeys to Brest-Litovsk – reached an agreement with Lenin that he'd continue to stall but, if the Germans resumed hostilities, he'd back Lenin. Yet, even when the Germans launched a new offensive on 17 February, Trotsky still delayed, hoping to provoke revolution in Germany. However, as the Germans advanced into Russia, he finally agreed peace had to be signed, but couldn't bring himself to sign a harsh treaty. A special party congress criticised his position so, on 23 February, with his pride wounded, he resigned as Commissar for Foreign Affairs.

The treaty, signed on 3 March 1918, was approved by the Seventh RSDLP (Bolshevik) Congress, which also changed its name to the All-Russian Communist Party (RCP). However, the treaty brought about the end of the Left SRs' participation in the government; and, because of a German advance on Petrograd, Russia's capital was moved to Moscow on 12 March 1918.

Trotsky's Red Army

While Trotsky had been in Brest-Litovsk, the Constituent Assembly – elected in mid-November, under a franchise which unduly favoured wealthier peasants – had met in Petrograd on 18 January. Because of communications problems, many areas had voted unaware the Provisional Government had fallen, or that the SRs had split into Left and Right parties. The SRs as a whole had won most seats, with 37% of the vote – but no party had an overall majority. Nonetheless, Left SRs represented many of the rural areas and, had knowledge of the split been known, would probably have won in many more, as they supported massive land redistribution. Together with the Bolsheviks, who'd won 23% of the vote, they formed the most sizeable bloc.

However, the Constituent Assembly refused to accept Sovnarkom or the decrees passed by the Congress of Soviets. Furthermore, the Kadets were implicated in various White Guard uprisings. Consequently, the Constituent Assembly had been dissolved by force. Its place was taken by the recently-elected Third All-Russian Congress of Soviets, which met for the first time on 23 January. In this, the Bolsheviks had won over half the seats – and the new CEC was made up of ten Bolsheviks, three Left SRs, along with one each for the Menshevik Internationalists, the Right SRs and the Mensheviks.

Trotsky's new post, confirmed on 13 March, was as Commissar of War, and Chair of the newly-formed Supreme Military Council – an advisory body formed, at his suggestion, of former Tsarist officers willing to work with the new Soviet government. It was headed by Bonch-Bruevich, the ex-Chief of Staff, who'd been persuaded to take this role by his Bolshevik brother. That Trotsky was given this post – at such an uncertain time – shows the high esteem in which he was held by leading Bolsheviks. His broad political approach, and 'his astonishing energy and ability to inspire people', made him ideal for such a role. Trotsky argued, in case of further attacks by the Germans, that the almost non-existent Russian army should be replaced by a new army 'strong in revolutionary enthusiasm' – seeing his main role as 'the "revolutionary education" of the masses in uniform'. Trotsky's role as Commissar of War would 'define his image as a hero of the revolution'.[29]

To 'arm the revolution', he formed an army out of the largely undisciplined Red Guards (numbering no more than 10,000 in early 1918) and some bands of partisans. His plan was to 'save the Soviet Republic' by transforming them – using 'Work, Discipline and Order' – into leaders who could help create an efficient fighting force from the untrained masses. Trotsky first appealed for recruits from amongst industrial workers, making Bolsheviks the inner core of every regiment. When, by late summer 1918, this proved inadequate, he resorted to conscription.[30]

Although initially using experienced former Tsarist officers as 'military specialists', he also appointed political commissars at every level of command, to ensure the loyalty of the officers and to politically educate the troops. He also imposed a rigid centralisation. Both aspects earned him animosity: from the Left SRs and the Mensheviks, and even from some Bolsheviks, such as Zinoviev – even though, by late 1919, he'd promoted almost 200,000 Red Army NCOs to officer rank. Particular opposition came from Stalin, and Voroshilov, the commander of the Tenth Army.

The Bolsheviks faced both White Guards and fourteen foreign armies – including from Britain, France, Japan and the US – as well as various non-Bolshevik socialist groups like the Mensheviks, SRs and anarchists. There was also the Czechoslovak Legion of Austro-Hungarian POWs. This had initially helped the Russian Army against the Germans, and Trotsky hoped to retain them – but the Legion wanted to help the Allies on the Western Front.

The Sword of the Revolution

When the Civil War began, Trotsky had been living with Sedova and their sons, in a four-roomed flat in Moscow's Kremlin, across a corridor from Lenin: the two families shared a dining room and bathroom, and Lenin frequently played with Trotsky's children. Meanwhile, Sokolovskaya remained in Petrograd with their two daughters, working for the Commissariat of Education, in charge of museums and ancient monuments.

However, Trotsky was by no means a 'desk soldier'; consequently, neither of his families saw much of him during the Civil War, as he spent most of the next two and a half years on his special armoured train, visiting the twenty-one fronts and sixteen armies under his control. From its first journey in August 1918 to the end of the Civil War in 1920, the train covered over 100,000 miles.

His train – soon known as the 'Guard of the Revolution' – became a symbol of the embattled revolution; and, eventually, of its victory. It was staffed by an extremely loyal crew – including around 25 crack troops, all dressed in identical leather uniforms. Trotsky maintained his dress standards during the Civil War, wearing a uniform consisting of 'a smart dull-green tunic, a cap and a greatcoat'. He also insisted on similar standards from others; that meetings began on time; and that reports were thorough. As he himself said: 'my own personal life was inseparably bound up with the life of that train. The train, on the other hand, was inseparably bound up with the life of the Red Army.'[31]

His train had several functions: printing and distributing a regular Red Army newspaper, along with educational and propaganda materials; and carrying supplies and awards for outstanding soldiers. Its main role, though, was for Trotsky – as the public face of the Red Army – to inspire and rally the troops. Sometimes, as part of his morale-boosting visits, as well as awarding medals (including the Order of the Red Banner, created by him in September 1918) to soldiers who'd excelled themselves, he even gave his own wrist watch or personal revolver. He brought Bolshevist ideas to hundreds of places, and 'Workers and peasants who listened to him were frequently entranced, and there was always an eagerness to set eyes on the great man'. In this role, he didn't hesitate to put himself on the front line, thus exposing himself to real risks – unusual in someone with such an important government post: 'There is much testimony to his and his crew's commitment to the Red cause, and much evidence of personal bravery'. All this helped make him immensely popular with the troops, as he gave the impression 'he was capable of sacrificing himself' for the revolution: it was this work which earned Trotsky the title 'the Sword of the Revolution'.[32]

Once arrived at a front, he used unconventional methods for decision-making, inviting 'those from the lower commanding force and from the ranks' to planning meetings, in order to get 'a picture of the situation that was neither false nor highly coloured'. This, however, upset those Bolsheviks who liked tight central party control. Although many of the practical details were put into effect by Bonch-Bruevich, he couldn't have done so without Trotsky's strong political support. As Kalinin is reported to have said: 'Leon Davidovitch is pulling the cart of civil war all by himself.' Trotsky also appointed brilliant strategists such as Antonov-Ovseenko, S. Kamenev, Tukhachevsky and Vatzetis who were in charge of the main fronts and battles. By May 1918, Trotsky's Red Army had 300,000 soldiers and, by the end of the Civil War, it numbered over five million.[33]

One controversial aspect of Trotsky's role in the Civil War concerns the use of harsh reprisals and terror. Desertion amongst conscripts, especially in the early stages of the war, was often severely punished – occasionally, he ordered the execution of every tenth man of units refusing to fight, including the political commissars attached to them; this was later used against him by his opponents. However, he also used personal persuasion – including, with only 'a single armed guard', winning over a crowd of dangerously demoralised soldiers shouting *'Death to Trotsky!'* At times, there were also harsh measures against civilians: for instance, where villagers had sided with the Whites and helped kill Red Army soldiers. However, he also urged leniency for captured White soldiers and, although holding officers' families hostage against betrayal or desertion, there's no evidence that any executions took place when betrayals nonetheless took place. In fact, it was 'more usual for Trotsky to intervene to get arrested officers released.'[34]

Military and Political Battles

Although Trotsky's decisions were usually proved correct, he also made mistakes; and, because he was mostly absent from government and party meetings – staying in touch by telegram – his enemies within the RCP were able to undermine him. The main fronts were the Eastern, Southern and Northern. In August 1918, the most immediate threat was on the **Eastern Front**, from Admiral Kolchak's White Guards, and where the Czech Legion had seized Samara, forcing the Red Fifth Army to retreat. Trotsky had been slow to see the danger there, seeing the German threats to Moscow and Petrograd as more important. When the situation deteriorated on the Volga, Trotsky rushed to Svyazhsk. Finding the front in a state of 'virtual collapse', he successfully rallied them with 'torrents of passionate eloquence…and personally led them back to the fighting line'. He ignored advice to move to a safer place, to avoid demoralising the troops. His strict discipline was shown when, after a court-martial, he had a local commander and political commissar shot for attempted desertion.

It was during this critical battle he encountered Larisa Reissner, a passionate revolutionary journalist – and the first woman to be appointed as a political commissar in the Red Army. After having had relationships with some of Russia's important young poets, she later became Radek's companion. Trotsky wrote about her with passion: 'With her appearance of an Olympian goddess, she combined a subtle and ironical mind and the courage of a warrior...' She likewise wrote warmly about him: 'With Trotsky – it was the sacred pathos of struggle; words and gestures recalling the best pages of the Great French Revolution.' These mutually-appreciative descriptions – apparently, she even persuaded Radek to deliver a message to Trotsky, stating she wished to have a child by him – and the fact that Trotsky spent nearly one month on this front, resulted in rumours that they'd had a brief affair. This alleged affair formed the opening frames of the 2017 Russian TV series, *Trotsky*.[35]

Trotsky managed to turn the situation around and, on 7–8 September, took part in a naval night raid on Kazan. However, he then ordered the execution of twenty soldiers for desertion – including several political commissars. When Bonch-Bruevich resigned, Trotsky appointed Vatzetis as the new Commander in Chief. Trotsky's methods led to much criticism at the Eighth Party Congress in March 1919. By then, the Civil War had just entered its most crucial stage, with the Soviet government controlling only central Russia. Although his general line was upheld, some of his policies were modified and only one-sixth of the delegates voted for him to be re-elected to the CC. From then on, Trotsky was often under political fire from his own party. However, by early May 1919, Kolchak's advance had been halted by General S. Kamenev and, by October, the whole of the Volga region was under Red Army control. Yet, when Kamenev insisted on pursuing Kolchak into Siberia, Trotsky sacked him. Gusev and other political commissars complained to Lenin and Stalin: Trotsky's decision was overturned, and he was proved wrong when Kamenev eventually inflicted total defeat on Kolchak.

In the summer of 1919, Trotsky focussed on the **Southern Front**, where the main threat came from Denikin's White Army, which was advancing on Moscow. The Tenth Army was based here – and it was here Trotsky made some of his most serious enemies, including Stalin, whom he'd appointed as the chief political commissar. Despite having numerical advantage, that front suffered several defeats, which Trotsky felt was because Stalin refused to implement the strategy he advocated. When Trotsky arrived, he ordered total reorganisation; Stalin supported Voroshilov, the local commander, in refusing to comply. Trotsky's opponents then started a 'whispering campaign' against him for executing local commissars. Stalin, aided by Zinoviev, tried to turn Lenin against Trotsky – initially with some success. Criticisms of Trotsky even appeared in *Pravda*. Once again, Trotsky was overruled – but this time, he was proved correct – but not until October 1919, by which time Denikin had almost reached Moscow. In July 1919, Trotsky's commander, Vatzetis, was replaced by Kamenev, while several others appointed by

Trotsky were demoted. Trotsky – exhausted and unwell – stormed out of the CC meeting, offering his resignation. This prompted Lenin to give him the so-called 'blank cheque', approving in advance any of Trotsky's orders.[36]

Coinciding with those threats on the Southern Front, there was also an increasing threat on the **Northern Front**, where Yudenich – armed and supported by British planes and tanks – had formed a White Army in Estonia: by October 1919, he had reached the outskirts of Petrograd. The situation was so dire that Zinoviev proposed abandoning Petrograd, and even Lenin agreed, in order to concentrate on Moscow's defence. Trotsky – for once supported by Stalin – disagreed, because of Petrograd's symbolic importance as 'the cradle of the revolution'. Trotsky rushed there in person, to find British tanks already in the suburbs, and the city and troops in panic. His attitude towards Zinoviev was brusque, if not outright contemptuous. Once again, his oratory roused both troops and civilians, raising the slogan 'We will not give up Petrograd!' He even commissioned a poet to write stirring verses to raise morale. In addition, he took on the role of regimental commander, personally leading soldiers into the thick of battle to stop the Reds retreating: 'I mounted the first horse I could lay hands on and turned the lines back.' Within a week, Yudenich had been beaten back and, on 7 November – his fortieth birthday – Trotsky returned to Moscow with news of their victory, where he received the Order of the Red Banner for his bravery. In December 1919, most of the foreign armies withdrew from Soviet Russia and, even though there were some mopping-up campaigns in 1920, against a White Army led by Baron Wrangel, it was clear the Revolution had been saved.[37]

The defence of Petrograd in October 1919 is one of several situations where Trotsky's real daring – both as tactician and as war commander – often made the crucial difference between victory or defeat. Consequently, Trotsky was acknowledged as the architect of the Red Army's victory. Lunacharsky, who commented on Trotsky's 'imperiousness' and his inability – or unwillingness – to be 'kind or attentive' to people, nonetheless concluded that not even Lenin 'could have coped with the titanic mission [Trotsky] took upon his shoulders... of being the unceasing electrifier of a weakening army, now in one place and then in another.'[38]

Trotsky and the Third International

Since 1915, Trotsky had joined Lenin in calling for the formation of a Third International, to replace the disgraced Second International. While travelling to the Civil War fronts on his train, Trotsky continued writing about the need to break the chains of imperialism intent on 'strangling Bolshevism in its cradle' – as Churchill is purported to have said in 1919, when calling for a 'crusade of fourteen nations' against Soviet Russia. In fact, even before the end of the First World War, Trotsky had been involved in preparations for this Communist International (Comintern).

On 2 March 1919, the Founding Congress of this Third International met in the Kremlin. Trotsky made a special effort to come from the front to be there and see history made. After Lenin delivered a report to the Congress, Trotsky – described by Arthur Ransome (the *Swallows and Amazons* author) as wearing 'a leather coat, military breeches and gaiters, with a fur hat with the sign of the Red Army in front' – made a stirring speech in which he declared that the thousands of Red Army soldiers and socialist workers who, so far, had died in the Civil War, had 'fallen not only for the Soviet Republic but also for the Third International'. He concluded his report with these words: 'We are ready to struggle and die for the world revolution!' On 6 March, on the last day of the Congress, Trotsky read out the *Manifesto of the Communist International to the Workers of the World*, which he had written, closing by stating that the Comintern was 'against imperialist barbarism, against monarchy, against the privileged estates, against the bourgeois state and bourgeois property, against all kinds and forms of class or national oppression'. Because of Trotsky's military commitments, Zinoviev was elected its first President; when the Congress closed, Trotsky rushed back to the front.[39]

Despite the defeat of revolutions in Germany and Hungary, by the end of 1919, the Civil War was virtually over. The Russian Revolution had – in large part because of Trotsky's efforts – survived both internal and external threats; and the Third International had finally been established. Trotsky was thus at the zenith of his political career. However, within three years – partly because of the economic policies he advocated after 1920 – he became increasingly isolated within the leadership of the RCP.

Chapter 7

The Commissar in Power, 1920–23

'Those who for a long time had been preparing to be my opponents – Stalin above all – were anxious to gain time... They conferred secretly...'[1]

Those words – written by Trotsky in exile in Turkey – reflect his surprise at not hearing about Lenin's first stroke, in May 1922, until three days later. As chief organiser of the November Revolution in 1917, and then the 'Sword of the Revolution' during the Civil War, Trotsky had reached the zenith of his political life. Yet events soon set him on the road to a slow process of political decline, culminating in his expulsion from the Soviet Union he'd done so much to help establish.

From 1920 onwards, Trotsky began to experience 'Defeat in Victory'. In 1920, he argued for centralisation, and for strict controls on the proletarian democracy he'd advocated so passionately for so long. Then, from 1921, he became an increasingly outspoken critic of party interference in the state and undemocratic actions that undermined socialist democracy. As Deutscher stated: 'At the very pinnacle of power Trotsky, like the protagonist of a classical tragedy, stumbled.' This was partly down to his aloofness from leading party members who, after the Civil War, began to adopt what Trotsky saw as a 'semi-bourgeois way of life', visiting each other's homes and holding drinking parties: 'If I took no part in the amusements that were becoming more and more common in the lives of the new governing stratum...it was because I hated to inflict such boredom on myself.'[2]

Yet, until 1923, Trotsky remained a key player in both the RCP and the government. At the start of 1920, he oversaw the mopping-up campaigns against remaining White armies that ended the Civil War. However, no sooner had this been done, when war broke out with Poland – leading to a significant policy difference between himself and Lenin. Once this military conflict had ended, Trotsky turned his attention to economic matters – and, once again, found himself in disagreement with Lenin. Though of much more significance for Trotsky's future was the fact that, following a series of strokes, Lenin was increasingly inactive from 1922 onwards.

From Civil War to Economic Reconstruction

The Civil War had forced the Bolshevik government to abandon plans for a form of 'state capitalism' and, instead, adopt the economic policy known as 'War Communism' – partly because, to aid the Whites, many factory and bank owners had closed down their enterprises. The new government thus took over industries and banks, and requisitioned grain from the peasants. By January 1920, though, with the Civil War almost over, the Soviet government began to consider restoring *soviet* democracy. However, a controversy broke out over how to rebuild the Russian economy which had been severely disrupted by six years of war, revolution and civil war. As early as December 1919, Trotsky proposed introducing universal labour service and central planning; and transforming the Red Army into a democratic militia system to facilitate economic reconstruction. With Lenin's support, he had presented this to the Seventh Congress of Soviets – yet, when these proposals had appeared in *Pravda*, there was widespread protest from the trade unions.

In January 1920, Lenin and Trotsky met Communist trade union leaders, with Trotsky stating that the newspapers weren't fully reporting the seriousness of the economic situation, which was: ' a hundred times worse than our military situation ever was'. Although Lenin spoke equally-strongly in favour, they failed to get union leaders to agree. Trotsky – with Lenin's support – then decided to use Red Army soldiers as workers in labour battalions, moving now-idle regiments into work such as timber-felling, mining, transport and farming.[3]

Trotsky saw this as a step towards getting acceptance for the conscription and direction of civilian labour. In addition – mirroring his use of Tsarist military specialists – Trotsky also proposed using industrial specialists who'd previously worked for capitalist firms: something he'd first raised during the Civil War. He also turned his attention to agricultural production, after realising many peasants responded to grain and livestock requisitioning by reducing the area farmed and slaughtering stock: 'My practical work had satisfied me that… to revive our economic life…we had to restore the home market in some degree.'[4]

He thus sent an 'Open Letter' to the CC, recommending the development of state farms and, in some areas, a move to collectivisation. However, very controversially, he also argued for replacing state requisitioning with a tax in kind, graduated to favour those who produced most. The only coercion would be forcing peasants to sow greater areas for grain. This was a complete reversal of war communism policies and, in early March, was opposed by

Lenin, the CC, and the Politburo. So, Trotsky dropped his ideas – which pre-figured Lenin's New Economic Policy by one year – instead arguing that, if war communism was to be continued, it should be made more efficient which, given the inability of the devastated economy to offer rewards, would need increased compulsion. His close friend, Joffe, commented later in a letter: 'it was Trotsky's major weakness that he did not persist in his wisdom, especially when to be wise was to be alone'. And, as Deutscher points out: 'One might add that on this occasion Trotsky, rebuked for his wisdom, plunged back into the accepted folly [of war communism] and persisted with it with an ardour which even the fools thought too foolish.'[5]

Nonetheless, Trotsky was appointed Commissar for Transport; as he saw the railways and waterways as key to economic recovery, he began to centralise – including restricting the influence of the two main transport unions. At the Ninth Party Congress, in March 1920, Trotsky argued for labour conscription, and for a sliding scale of rations for industrial workers, to encourage greater output. He made it clear that, as the transition from capitalism to socialism would be a long and difficult process, compulsion of some kind would be an essential part of the construction of a workers' state for some time as: 'We are making the first attempt in world history to organise the labour of working people in the interests of the working majority: but that, of course, does not mean the destruction of the element of compulsion.'[6]

A minority of delegates – the left wing Democratic Centralists (or Decemists, led by Vladimir Smirnov) and the Workers' Opposition (led by Alexandra Kollontai and A. G. Shliapnikov) – opposed these ideas, and Trotsky argued against them. Ironically, within just a few years, he would ally with these people against Stalin. Then, at a trade unions' congress, Trotsky argued again for the militarisation of trade unions; for a central authority to direct industry; and for the use of 'bourgeois' specialists. Although there were soon signs of improvement as a result of some of these policies, Trotsky's actions led to considerable party and trade union opposition.

War with Poland

However, a new threat came from Marshal Pilsudski's Poland. Soviet Russia – as urged strongly by Trotsky – had already recognised the independence of Estonia and Latvia, and was negotiating a similar treaty with Lithuania. It was also offering generous terms to Poland, but Pilsudski kept them secret from the Polish people – leading Trotsky to argue for the resumption of open diplomacy. At the end of April – once Pilsudski was sure the Whites, who opposed Polish independence, were defeated – the Polish army launched a big invasion. Trotsky left Moscow on 7 May for the front, to stop further retreat. Quickly realising the Red Army was facing a professional regular army, he decided many more skilled officers were needed at even the most junior levels. Consequently, many Army Commanders became Divisional Commanders, and so on down the ranks – though all officers so affected retained their original rank and salary. By mid-June, he had stabilised the situation. By the end of June – despite also having to deal with Baron Wrangel's White forces in the Crimea, in what proved the final conflict of the Civil War – Trotsky had pushed the Polish army back to the ethnic Soviet-Polish boundaries.

Yet, in July, a disagreement with Lenin arose over how to respond to Britain's proposal for ending the war, by establishing the 'Curzon Line' as an agreed border. Trotsky argued for acceptance; Lenin, however – desperate to end Soviet Russia's isolation – wanted the Red Army to advance on Warsaw, to help spark a revolution in Poland, which could then act as a bridge across which Soviet Russia could join up with revolutionaries in Germany and other countries. Trotsky opposed 'exporting revolution on bayonets', arguing it would increase nationalism, not revolution, as Tsarist oppression of Poland meant an invading Red Army would be resisted. However, apart from – briefly – Rykov, Trotsky was alone in arguing thus, and the Politiburo decided on advance to Warsaw. As instructed, Trotsky issued the orders to advance but, when ordered to supervise the offensive, he refused.

By mid-August, following some serious defeats – down, in part to Stalin (the chief political commissar of the southern army) – the Politiburo wavered. In September, following a visit to the Polish Front, Trotsky persuaded them to vote for an immediate provisional peace. However, when Poland's terms for peace were presented on 12 October – demanding territory 200km to the east of the Curzon Line – the Politburo considered resuming the war. Trotsky threatened to resign, so an armistice was signed on 18 October. Trotsky then left to oversee the final defeat of Wrangel and the French forces supporting him, which took place on 7 November 1920. To symbolise the end of the Civil War, Trotsky's special trains were disbanded.[7]

Clare Sheridan

It was during this period that Service – apparently on the basis of previously-unseen documents – claims Trotsky had an affair with Clare Sheridan, the British sculptor. Sheridan – a cousin of Winston Churchill – had met Trotsky's brother-in-law, Kamenev, while he was on a diplomatic mission to London. They had an affair, and Kamenev then invited her to Soviet Russia to make busts of the leading revolutionaries. The UK authorities refused her a visa; so, without one, she sailed with Kamenev to Stockholm, where he got her an Estonian visa. On 20 September 1920, Sheridan arrived in Moscow.

She stayed in the Kremlin, doing busts of Lenin, Dzerzhinsky, Kamenev – and Trotsky. She allegedly had affairs with more than one of those sitters – her relationship with Kamenev is thought to have started the problems with his first wife, Olga Bronstein, Trotsky's sister. Whether or not Trotsky was flirtatious and particularly attracted by beautiful women, it is certainly true that several beautiful women were drawn to him after the November Revolution brought him to fame. After meeting Trotsky for the first time, Sheridan commented in her 1921 book, *Russian Portraits*: 'He interested me very much. He is a man with a slim, good figure, splendid fighting countenance, and his whole personality is full of force.' She began sculpting Trotsky on 18 October, and later wrote several passionate descriptions of him: 'When he talks his face lights up and his eyes flash. Trotsky's eyes are much talked about in Russia, and he is called "the wolf"....' Service claims Sedova mentioned this affair in 1940; and that, in the 1930s, his 'entourage' suspected they'd had an affair. Whatever the truth, Trotsky dedicated a painting of himself to Sheridan, and invited her to stay in Soviet Russia and set up a studio. However, she declined, arriving back in Britain on 23 November 1920.[8]

The 'Trade Union Question'

Although from April 1920 onwards, Trotsky had mainly been preoccupied with military matters, he'd continued to push through reforms to improve Russia's still-chaotic transport system. In September, he set up Tsektran, a new trade union for all transport workers, which was to be under central Party control, with himself as Chair. As soon as the Polish War was over, he pushed for similar changes with other trade unions. However, Lenin changed his mind about centralising control over the trade unions, and worked instead to reestablish their 'proletarian democracy'. This issue was Trotsky's third serious disagreement with Lenin – Trotsky later wrote: 'One cannot deny that the so-called discussion of trade-unions clouded our relationship for some time.'[9]

At the Ninth RCP Conference, in late September, Trotsky was only allowed to speak on military matters; while Zinoviev successfully moved a resolution which said Trotsky's trade union reforms were only temporary, and that normal trade union life would soon resume. In November, the clash between Trotsky and Zinoviev became more open, with Trotsky stating that labour conscription, and the appointment, rather than election, of trade union leaders, would continue. At the 8 November 1920 CC meeting, Trotsky argued trade unions should act as administrative organs of the state. This was opposed by Tomsky, the RCP trade union leader: Lenin distanced himself from Trotsky, stating the era of Labour Armies was over. The CC supported Lenin – but only by 1 vote; so a Commission on Trade Unions was set up under Zinoviev, to report back to the CC on 8 December. Trotsky was given a seat on the Commission but, because he was not given as much access to the press as Zinoviev, he resigned in early December.

Lenin tried to achieve a consensus, but Trotsky refused to sign the Trade Union Commission's Report, and successfully argued for a full party debate, in advance of the Tenth Party Congress, due in March 1921. On 30 December, Trotsky spoke at the Eighth Congress of Soviets, calling for a fusion between trade unions and industrial administrators, in order for rapid industrial recovery. In a pamphlet, *The Path to the United Economic Plan*, he denied his ideas of making trade unions part of the state system meant he was a 'super-centraliser' – in fact, he argued for a high degree of autonomy for enterprises, though within a firm central economic plan. However, Trotsky later acknowledged what he saw as Lenin's 'unerring political instinct' in the trade union question: 'Whereas I was trying to get an ever more intensive effort from the trades unions…Lenin, guided by political considerations, was moving towards an easing of military pressure.'[10]

Zinoviev proposed that elections for the Tenth Congress should be on the basis of platforms – and, in Petrograd, he put forward Lenin's 'Platform of the Ten', based on the Trade Union Commission's Report. In reply, Trotsky got the Moscow party to support his ideas. Across the country, regional party committees voted against Trotsky's proposals, and Zinoviev launched a bitter attack on Trotsky's recent actions. However, on 28 February – just before the Tenth Party Congress – the Kronstadt Rebellion began. The programme of these rebels called for a 'renewal of the Revolution' and the restoration of multi-party democracy. They also called for 'freedom of the spoken and printed word for all revolutionary parties and groupings; freedom for the trades unions; the release of revolutionary political prisoners….'[11]

This uprising saw opponents of the RCP – Left and Right SRs, Mensheviks and anarchists – join with the rebels. In addition, some dissident

David Bronstein, Trotsky's father c. 1900. (Public Domain)

Anna Bronstein, Trotsky's mother c. 1900. (Public Domain)

Above left: The South Russian Workers' Union: Aleksandra Sokolovskaya, with Trotsky on her left and brother Ilya Sokolovsky on her right, and G. Ziv (centre), Nikolaev 1897. (Public Domain)

Above right: Trotsky in 1897, aged 18. (Public Domain)

Trotsky's police mug-shots, c. 1900. (Public Domain)

Sokolovskaya and Trotsky, in the summer of 1902. (Public Domain)

Trotsky in his cell in the Peter and Paul Fortress, 1906. (Public Domain)

Trotsky with Zina in 1906 - during the trial. (Public Domain)

Above: Trotsky in Vienna, c. 1913. (Public Domain)

Left: Trotsky with Nina in France, 1915. (Public Domain)

Right: Trotsky's
French passport,
1915 - used
to attend the
Zimmerwald
Conference. (Public
Domain)

Below: The British
government's
Order for Arrest
of Trotsky and
other Russian
revolutionaries,
March 1917.
(Public Domain)

Signature du Titulaire:

Léon Trotsky

1. *Order for Arrest of Trotsky and Other Socialists*

London March 29 1917.

Britannia,

Halifax, N.S.—

101. Following are on board CHRISTIANAFJORD and should be taken off and retained pending instructions. TROTZKY VOSKOFF GLADNOWSKI MUCHIN and others. These are Russian Socialists leaving for purpose of starting revolution against present Russian government for which TROTZKY is reported to have 10,000 dollars subscribed by Socialists and Germans.

2.40.p.m.

Devonshire,[1]

N.C.O.

1. *H.M.S. Devonshire*, the British warship that provided the boarding party that arrested Trotsky, and the "N.C.O." was the "Naval Control Officer."

Trotsky, Commissar for Foreign Affairs, at his desk, 1918. (Public Domain)

Trotsky (with walking stick) and Kamenev (far right) during the Brest-Litovsk negotiations, in January 1918. (Public Domain)

Trotsky (back row), accompanied by the other Soviet delegates to the Brest-Litovsk negotiations: sitting from L>R: Kamenev, Joffe, Anatastasia Bitzenko, 1918. (Public Domain)

Trotsky and his famous armoured train, visiting the Western Front during Civil War, winter 1918/19. (Public Domain)

Left: Larisa Reissner, c. 1924. (Public Domain)

Below: Trotsky, Lenin and Kamenev in discussion, during the Second Congress of Comintern, July 1920. (Public Domain)

Above: Trotsky (4th from left) in 1920, at the Second Congress of Comintern. To his left is Alfred Rosmer; two to his left is Zinoviev; next to him is Bukharin; two to the left of him is Radek.

Right: Clare Sheridan, sculptor, c.1921. (Public Domain)

Радек.

Above left: Clare Sheridan's bust of Trotsky, 1920 (it was on his bookcase in the study in Mexico). (Public Domain)

Above right: Trotsky, with Christian Rakovsky, 1924. (Public Domain)

Left: Karl Radek, c.1925. (Public Domain)

Above: Olga Kamenev, Trotsky's younger sister, in 1927 - when she was Chair of the Society for Cultural Relations. (Public Domain)

Below: Trotsky and members of the Left Opposition on their way to exile in 1928, after their expulsion from the RCP: L>R Front - Serebryakov, Radek, Trotsky, Boguslavsky, Preobrazhensky; Back - Rakovsky, Drobnis, Beloborodov & Sosnovski. (Public Domain)

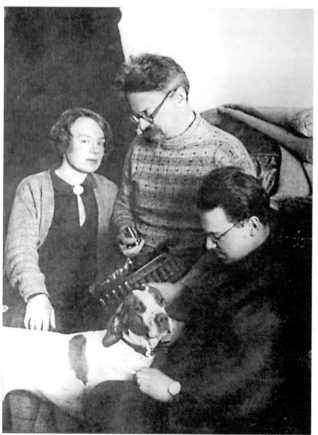

Above: Trotsky and some of the Left Opposition in Moscow, 1927. I Smirnov is on Trotsky's right; I Smilga is on his left; Man Nevelson, Trotsky's son-in-law, is back row, 2nd from left. (Public Domain)

Left: Trotsky, Natalia Sedova and Lyova, Alma-Ata, 1928. (Public Domain)

Above: Trotsky's house in Büyükada. (Public Domain)

Right: Trotsky speaking in Copenhagen, November 1932. (Public Domain)

Above: Trotsky and Sedova, arriving in Mexico, 24 January1937. Frida Kahlo is behind Sedova. (Public Domain)

Below: Trotsky and Sedova, with Diego Rivera on the right, 1937. (Public Domain)

Above: From L to R: Jean van Heijenoort, Albert Goldman [lawyer], Trotsky, Sedova, Jan Frankel, April 1937 - during hearings of the Dewey Commission. (Public Domain)

Right: Frida Kahlo, 1932. (Public Domain)

Sedova and Trotsky in
1937. (Public Domain)

Trotsky with Andre
Breton, the French
Surrealist writer and
poet 1938. (Public
Domain)

Communists also joined them – though not the Decemists or the Workers' Opposition. By then, although the bulk of the working class still remained committed to the November Revolution, they were increasingly unhappy with several Communist policies and practices. Deutscher, in fact, states that: 'If the Bolsheviks had now permitted free elections to the Soviets, they would almost certainly have been swept from power.' Although, as he also argues, the RCP clung to power, not for its own sake, but because it identified the fate of Soviet Russia with itself, seeing itself as the only force in 1921 capable of 'safeguarding the revolution'.[12]

When negotiations between the government and the rebels broke down, Trotsky, as Commissar of War, was ordered to issue a final warning that if weapons were not surrendered, the rebels couldn't count on the 'clemency of Soviet power'. On 7 March, the military assault began, under Tukhachevsky, ending ten days later. Though Trotsky took no further part in it, or in the harsh repression which followed, his democratic revolutionary integrity would be questioned by many over the next twenty years. At the victory parade, Trotsky made a comment which reflected the general mood of the RCP, terming the rebels as 'our blinded sailor-comrades'.

In 1938, Trotsky clarified his role, saying excesses in revolutions are inevitable, as each revolution is 'an "excess" of history': 'Whoever so desires may on this reject revolution in general. I do not reject it. In this sense I carry full and complete responsibility for the suppression of the Kronstadt rebellion.' He argued those Kronstadt sailors were not like those who'd been involved in the November Revolution or Civil War, and had played little part in those events: '…Communist in name only, [they] produced the impression of parasites in comparison with the workers and Red Army men of that time.' However, whether Trotsky's view was accurate – or merely political character assassination – is disputed by historians.[13]

The Tenth Party Congress

On 14 March – with the Kronstadt Rebellion approaching its final stage – Zinoviev introduced the debate on the Trade Union Question. Trotsky defended his views, saying that, if there was a temporary clash between workers' 'passing moods' and the party, the party had the right to assert its power. More seriously, he attacked Zinoviev and Kamenev for abuse of party rules in order to 'win' the argument; and criticised Lenin for siding with Zinoviev. Lenin was furious, saying to some of his closest supporters: 'I have been accused: "You are a son of a bitch for letting the discussion get out of hand". Well, try to stop Trotsky! How many divisions does one have to send against him?' Afterwards, several senior party officials who supported Trotsky's arguments were removed from important party bodies. More significantly, in elections to the CC, Trotsky only managed to come 'a humiliating tenth'[14]

However, the Kronstadt Rebellion, and several serious peasant uprisings against grain requisitions, had shown how politically isolated the RCP was within Soviet Russia. In addition – as French encouragement of the Polish invasion had shown – the Soviet Republic was still surrounded by hostile capitalist states.

Consequently, Lenin came round to Trotsky's earlier suggestion of replacing grain requisitioning with a tax – yet another example of both men arriving at the same conclusions, but not always at the same time.

In fact, as early as 8 February – after discussions with peasant leaders and *before* the Kronstadt Rebellion – Lenin had proposed what became known as the New Economic Policy (NEP) which went even further than Trotsky's earlier proposals, calling for relaxation of some state controls on the economy, and allowing a partial revival of capitalism. This was essentially a return to the 'state capitalism' the Bolsheviks had originally wanted in 1917, before the Civil War had forced them to adopt full control of the economy via 'War Communism'. However, before the Kronstadt Revolt, the majority of RCP leaders had opposed this.

As the partial-revival of capitalism was seen as dangerous, Lenin proposed that, temporarily, other parties in the *soviets* should be banned. He further argued for a temporary ban on factions within the RCP, to prevent banned parties from reappearing within the RCP itself and becoming vehicles for counter-revolution. During the Civil War – despite periodic restrictions when some parties assassinated Bolshevik officials or seemed to be supporting the Whites – this had never been proposed. Significantly, though, this was not an argument, in principle, for a one-party state. Lenin now called for firm party unity around the official platform and policies of the CC. Trotsky agreed, and disbanded the group which had formed around him during the recent controversies: this had included Bukharin, Preobrazhensky, Rakovsky, Pyatakov and Sokolonikov. Tragically, these restrictions on factions were the very weapons Stalin would soon use to oust Trotsky and make himself the sole dictator of the Soviet Union.

The debates over trade unions and economic policy show both Trotsky's strengths and weaknesses – a strongly-logical administrative approach to problems, but, at times, an inability to see the likely political reactions. Apart from angering trade union members, his policies contributed to the further growth of the left wing Workers Opposition and the Decemists. These groups also opposed Lenin's NEP, and were the first to grasp the drift towards an increasingly privileged bureaucratic elite taking over the party. Ironically, given that within two years he would be putting forward many of their criticisms, Trotsky opposed them at the Tenth Party Congress, accusing them of placing '…the workers' rights to elect representatives above the party', and arguing that 'The party is obliged to maintain its dictatorship, regardless of temporary wavering in the spontaneous moods of the masses.' Lenin was not prepared to go this far in justifying a departure from the norms of *soviet* and workers' democracy, hence his opposition to undermining the independence of trade unions – even if it annoyed administrators like Trotsky.[15]

Partly as a result of Trotsky's passionate denunciation of their views as having 'anarcho-syndicalist tendencies', these minority left wing groups were overwhelmingly defeated, with Lenin threatening them with expulsion if they continued their activities – although he failed to get CC agreement on that point. This situation was genuinely tragic for revolutionaries like Trotsky – as Deutscher commented: 'By 1921 the Russian working class had proved itself incapable of exercising its own dictatorship...Having exhausted itself in the revolution and the civil war, it had almost ceased to exist as a political factor.'

After 1921, the really determining section of the party was increasingly reduced to the few thousand veterans of revolution, who Lenin called the 'Old Guard'. Following the risky change to NEP, unity amongst this Old Guard – especially at the very top – came to be seen as vital. After the Congress endorsed the NEP on 15 March, Trotsky took a two-month break – his first since returning to Russia in May 1917. He went to the countryside outside Moscow, spending his time writing, and indulging his love of fishing and hunting.[16]

The Gosplan Controversy

Following his holiday, Trotsky returned to Moscow and the four small rooms he and his family occupied in the Kremlin. The Trotskys – unlike some of their near-neighbours, such as the Radeks and the Kamenevs – maintained their usual modest lifestyle. In fact, because of the privations in 1920s Soviet Russia, it was more modest than they'd enjoyed in Paris or Vienna, as food was at times short even in the Kremlin. Their sons were often without either parent for much of the day as Sedova worked as a conservationist of artefacts of historical significance and then took over responsibility for wounded Red Army soldiers.

The boys also saw less of their step-sisters who'd remained in Petrograd after the government had moved to Moscow. Nonetheless, both Trotsky's daughters remained committed to his politics, and both were excited to take up posts for the Soviet government. Because of work commitments, Trotsky missed both of their weddings – whilst younger daughter Nina was able to forge an independent life, Zina continued to miss her father. Not long after moving into the Kremlin – Trotsky's father – then aged seventy – paid a visit. He'd walked to Moscow, having lost his farm during the Civil War; as Sedova recalled: 'Father and son greeted each other warmly... he said... "We fathers slave away all our lives to put something by for our old age, and then the sons come along and make a revolution."' Trotsky found him a job as manager of a state grain mill, where he worked until his death from typhus in spring 1922.[17]

Trotsky now wondered if the end of the Civil War was 'an anticlimax in his fortunes' and that the 'heroic phase' of the revolution was over. As the Red Army was demobilised – reduced to one-third of its size – and the economic problems forced him to drop plans of transforming it into a democratic and socialist militia, he focussed on its training. Under his direction, the young commanders of the Civil War went on to become brilliant marshals in the Second World War. To inspire Red Army troops with an understanding that they were defenders of the revolution, he devised new regulations and colourful pageantry: 'On May Day and on the anniversaries of the revolution...he rode on horseback...To his greeting "Salute, Comrades!", the troops replied: "We Serve the Revolution!"... There was as yet no mechanical pomp or ceremony.'

But, by 1921, war-ravaged Soviet Russia was tired of heroism, and Trotsky – though he could still thrill the crowds with his speeches – began to lose the 'intimate contact with his audiences' he'd formed during the Civil War.[18]

His main concern remained the need for clear economic planning. On 7 August 1921, Trotsky presented a paper to the CC pointing out the erratic nature of planning. Despite a decision in February 1921 to establish Gosplan (the State Planning Commission), it was only formally constituted in April 1921, and its terms of reference were unclear. Trotsky's main argument was planning had to be based on close monitoring, and that it had to be 'put together around large-scale nationalised industry as a pivot'. As signs of economic recovery under NEP emerged, Trotsky wanted to ensure the socialist part of the economy wasn't swamped by the private. On 4 February

1922, he argued for less party interference and more reliance on economic experts and specialists.[19]

Although Lenin disagreed, Trotsky presented his ideas to the Eleventh Party Congress, which met on 27 March 1922. He argued that although the overall economy was socialist, 'capitalist methods of calculation' were still needed, to make the most efficient use of resources. He also argued this would require sacrifices by workers via 'primitive socialist accumulation'. He rejected attacks by the Workers' Opposition that this was exploitation of workers, stating workers weren't being exploited by a different class, but would be making sacrifices for their own class and revolution. He upset many party officials by saying interference in administration by different levels of the party was exhibiting the 'worst elements of bureaucratism'. While the party was the ruling party, it did 'not at all mean the Party directly administering every detail of every affair'.[20]

Zinoviev led the opposition to Trotsky's suggestions, which were rejected. It was also at this Congress that Zinoviev proposed Stalin for the new post of General Secretary of the RCP – Lenin, though doubtful about Stalin's suitability for such a post, eventually agreed. As this was essentially an administrative post with no obvious political significance, none of the other leaders was interested in doing the job. However, it would give Stalin ultimate control over the appointment or dismissal of key party personnel, including party secretaries.

After the Congress, Lenin – trying to rebuild bridges – proposed Trotsky as one of his three deputies. Trotsky refused, as he would have become responsible for implementing an economic approach he felt lacked focus. Another possible reason for his refusal was that he was generally seen as Lenin's 'second in command', so he didn't need to have it formalised. Instead, with the Commissariat of War no longer so central, Trotsky used his 'free' time to seriously consider economic matters; to complete his book, *Literature and the Revolution*; and to focus on the Communist International: 'While the Politburo was expressing its disapproval of his [Trotsky's] aloofness, he was surrounded by books and immersed in his writing'.[21]

Then, on 25 May 1922, Lenin suffered a severe stroke and was out of action until mid-July. When Lenin returned to work, he was horrified to discover that Zinoviev, Kamenev and Stalin – in what became known as the 'triumvirate' – were working to remove Trotsky from his leading positions. The first sign of that was that they delayed telling Trotsky – himself recuperating from a foot injury, sustained on a fishing trip – about Lenin's stroke for three days. Although Lenin blocked these moves, Trotsky was increasingly sidelined by party officials. This was partly down to his inability to understand the importance of establishing friendly – as opposed to professional – relations with the other leaders: something Stalin understood much better. Nonetheless, believing he was right, Trotsky – largely unaware of his increasing isolation at the top of the party – continued to push his ideas about giving Gosplan more control.[22]

Increasingly, Trotsky – who, in the first half of 1922 had been 'the Bolshevik disciplinarian' – found himself in conflict with the party's disciplinarians. Ironically, having attacked the Workers' Opposition and the Decemists – who'd been the first to argue for a more socialist direction to economic policy, the restoration of inner-party democracy, and against growing state and party bureaucracy – Trotsky was now putting forward views similar to theirs. Essentially, Trotsky began grappling with the dilemma – which also affected the party as a whole – between authority and freedom: 'He sought to strike a balance between Bolshevik discipline and proletarian democracy; and the more the balance was tipped in favour of the former, the more he was inclined to uphold the latter.' As that balance was increasingly upset by developments after 1921, Trotsky began putting the claims of inner-party democracy above those of discipline. As Stalin came to personify the growing bureaucracy and drift towards totalitarianism, Trotsky increasingly represented a 'workers' democracy' standpoint.[23]

Lenin Reconsiders

Although increasingly isolated at the top, for the party as a whole – and the world – Trotsky was still seen as standing shoulder to shoulder with Lenin, as one of Russia's two main revolutionaries. In November 1922, with Lenin still not fully recovered, and Trotsky absent from Moscow, the CC proposed weakening state control over foreign trade, allowing rich peasants to sell their produce abroad for higher prices. Trotsky and Lenin were horrified, seeing the state monopoly of foreign trade – one of the 'commanding heights' of the Soviet economy – as vital for moving to a fully-socialist economy, by stopping foreign capital subverting moves to socialism. In mid-December, Lenin wrote to Trotsky, to ask him to oppose this, commenting: 'I think we've reached complete agreement. I ask you to announce our solidarity at the plenum [of the CC].' In the end, this wasn't necessary as the CC, as soon as they knew Lenin was against, dropped their proposal.[24]

Trotsky then resumed his arguments in favour of giving Gosplan more powers and, in late December, Lenin wrote a letter to the Twelfth

Party Congress, broadly supporting this. Lenin – shocked by the level of party and state bureaucracy on his return to work – discussed this with Trotsky. According to Trotsky, in a private conversation, Lenin accepted 'organisational changes' were needed – including within the CC's Orgburo, supervised by Stalin: '"Oh, well", Lenin went on, obviously pleased that we had called the thing by its right name, "if that's the case, then I offer you a bloc against bureaucracy in general and against the Organizational Bureau in particular"….' Though Thatcher disputes whether there was such 'a firm Lenin–Trotsky alliance', it seems Lenin then proposed establishing a special commission, with himself and Trotsky as members, to weaken Stalin's bureaucratic grip and for: 'creating such conditions in the party as would allow me [Trotsky] to become Lenin's deputy, and, as he intended, his successor to the post of Chairman of the Soviet of People's Commissaries.'[25]

However, Lenin then suffered another stroke – and growing political unease led him, between 23 and 25 December 1922, to dictate what became known as his *Political Testament*. This assessed all the main leaders, and raised particular concerns about the relationship between Trotsky and Stalin, which he feared could lead to a serious split in the party. In it, Lenin noted Stalin, as General Secretary, had: 'concentrated enormous power in his hands' but worried he did not know 'how to use that power with sufficient caution'. As regards Trotsky, after referring to 'his exceptional abilities', Lenin expressed concerns over 'his too far-reaching self-confidence and a disposition to be too much attracted by the purely administrative side of affairs'. On 4 January 1923, angered by Stalin's extreme rudeness to Krupskaya, Lenin added a *Postscript*, recommending Stalin be removed from his position as General Secretary. A few days earlier, he'd asked Krupskaya to tell Trotsky his feelings towards him hadn't changed since they'd first met in London in autumn 1902.[26]

At the end of January 1923, Lenin wrote an article criticising the work of another body supervised by Stalin. The Politburo opposed printing it in *Pravda* but, supported by Kamenev, Trotsky got it printed. Stalin then proposed Trotsky become one of Lenin's deputies, in charge of the Council of Labour and Defence. Trotsky again declined, pointing out that Gosplan needed to give precedence to long-term planning over short-term financial considerations, and that the Politburo's interference was undermining effective economic planning. Trotsky's refusal was a mistake – his 'arguments were cogent but reflected a tactical rigidity. He was turning down a chance to dominate the Soviet government while Lenin was away. His repeated refusals made him appear haughty – something his enemies were quick to exploit.'[27]

Yet Trotsky continued to argue his case and, by 13 February, the Politburo began to support him. It was at this point a 'whispering campaign' against Trotsky emerged, claiming he'd opposed Lenin at almost every turn. Trotsky countered this by a letter to the CC on 23 February – thus giving his opponents time to organise their response. The CC then agreed Trotsky's proposals should be debated at the Twelfth Congress. On 2 March, Lenin wrote what was to be his last article – *Better Fewer, but Better* – about how careerists were joining the party, and thus the need for expulsions.

The Georgian Affair

By then, Trotsky and Lenin had been brought even closer together by the 'Georgian Affair'. Stalin, as Commissar for Nationalities, was in charge of transforming the RSFSR into a more centralised Union of Soviet Socialist Republics (USSR). However, Lenin became concerned at attempts to weaken the autonomy of the constituent republics, and was particularly alarmed by reports of Stalin's brutal suppression of his political opponents in Georgia. On 5 March, Lenin wrote to Trotsky, asking him to attack Stalin's treatment of the Georgians at the forthcoming CC: 'Dear Comrade Trotsky: ...If you were to agree to undertake the defence, my mind would be at rest.... With best comradely greetings, LENIN.' Trotsky – himself confined to bed with lumbago – asked if he could discuss it with Kamenev. Lenin immediately wrote back, urging Trotsky not to give Stalin – or any of his associates – advance warning of the attack to come, warning that Kamenev 'will immediately show everything to Stalin, and Stalin will make a rotten compromise and then deceive us'. Fearing he was about to die – his next stroke was imminent – Lenin informed Kamenev he was breaking off all relations with Stalin, because of his rudeness to Krupskaya, who had been collecting evidence about Georgia for Lenin.[28]

As so often before, Trotsky's foresight had initially condemned him to political isolation. Yet, strangely, Trotsky hesitated – even though Lenin saw Trotsky's earlier concerns as being right, and wanted his own views published before the Twelfth Congress, due to begin on 17 April. Instead, believing Stalin and the rest of the triumvirate were beaten, and still expecting Lenin to recover, Trotsky handed over Lenin's dossier to Kamenev on 6 March. Trotsky also agreed with Stalin – who said he'd mend his ways – that only leading provincial delegates should be given a summary of Lenin's views. Trotsky even said he wouldn't support Lenin's call for Stalin to be dismissed as General Secretary. Four days later, on 10 March, Lenin suffered his third and final stroke, leaving him paralysed and speechless most of the time until his death in January 1924.

Stalin and his supporters relaxed – especially after persuading Trotsky to say nothing about Georgia and Lenin's views at the Congress. As Deutscher said: 'Hindsight makes Trotsky's behaviour appear incredibly foolish...Years later he remarked wistfully that if he had spoken up at the twelfth congress, with Lenin's authority behind him, he would probably have defeated Stalin there and then...'

As well as Lenin's support making him feel secure, Trotsky also fatally underestimated his rival – 'the wilful and sly but shabby and inarticulate man in the background' – seeing it as something of a bad joke that such a man should be his rival. He was not prepared to stoop to their level of intrigue. However, his conduct can be seen 'as awkward and as preposterous as must be the behaviour of any character from high drama suddenly involved in low farce'. However, objective changes also aided his opponents: 'Some of my friends used to say to me: "They will never dare to come out against you in the open. In the minds of the people you are too inseparably bound to Lenin's name. It is impossible to erase the October revolution, or the Red army, or the civil war."' Trotsky didn't believe that to be the case, as: 'In the final analysis the fate of personal authority is determined by the deeper processes going on in the masses.'[29]

The start of the Twelfth Congress – the first without Lenin – showed Trotsky's position in the party as a whole: almost every one of the usual messages from party cells, trade unions and student groups from across the country, mentioned Lenin and Trotsky in the same breath. While a few mentioned Zinoviev and Kamenev, hardly any mentioned Stalin – making it very clear whom the party would have chosen as Lenin's successor. Consequently, behind the scenes, the triumvirs spoke to delegates, warning them of signs of Trotsky's 'ambition', and arguing the case for a collective leadership of 'lesser' men.

Although Lenin had told the Georgian delegates Trotsky would explode a 'bomb' against Stalin, Trotsky kept his promise to Stalin to say nothing when the Georgian Affair was debated. Although Bukharin and Rakovsky supported the Georgians' call for Lenin's notes to be read out, Stalin was able to deflect this. Instead, Trotsky argued for central planning, with each factory to be 'profitable' – even if it meant redundancies – with profits funding further state investments. To oversee all this, he once again appealed for Gosplan to be given more powers; and, once again, he stressed – openly – how, initially, it would have to be the industrial working class which would shoulder the main burden of industrial reconstruction. Though, 'in Trotsky's scheme of things there was no room for any sudden "abolition" of N.E.P., for prohibition of private trade by decree' or 'for the violent destruction of private farming.' Not surprisingly, this didn't go down well with the party or workers; and, once again, Zinoviev, on behalf of the triumvirate, opposed this. As Deutscher commented: 'He could not help saying the most unpopular things once he was convinced that what he had to say was of vital importance and that it was his duty to say it.'[30]

Zinoviev, speaking of Lenin's illness, then called for strict party unity around the 'Old Guard', stating that any criticism of the party line, even left wing criticism, would be essentially 'Menshevik' criticism. Nothing like this had ever been said before and, although specifically directed at the Workers' Opposition, the real target was Trotsky. The Workers' Opposition, and other dissenters, hit back, attacking such 'papal infallibility'; calling for the triumvirate and the ruling clique to be disbanded; attacking Stalin's persecution of critics; and calling for the end of the 1921 ban on factions. Yet, Trotsky instead said – given the continued absence of Lenin – he fully supported the need for unity. Thus, at this most crucial turning point, Trotsky failed to protect himself from what was to come:

> 'He missed the opportunity of confounding the triumvirs and discrediting Stalin. He let down his allies...He kept silent when the cry for inner-party democracy rose from the floor...
>
> 'Finally, Trotsky directly strengthened the triumvirs when he declared his "unshaken" solidarity with the Politburo and the Central Committee....'[31]

The Left Opposition

When the new – and enlarged – CC elected by the Congress met, it reappointed Stalin as General Secretary; Trotsky didn't propose a different candidate, even though he knew Lenin would have done. Of its forty members, only Rakovsky, Radek and Pyatakov were his friends; whilst in the Politburo – comprising himself, Lenin, Zinoviev, Kamenev, Stalin, Bukharin and Tomsky – even Bukharin, in the process of moving from the left to the right in the party, was increasingly drawn to the triumvirs. Thus Stalin, and the other two triumvirs, dominated the Politburo and through that body, the CC and the Central Control Commission (CCC). In particular, Stalin made full use of his power to nominate and appoint officials – especially party secretaries, who increasingly decided delegates to congresses. There was now only one way Trotsky could have counteracted these developments – by appealing over the heads of the 'Old Guard' to rank and file party members. Something that, considering his support for unity, he could not do. For the time being, he was forced to wait for an opportunity to resist.

Such an opportunity came in the summer of 1923, when food shortages – and the reappearance of unemployment in some sectors – led to a series of strikes. Although the leaders of the Workers' Opposition and the Decemists, wishing to avoid expulsions, didn't support these protests, some of their splinter groups – such as the Workers' Group and the Workers' Truth – did. This took the party elite by surprise, and it looked like a general strike was in the offing. This was the most serious political crisis since Kronstadt.

Yet at this crucial time, Trotsky and Sedova were both ill: Sedova with a bad case of malaria. As a result, doctors recommended both should rest, and the Politburo told Trotsky not to engage in 'internal party conversations'. However, in September, with even some left wing Communists renaming the NEP as the 'New Exploitation of the Proletariat', Dzerzhinsky, in charge of the GPU – as the security police were now called – suggested insisting all party members denounce any member who engaged in 'aggressive action' against the leadership. Although Trotsky didn't object to these dissidents being imprisoned for their activities, this was a demand too much. He also argued that the causes of the protests could only be dealt with by proper economic planning – as approved by the Twelfth Congress, but still largely unimplemented – in order to speed up economic recovery, so facilitating higher wages and more consumer goods.[32]

Zinoviev and Stalin, however, insisted on increased party control and firm action against 'factional' activity. Taking advantage of Trotsky's absence, they extended party control of the Red Army, and significantly reduced the use of military specialists. When Trotsky returned, there was the predictable explosion, with Trotsky threatening to resign from the CC and all his government posts – but the Politburo wouldn't accept this. Trotsky also criticised Stalin's use of inappropriate methods to extend party control of the economy. On 8 October, Trotsky sent an 'Open Letter' – dictated whilst he was still ill – addressed to the CC, but only intended for the Politburo, claiming Stalin had 'selected' most of the delegates to the Twelfth Congress; that he was removing Trotsky's supporters; and that local party secretaries were increasingly being appointed rather than elected: 'The appointment of provincial Party committee secretaries is now the rule…Participation by the Party rank and file…is becoming more and more illusory.'[33]

Then, on 15 October 1923, forty-six leading communists, several of whom – Preobrazhensky, Pyatakov, and Antonov-Ovseenko (then chief political commissar of the Red Army) – were associated with Trotsky, sent their *Letter of the Forty-Six* to the Politburo, asking for their concerns to be passed to the CC and the party as a whole. Their 'Letter' – or 'Platform', as it became known – basically echoed Trotsky's economic planning ideas, but went further by also demanding the ending of the ban on party factions, in order to allow full debate on important issues: 'The inner party struggle is waged all the more savagely the more it is waged in silence and secrecy.' Members of the Workers' Opposition and the Decemists were also involved in this clear political platform, which became known as the '1923 Opposition'.[34]

Though the CC discussed the 'Letter', it was kept secret from the party as a whole and, on 19 October, the Politburo accused Trotsky of being responsible for this factionalism, and of trying to separate the Soviet apparatus from the Party. It then referenced all the occasions on which he'd opposed Lenin – though failing to mention all those where they'd agreed. The CC then sent agents to party cells, warning them not to discuss the unpublished 'Letter', but calling on them to denounce it! Trotsky responded on 23 October, denying he'd in any way orchestrated this loose coalition. Though it seems likely he knew what they were planning, he was scrupulous in observing the ban, and the triumvirs never presented any evidence to the contrary. Trotsky then reminded them Lenin had agreed with him over giving Gosplan more freedom to decide economic matters, and that on 2 June 1923, Krupskaya had circulated Lenin's letter, stating just that, to all Politburo members. In a letter to Zinoviev, she later objected to the triumvirate's attempts to blame Trotsky for the growing split in the party, saying 'I ought to have shouted that this was a lie'.[35]

On 26 October, the CC reiterated that factional discussion on the basis of platforms was forbidden. However, it also resolved, on 7 November – the sixth anniversary of the revolution – to move towards restoring internal party democracy, by opening the pages of *Pravda* and other newspapers, and inviting party members to express their views on issues they were concerned about. Initially, only Moscow was given this freedom. The triumvirs allowed the Forty-Six to visit party cells to argue their case – and received a resounding shock: party cells received official leaders with hostility, whilst acclaiming 'Opposition' representatives. Research has shown that between 25% and 50% of workers' cells in Moscow approved of Trotsky's calls for reform; while of the military cells, at least 30% backed Trotsky; and amongst the Communist Youth (Komsomol) cells and university cells, support for him was even higher.[36]

The triumvirs panicked, ordering the garrison cells not to vote on the statement of the Forty-Six, and dismissing Antonov-Ovseenko from his post. Shortly after, other critics were demoted or disciplined, and the committees of party cells that had backed the Forty-Six were dismissed and reorganised. The Politburo then decided to take the steam out of the situation by seriously considering appointing Trotsky as head of Gosplan; 'borrowing' some of Trotsky's and the Forty-Six's demands; and promising a 'New Course' which would allow full freedom of expression and criticism for party members. At this crucial time, Trotsky himself was still suffering from a prolonged bout of 'flu' and malaria contracted during a hunting trip in late October 1923, so several Politburo meetings were held in his flat: '"Those were hard days", my wife writes in her memoirs, "days of tense fighting for Lev Davydovitch at the Politburo against the rest of the members. He was alone and ill...After each of these meetings, L. D.'s temperature mounted; he came out of his study soaked through..."'[37]

In 'On Building the Party', the Politburo set out new guidelines on internal party democracy; Trotsky, however, insisted the rule against factionalism shouldn't automatically be applied to 'disciplined' party members who presented collective statements. On condition his reservations be recorded, Trotsky signed the text on 5 December. However, the day before, *Pravda* had published an essay by him, setting out his general concerns about bureaucracy. This was followed by other articles which eventually appeared in his pamphlet, *The New Course* – containing the essence of 'Trotskyism'. On 11 December, *Pravda* published his 'Open Letter to Party Meetings', which denounced – with his usual passion and sense of urgency – increasing 'bureaucratic degeneration', and warned the rank and file that the leadership already seemed to be trying to 'nullify bureaucratically' the newly-announced 'New Course'. He even suggested the older leadership was out of touch with younger communists, and was in danger of degenerating into reformism: 'It is only by a constant active collaboration with the new generation, within the framework of democracy, that the Old Guard will preserve itself as a revolutionary factor.' This looked very much like factionalism – and, by seeming to break the recent agreement, was bound to anger the rest of the Politburo.[38]

Their anger increased when, read out to party meetings, it met with enthusiastic responses – even from members of dissident groups that Trotsky had voted against. But he'd left it too late – in the nine months since the Twelfth Congress, Stalin had taken a much firmer grip on local parties. Consequently, although many party meetings were overwhelmed by supporters of the 'Opposition' and passed resolutions in favour of Trotsky's 'Open Letter', it was the branch secretaries – appointed by Stalin – who passed on, or suppressed, the outcome of meetings, and then packed subsequent meetings with supporters of the triumvirs.

This aspect proved crucial, as the Politburo had ruled that the debate would be concluded at the Thirteenth Party Conference in January 1924. Before then, branch secretaries influenced the indirect election of delegates, by concealing votes, to make sure it was supporters of the triumvirs, not of the 'Opposition', who would attend the Conference: 'The Forty-Six claimed, without meeting with denial, that at the regional conference, which was the tier above the primary cells, they had obtained not less than 36 per cent of the vote; yet at the gubernia conference, the next tier, that percentage dwindled to 18.' On that basis, it would appear 'the opposition had behind it the great majority of the Moscow organization'.[39]

Trotsky was also concerned over Stalin and Zinoviev's interference with *Pravda* when reporting party discussions. When two journalists resigned over such editorial interference, Stalin appointed replacements loyal to him and Zinoviev. Trotsky's main supporters – such as Rakovsky, Krestinsky and Joffe – were then appointed to posts abroad, while lesser figures were demoted or even dismissed. This sort of behaviour was what Trotsky had disliked about the early Bolshevik Party, and what some in the IDO had feared might reappear after the merger.

However, Trotsky was especially concerned about what he saw as the signs of a 'Thermidorian reaction' – as had happened in the French Revolution after 1789, when the initial revolutionary phase was stalled, and then reversed, by more conservative elements. As a result of the NEP, many wealthy peasants (*kulaks*) had emerged, along with wealthy middlemen (known as 'NEP-men') in the towns. The fear – in a one-party system – was that these new capitalist elements would use their wealth to infiltrate the party and influence its policies, and so bring about a quiet counter-revolution. Hence the great importance Trotsky placed on Gosplan – and why he now stressed the need for open debate within the party to combat such tendencies.

The response of the Politburo was quick – Trotsky was denounced in *Pravda* for breaking the agreement; for going above the heads of the CC to the rank and file; and for trying to set younger party members against the 'Old Guard'. *Pravda* also alluded to his past associations with the Mensheviks – seen ever since 1917 as a petit bourgeois party. Trotsky's response – sent to *Pravda* on 23 December, but not published until 28 December – added to the tensions, by hinting at the substitutionism he'd warned about in 1904; arguing that the ban on factions was being used as a ban on debate; and warning against the danger represented by 'conservative bureaucratic factionalism'. On the last day of December 1923, the Politburo hit back with an article in *Pravda*, claiming Trotsky's article was 'a direct confession that he had set up a faction' and that, although Lenin had come round to Trotsky's arguments for strengthening Gosplan's role, he had also said Trotsky should not be its president.[40]

Trotsky's gifts – which included a strong sense of drama – were best suited to the 'heroic' phases of the revolution and the Civil War. By 1921, the people were exhausted, and Trotsky's romantic rhetoric and revolutionary exhortation were out of kilter with the new times. After 1921, what was needed was Lenin's quiet, unobtrusive personality, which was more attuned to the people's political moods. Thus, by the end of 1923 – with Lenin inactive – Trotsky was isolated at the top levels of the RCP. This isolation would intensify in the next six years, at the end of which he would be expelled from the Soviet Union.

Chapter 8

Fighting Against His Time, 1924–28

> '…when the struggle is one for great principles, the revolutionary can only follow one rule: *Fais ce que dois, advienne que pourra.*'[1]

This comment – 'Do what you must, come what may' – written in exile in Turkey, explains why, after 1923, Trotsky continued his resistance, despite mounting attacks on him, gradual political decline and increasing ill health – the latter probably exacerbated by the strain and depression resulting from political struggle, and growing awareness of his isolation. Yet his work routine remained exhausting – as noted by Sedova: 'Leon Davidovitch always had an inordinate capacity for work. He lived under great pressure, dealing with twenty different matters at once…No wonder that his health began to suffer:….'[2]

His deteriorating health necessitated frequent long absences from Moscow, seriously weakening him as the Opposition's most authoritative spokesperson. His political influence was further weakened by the 'cult of Lenin', beginning immediately following Lenin's death, whereby his opponents decided to revere Lenin's every word – including those written during pre-1917 disputes with Trotsky – and to rename Petrograd as Leningrad. Strangely, Trotsky was reluctant to contradict this, and showed 'almost inexplicable forbearance in refraining from any sort of protest against the partial suppression of Lenin's will.'[3]

Though Trotsky had, since his youth, seen 'intellectual recognition' as 'immeasurably more important than official posts or political status', he was further weakened by his 'constructive dismissal' as the Commissar of War. He also failed to judge the most opportune times to engage in the unfolding political struggle – Stalin, dismissed by Trotsky as a 'nonentity', proved more skilful. Unlike the lead-up to the November Revolution, Trotsky seemed to lack 'guile in struggle after struggle'. By publishing *The New Course*, 'he had thrown away the advantages of stealth. And having started an ill-prepared offensive, he omitted to give it his all'.[4]

Trotsky's Left Opposition

As Trotsky formed the 'Left Opposition' at the end of 1923, Stalin used his growing power over the party machine to stifle criticisms, and to isolate Trotsky and his supporters before the Thirteenth Party Conference. On 14 January – with Trotsky absent because of ill health – the CC condemned Trotsky's actions, and a Military Commission was set up to examine the work of his Commissariat of War. Stalin also ensured most Left Opposition supporters failed to get selected as Conference delegates.

Continuing ill health meant Trotsky was unable to attend the Conference, which began on 16 January – leaving Pyatakov, Preobrazhensky, Radek and V. Smirnov to speak for the Opposition. With only three delegates supporting Trotsky, the Conference formally condemned the views of Trotsky and the Forty-Six as a 'petty bourgeois deviation from Leninism', accusing them of 'ultra-factionalism' and disloyalty to the Politburo. Promises of more internal party democracy were ignored; instead, more Oppositionists were demoted or dismissed from posts of responsibility. The Conference ended on 18 January; that same day, Trotsky – on doctor's orders – left Moscow for a two-month rest cure at Sukhumi, on the Abkhazian coast of the Black Sea. Three days later, on 21 January 1924, Lenin died.

As soon as Trotsky received news of Lenin's death – despite suffering from a high temperature – he cabled he was returning immediately for the funeral. Stalin, however, said he'd not be back in time, and it was now particularly important for Trotsky to get well as soon as possible. Consequently – after cabling a brief stunned tribute to Lenin – Trotsky continued his journey, aware that, without Lenin's support, his ability to resist had been drastically reduced. However, the funeral didn't take place until 27 January, with Stalin and the others as the chief mourners. Though Trotsky's instinct had been to write a letter of condolence to Krupskaya, he didn't, 'afraid that [his words] would only sound conventional'. Despite this surprising failure, in a letter to Trotsky – written shortly after Lenin's funeral – Krupskaya wrote: 'The attitude of V. I. towards you at the time when you came to us in London from Siberia has not changed until his death. I wish you, Lev Davydovich, strength and health, and I embrace you warmly.'[5]

Trotsky's absence from the funeral was seen by many senior party members as disrespectful – and greatly surprised his friends, and his son, Lyova. As Sedova later wrote, Lyova revealed in a letter how, despite a heavy cold and a very high temperature: 'he went in his not very warm coat to the Hall of Columns to pay his last respects, and waited, waited, and waited with impatience for our arrival. One could feel in his letter his bitter bewilderment and diffident reproach.' More damaging to Trotsky's chances, was the triumvirs' decision to widen party membership: the next four months saw almost 250,000 new members – most of this 'Lenin Levy' were politically immature or simple careerists.[6]

While recovering at Sukhumi, the new Military Commission visited him, informing him of certain 'personnel changes' – including replacing Efraim Sklyansky, who'd been his loyal deputy throughout the Civil War, with one of Zinoviev's supporters. Debilitated by illness, and feeling the revolution was on the ebb and reaction on the rise, Trotsky concentrated on getting his huge archive in order, preparing his collected works for publication, and writing letters and articles. He also drafted most of his book, *On Lenin*, which came out in 1925, and was intended to counter the ever-growing misrepresentations of the triumvirs about his relations with Lenin.

Yet, Trotsky – who arrived back in Moscow a few days before the Thirteenth Party Congress met on 24 May – still had a chance of avoiding his fate, as Krupskaya had just revealed Lenin's *Testament* to the CC, and wanted it read out to the Congress. However, the CC only agreed to it being revealed to senior Congress delegates, the day before the Congress. Nonetheless, its clear recommendation that Stalin be dismissed should have ensured he would never succeed Lenin as leader of the Communist Party. If Trotsky, Zinoviev and Kamenev had come together then – as they did in 1926 – Stalin and Bukharin would almost certainly have been defeated. However, Trotsky remained silent, while Zinoviev and Kamenev argued the party needed to stick together following Lenin's death. So – despite strong protests from Krupskaya – the CC decided not to remove Stalin as General Secretary, and not to publish Lenin's *Testament*.

At the Congress, Zinoviev called on Trotsky to 'recant' his 'petit bourgeois deviation'. Trotsky – who otherwise stayed silent – refused, pointing out it was the duty of a revolutionary to draw attention to dangers and errors. He further argued, since many of his views on Gosplan had now been adopted, they couldn't be termed a 'petit bourgeois deviation', stating 'I cannot say so, because I do not think so'. However, he then made a serious tactical mistake by stating no one could be 'wrong against the party', and that he would accept any discipline the Congress decided on: 'In the last analysis, the party is always right....' Some have seen this as 'the most inept speech of his career'. The Congress – before which Trotsky appeared as 'bent but unbroken, disciplined but unrepentant' and seemingly 'all the more defiant' – duly endorsed the Thirteenth Conference's verdict. He was then threatened with expulsion if he engaged in any further political controversy. His Left Opposition had thus been defeated, so ending the first stage of the power struggle.[7]

'Losing' the Communist International

Although increasingly isolated within the RCP leadership, Trotsky – as the author of its stirring manifestoes and the hero of its first four congresses – had significant support within the Communist International. Most European communists were shocked by the attacks on him: 'To them Trotsky had been the embodiment of the Russian revolution, of its heroic legend, and of international communism.' During 1923, the German, French and Polish Communist parties – Comintern's three biggest parties – had protested about the campaign against him. However, the triumvirs – anxious to end Trotsky's support within Comintern – 'disciplined' those communists still supporting him.[8]

By May 1924, Zinoviev – as Chair of Comintern – managed to get the leaders of all foreign communist parties – except one – to support the judgement passed on Trotsky and 'Trotskyism'. The one exception was the French CP, whose leader, Boris Souvarine, announced their CC had voted twenty-two to two to protest against the attacks on Trotsky. Within a month, Souvarine had been expelled from the French CP.

In June, the Fifth Congress of Comintern met in Moscow and endorsed Trotsky's excommunication. Although writing his last *Manifesto* for the Comintern, Trotsky was not re-elected as a full member to its ECCI – ironically, Stalin took his place.

The Power Struggle Intensifies

The next stage of the power struggle began on the eve of the seventh anniversary of the November Revolution, with the publication of Trotsky's 1917 speeches and writings – prefaced by his new article, *Lessons of October*. In it, Trotsky – debarred from commenting on contemporary political issues – used history to show how close his views were to Lenin's. He also revealed how Zinoviev and Kamenev had opposed Lenin on several critical issues – including the armed uprising in November 1917. Trotsky always denied he'd written *Lessons of October* in order to reopen a factional struggle – though 'it is hard to see what purpose it had other than to denounce those who had dared brand him "petit bourgeois"'.

Whatever his motives, its publication 'at once stirred up a storm'. The triumvirs – aware it undermined their depiction of Trotsky as a 'Menshevik' – launched a coordinated 'literary debate' against 'Trotskyism'. Dozens of articles – often personally abusive – appeared in the press, focussing on his initial links with the Mensheviks; his early disagreements with Lenin; and denying his leading role in the November Revolution. Kamenev, Zinoviev and Bukharin attacked Trotsky in speeches and articles, calling for an 'ideological struggle against Trotskyism'; while Stalin organised party cell meetings to criticise and condemn Trotsky – even claiming a previously unheard of 'Centre', not the MRC, had masterminded the November insurrection. They also warned Trotsky's theory of 'Permanent Revolution' – an 'insult' to Soviet Russia's self-sufficiency – risked undermining peace and stability.[9]

Despite these attempts to erode his reputation, Trotsky – whose illness had flared up yet again, confining him to bed – remained silent. Even when groups of workers wrote to the CC, criticising the anti-Trotsky campaign as 'harmful and unworthy of the party', and friends such as Rakovsky and Joffe urged him to respond: 'L. D. kept silent. But what it cost him to maintain that silence!' Friends who visited him, commented on how pale and tired he looked. For Sedova, still working at the Commissariat of Education, going to work during these attacks was 'like running a gauntlet' – though there was unquestionable sympathy from most of her colleagues.[10]

A joint CC/CCC meeting was announced for 19 January 1925, to discuss Trotsky's removal as Commissar of War. Trotsky – too ill to consider attending – restrained followers like Antonov-Ovseenko, who urged him to appeal to the military cells. Instead, on 15 January, he pre-emptively resigned: thus cutting himself off, without a fight, from an important political base. As he himself wrote: 'Next to the traditions of the October revolution the epigones feared most the traditions of the civil war and my connection with the army.' His resignation letter stressed he had adhered to the decisions of the Thirteenth Party Congress; had not written his essay as an attempt to revive factional debates; and that he was prepared to take on whatever new role the party decided.[11]

His resignation was accepted, though Stalin didn't support Zinoviev and Kamenev's call for Trotsky to be expelled from both the Politburo and the CC. However, Trotsky was given a final warning that any renewed controversy would result in his expulsion from those bodies. Only two CC members, Rakovsky and Pyatakov, voted against. Almost immediately, the triumvirs launched a new campaign to 'explain' to the general public the 'anti-Bolshevik' character of 'Trotskyism'. Trotsky then left for the Caucasus, once again on doctors' orders, to recuperate.

An Interval

There was then a lull in inner-party struggle until the summer. During it, Trotsky effectively disbanded the Left Opposition, telling his bewildered supporters: 'We must not do anything at this moment, we must not come out into the open in any way.' He returned to Moscow in May 1925, and accepted new, relatively unimportant, posts on the Supreme Council of the National Economy (*Vesenkha*). His return coincided with Stalin – supported by Bukharin – revealing, for the first time, his idea of 'Socialism in One Country', directly opposing Trotsky's continued adherence to 'Permanent Revolution.'[12]

However, having defeated Trotsky, a rift within the triumvirate and the Politiburo emerged: partly triggered by Bukharin's call for peasants to 'enrich' themselves. Although the Fourteenth Party Conference, held at the end of April, had condemned that phrase, it had also reduced the tax burden on peasants, and made it easier to lease land and to hire – and fire – rural labour. Zinoviev and Kamenev began criticising socialism in one country as 'anti-Leninist'. As Zinoviev and Kamenev began moving left, the Centre – led by Stalin – was joined by Bukharin and the Right. These divisions came into the open during the summer, with Zinoviev attacking the growing dominance of Bukharin's rightist views, and arguing that the Conference's decisions were a 'retreat' from socialism.

Essentially, Stalin argued the new Soviet state – though isolated and surrounded by hostile capitalist states – could construct socialism on its own. However, it was vital to maintain peace and stability – particularly crucial was the NEP's alliance (*smychka*) between the industrial workers and the peasantry. As Trotsky clung to the belief economically-backward Russia needed assistance from sympathetic developed countries to progress to socialism, he was accused of lack of faith in Russia and its people. Yet Stalin's new policy was in complete contradiction to previous Bolshevik beliefs: 'He [Lenin] and his comrades knew that the emancipation of the workers could only result from the joint efforts of many nations…This conviction permeated all Bolshevik thinking and activity until the end of the Lenin era.'[13]

Nonetheless, in his essay *Towards Capitalism or Socialism,* Trotsky argued steps *towards* socialism could – and should – be taken. Yet he also warned about the relative technological backwardness of Soviet Russia, the threat posed by the USA's advanced capitalism, and how the privately-owned elements of the NEP economy could frustrate socialist economic policies. He thus began arguing for moves to strengthen socialist industrial planning. He also called for Comintern to adopt a more revolutionary line, in order to end Soviet Russia's isolation.

During the summer of 1925, there was another attempt to remove Trotsky from the CC, after Max Eastman – an Opposition supporter – had referred to Lenin's *Last Testament* in his book *Since Lenin Died*, giving a sympathetic account of Trotsky's positions since 1924. The triumvirs demanded Trotsky deny Eastman's claims – he did so, as urged by several of his close supporters, to avoid disciplinary actions. By then, several groups of Trotsky's supporters were meeting regularly in Moscow: these included Radek, Preobrazhensky, Pyatakov, Rakovsky, Antonov-Ovseenko, Muralov and Ivan Smirnov – leading Oppositionists, as well as his friends. While, in Leningrad, a group of about 30 Oppositionists – centred around Sokolovskaya – also maintained regular contacts. Elsewhere, though, with Trotsky avoiding political controversy, many Opposition groups began to disperse. However, during September, Trotsky once again became concerned about the danger of a Thermidorian counter-revolution. He revealed his thoughts to his friend, Skylansky: 'A victorious counter-revolution may develop its great men. But its first stage, the Thermidor, demands mediocrities who can't see farther than their noses.'[14]

In October 1925, Krupskaya joined Zinoviev and Kamenev in a joint statement, calling for free debate within the entire party on all issues. However, with the Centre and Right united behind him, Stalin blocked that – and the Left were then warned not to make any public criticisms of official policy. Soon after, though, at a Moscow Party meeting, Kamenev spoke about a 'pro-kulak' deviation; while, in November, Zinoviev's Leningrad party began attacking Politburo policies. Stalin immediately began removing Kamenev's supporters from their positions in the Moscow party. He had less success in Leningrad, though, where Zinoviev had a strong political base – bolstered by his also being President of the Comintern, and now having Krupskaya's support.

Trotsky, meanwhile, engrossed himself in his economic duties and literary work: partly because he was full of 'contempt for his opponents' and disgusted by their 'polemical methods and tricks'; but also because, as his private diary shows, he found Zinoviev and the Leningraders 'vulgar'. Yet Zinoviev and Kamenev were now advocating views very similar to those of his Left Opposition of 1923–24. Though he considered forming a bloc with Zinoviev, he didn't do so, believing Zinoviev didn't fully appreciated the need for proper industrial planning to develop the socialist parts of the economy. On 18 December 1925, the Fourteenth Congress opened: Trotsky had a consulting vote only, and it was to be the last he was to attend. During it, there was a fierce debate between the differing groups, with Zinoviev warning about bureaucratic degeneration, and even referring to Lenin's *Testament* and his warnings about Stalin's abuse of power. The party was more divided than ever – reflected in Zinoviev being allowed to present a counter-report, which revealed the strength of the 'Leningrad Opposition' and its attacks on Stalin's policies and increasing power. Yet Trotsky remained silent.[15]

He even remained silent when Krupskaya spoke about her opposition to the campaign against 'Trotskyism'; when Zinoviev revealed how he and Stalin had broken party rules in order to dismiss Trotsky's supporters; and when several leading Communists said they were disgusted by the slanders hurled against Trotsky, with Lashevich stating Trotsky 'had not been altogether wrong in 1923'. However, Trotsky's silence, plus the fact that – though unable to 'select' the Leningrad delegates – Stalin had ensured a majority of delegates supported him and Bukharin, meant Stalin survived that potentially fatal Congress. The new CC and Politburo both had Centre-Right majorities.

Nonetheless, Zinoviev continued his opposition in Leningrad where, unlike Trotsky, he had been determined 'to lay his hands on instruments of personal power'. These included control of the Leningrad *Pravda*. Also, Zinoviev – again unlike Trotsky – had always been a Bolshevik. Finally, when the new CC proposed to take disciplinary measures against Zinoviev and his supporters, Trotsky at last spoke up – and opposed this. Although Bukharin failed to persuade Trotsky not to support Zinoviev, he and Trotsky resumed a friendly but private correspondence. The end of the year thus saw intensified factional struggle, with a renewed campaign against Trotsky – Zinoviev was himself now accused of 'Trotskyism'. This campaign included, for the first time, an anti-semitic element, encouraged by Stalin who, unlike Trotsky, was 'anything but fastidious in the choice of means'.[16]

The United Opposition

In early January 1926, Stalin finally ousted Zinoviev from control of the Leningrad party, removing 'Zinovievists' from their positions with no significant opposition. Yet Trotsky didn't offer Zinoviev and Kamenev his support until a CC meeting in April. In secret talks held afterwards, the two ex-triumvirs revealed their growing fears regarding Stalin's methods and policies. With some support from Krupskaya, and a few other prominent party members, Trotsky joined with Zinoviev and Kamenev to form a United (Joint Left) Opposition. Zinoviev and Kamenev then publicly stated Trotsky had been right to warn about the dangers of growing bureaucracy; while Trotsky announced that, when criticising bureaucracy, he'd aimed at Stalin, not the other two triumvirs. However, by then, this new unity was almost too late to resist Stalin's growing power.

At this point, though, Trotsky resigned most of his posts and left – travelling under the name of 'Kuzmyenko' – for Germany, hoping doctors there could discover the cause of his continuing health problems. One surgeon recommended removing his tonsils – this was done without anaesthetics: 'It was a most unpleasant sensation to lie on the table and choke in one's own blood.' Whilst recovering, he and Sedova joined May Day celebrations in the Alexanderplatz, enjoying the ability to be in a crowd without attracting attention; and later going to a wine festival. Whilst in Germany, he wrote about the General Strike in the UK, expressing his fear that Stalin's 'socialism in one country' approach was leading the Soviet Union away from a truly revolutionary international stance. Just before making preparations to return to the Soviet Union, he was informed by German police that they'd foiled a White Russian assassination attempt on his life.[17]

On his return, he met Zinoviev and Kamenev, and they decided to take the political issues to the party's rank and file. Zinoviev and Kamenev were hopeful about the support the United Opposition had within the wider party, and thought all that was necessary was for them to appear 'on the same platform'. Trotsky, though, was much more cautious: '"The spirit of the times has changed", he retorted. "The masses are no longer the same as in 1917. They are tired…The working class is confused and afraid of changes that might make things even worse than they are…"' Zinoviev and Kamenev also warned Trotsky that Stalin was plotting his 'physical removal'. In 1935, Trotsky wrote in his diary: 'Zinoviev told me, not without embarrassment, "Do you think that Stalin has not discussed the question of your physical removal?"'[18]

In July, a joint CC/CCC meeting criticised Mikhail Lashevich – the Deputy Commissar of Defence, and a long-time supporter of Zinoviev – for having addressed around 70 party members in a *dacha* outside Moscow. Stalin, who saw Zinoviev as his main threat, proposed removing Zinoviev from the Politburo – but not Trotsky, hoping this would split this new emerging Opposition. Trotsky and Zinoviev reacted by formally announcing their new alliance, describing its position as the 'Bolshevik Left'. They then read out their prepared *Declaration of the Thirteen*, stressing the need for restoring party democracy; for changing economic policies to both strengthen the socialist elements of the economy and to stem the rise of bureaucratism; and for adopting a more revolutionary international policy. During that meeting, Dzerzhinsky delivered a vehement two-hour long attack on the Opposition: at the end, he stormed out, banging the doors behind him – and suffered a fatal heart attack in the antechamber. Thus began the next stage of the increasingly bitter power struggle – which lasted about eighteen months.

Stalin began his attack with strong criticisms of Trotsky's views, and then concentrated his fire on Zinoviev and Lashevich. On 23 July, Zinoviev was expelled from the Politburo, while Lashevich was expelled from the CC, and from his post. Stalin then focussed on getting Trotsky expelled from the Politburo, explaining in a letter to Molotov that Trotsky's determination to continue the struggle would be: '...all the worse for him'. Stalin's control of the party and the press meant he was able to ban party meetings; dismiss supporters of this latest Opposition; and prevent the Opposition's arguments reaching ordinary party members.[19]

After a summer break, Trotsky returned to the struggle in September, writing to the Politburo, warning of the possible rule of an autocrat if the party wasn't reformed and democratised. Then, at the end of September, using their right – as members of the CC – to address any party organisation, Trotsky and the others decided to appeal directly to party members. It's estimated the United Opposition had, at most, around 8,000 supporters: almost equally split between Trotskyists and Zinovievists. In addition, a few hundred remnants of the Workers' Opposition and the Decemists joined their ranks. Most party members, however, followed the lead of the Politiburo, or remained largely passive.

Meetings were held mainly in working class districts, often in tiny rooms, and sometimes in outbuildings and woods – with students keeping watch outside. Yet Stalin's control over the party machine meant they had little success. Even at meetings where Trotsky's views received much applause, the Moscow party organisers – appointed by Stalin – ensured the Opposition lost the votes at the end of those meetings. Outside the capital, Opposition speakers were often shouted down or even physically attacked – sometimes by organised brigades, brought in by lorry, using clubs to break up meetings.

Not surprisingly, some Oppositionists called on their leaders to declare their organisation to be a new party. These more radical views alarmed Trotsky himself, and his new allies. This, and awareness of their increasing isolation, led Zinoviev and Kamenev – fearing expulsion from the only legal party – to slowly drift away from Trotsky, seeking, instead, a compromise with Stalin. On 16 October, to keep the Opposition together, Trotsky reluctantly signed a joint statement with Zinoviev – admitting their recent behaviour had been factional, and agreeing to end their appeals to party members. They also dissociated themselves from those calling for the formation of a new party, and from those foreign communists who'd been expelled from their parties for supporting the United Opposition. Nonetheless, they stood by their principles, and made it clear they would continue their criticisms of official policy – but only within the CC.

However, while preparations were being made for the Fifteenth Party Conference, on 18 October, Max Eastman published the full text of Lenin's *Testament* in the *New York Times*; while the OGPU discovered Opposition leaflets were still circulating in Odessa. Trotsky – who'd given Eastman the gist of the *Testament*, without handing over the document – denied any involvement, but was forced to repudiate Eastman's revelations as a fraud. At a stormy Politburo meeting on 25 October, Stalin condemned the United Opposition as a 'social democratic deviation'. It was then, in one of the most dramatic episodes of the power struggle, that Trotsky – having accused Stalin of breaking the political truce – warned the party where, if it didn't change course, it was heading: '"The First Secretary poses his candidature to the post of the grave-digger of the revolution!" Stalin turned pale, rose, first contained himself with difficulty, and then rushed out of the hall, slamming the door.'[20]

The meeting then broke up in anger and confusion. Even some of Trotsky's supporters were shaken by what he'd said. According to Sedova, Pyatakov – 'very pale and shaken' – was the first to return to their home after that Politburo meeting, followed by Muralov and I. Smirnov. Pyatakov then burst out: 'And why, why did Lev Davidovitch say this? Stalin will never forgive him until the third and fourth generation!' When Trotsky returned – exhausted but calm – he brushed Pyatakov's fears aside; but, as Sedova noted, they now understood the breach between Trotsky and Stalin was 'irreparable'. Two days later, Trotsky – by then also suffering from insomnia, which even sleeping pills failed to cure – was expelled from the Politburo, while Zinoviev was removed as Comintern President. At the Fifteenth Party Conference, which began on 26 October, the United Opposition were allowed to put their case. Though Zinoviev began to backpedal, Kamenev stood more firmly by his criticisms, saying (incorrectly, as it turned out): 'Witch trials cannot be staged now...You cannot burn us at the stake.'[21]

Trotsky then spoke – in what Deutscher described as:

> '...one of his greatest speeches, moderate in tone, yet devastating in content, masterly in logical and artistic composition, gleaming with humour...' – making it clear it was because they believed the party could make the necessary policy changes, that they did not advocate forming a new party. However, he reaffirmed it was his duty, as a revolutionary, to point out errors and dangers: 'He who believes that our state is a proletarian state, with bureaucratic deformations...must struggle, by Party methods and along the Party's path, against that which is false.' His speech was so effective that Larin, who spoke next, exclaimed: 'This was one of the most dramatic episodes of our revolution...the revolution is outgrowing some of its leaders.'[22]

Although Stalin failed to persuade the Conference to insist that the Opposition leaders recant their view, it confirmed the removal from the Politburo of all three Opposition leaders. Although they remained on the CC, they were threatened with further consequences if they resumed the controversies. These signs of growing isolation, and fear that the RCP might disintegrate, led Krupskaya to distance herself from Trotsky and the United Opposition and to make peace with Stalin. This was a significant blow to the Opposition.

Trotsky, however, further developed his concerns about a Thermidorian counter-revolution, with Stalin in the role of 'grave-digger'. Yet he didn't believe Thermidor was inevitable – despite clear signs of the party's drift to the right. Nonetheless, this 'possibility of Thermidor' placed a huge responsibility on himself and the Opposition to continue the struggle – even if it were to cost him his life. History would soon show that such a fate indeed awaited him and those associated with him, whether political allies or family members. Yet, as he saw it, a revolutionary Marxist should not bow down before the reactionary mood of the party or the masses – even if this meant, for a time, they became isolated.

During the rest of 1926, newspaper attacks on the United Opposition continued; ordinary members lost their jobs; while many more senior Oppositionists were banished to remote parts of the Soviet Union. Trotsky fought on but, at first, confined his activities to writing letters to the Politburo, protesting about these intolerable aspects of the inner party regime. However, Zinoviev and Kamenev remained quiet. The winter of 1926–27 was thus relatively calm, with Trotsky concentrating on developing his theory of the 'Soviet Thermidor', concluding that the main threat came from Bukharin and the Right, not Stalin; and editing volumes of his *Works*. However, 1927 would turn out to be the decisive one as regards Trotsky's – and the Soviet Union's – fate.

In April 1927, the power struggle was re-ignited by political controversy over the massacre – launched by the leader of the Chinese nationalist Guomindang (GMD) – of communists and their allies in Shanghai. Previously, the Soviet government had advised the Chinese Communist Party (CCP) to join the GMD in a United Front. Trotsky had first criticised this in 1926 and, in March 1927, had tried unsuccessfully to get the Opposition to raise this issue. News of this massacre led to another clash between Trotsky and Stalin, which then spilled over into the press. Trotsky wrote an article which *Pravda* refused to publish. Trotsky complained, sent his article to the Secretariat for distribution to all CC members and, backed by Zinoviev, called for a closed CC meeting to discuss the China crisis.

Unsurprisingly, the Politburo rejected their call. Stalin then persuaded Krupskaya to write to Zinoviev, suggesting he cease his support for such a discussion. Trotsky thus had to reply on his own – he did so by not just criticising official foreign policy since 1923, and accusing Stalin and Bukharin of 'betraying Bolshevism' and 'international proletarianism', but also by linking the lack of a genuinely revolutionary approach to Stalin's theory of socialism in one country. This issue thus became connected to his fears of a creeping Thermidorian counter-revolution in the Soviet Union. He later wrote about how important he had seen this particular political struggle: 'We went to meet the inevitable débâcle, confident, however, that we were paving the way for the triumph of our ideas in a more distant future.'[23]

In May 1927, Trotsky also sent the ECCI of Comintern a statement on China, expressing his fears regarding the alarming drift to the right in the RCP since 1923: 'The attempt to represent the struggle against the Opposition as a struggle against Trotskyism is a woeful, cowardly way of masking the right deviation...' He was allowed to address the ECCI, summarising the main points of his unpublished article. Stalin spoke shortly after, accusing Trotsky of violating the terms of the October 1926 truce, and of starting a new factional struggle. On 25 May, Trotsky and his supporters published their *Declaration of the Eighty-four*, which he circulated to Comintern delegates the following day. Then, in early June, Zinoviev wrote an article, The *Declaration of the Eighty-four and Our Tasks*, claiming the Opposition was too strong to be suppressed, even if Stalin removed its main leaders. They hoped this *Declaration* would get thousands of signatures to ensure a full debate in the run-up to the Fifteenth Party Congress.[24]

On 24 June, at a CCC meeting, Trotsky repeated his criticisms of the policy on China, and explained at some length what he meant by the dangers of a Thermidorian counter-revolution. He argued that, instead of expelling people, the CCC should try to 'create a more healthy and flexible regime in the Party'. Stalin was furious when the CCC ruled that the latest *Declaration* was not a breach of discipline, and seemed prepared to concede the Opposition's right to address party meetings. Stalin failed to push through Trotsky and Zinoviev's expulsion from the CC, so he postponed the Fifteenth Party Congress, due to meet in November. On 27 June, at another CCC meeting, Trotsky was urged to unite behind the leadership in a struggle against bureaucracy but, on 28 June – ignoring Zinoviev's objections – Trotsky issued another declaration which, as well as repeating his opposition to policy on China, also attacked Stalin's economic policies for causing shortages of food and industrial products. Trotsky now felt increasingly confident that, with Stalin's failures exposed, the United Opposition would win the day.

However, by then, there was a 'war scare' in the Soviet Union, after Britain's Conservative government broke off diplomatic relations. It was thus easy for Stalin to portray the Opposition as aiding capitalist Britain by their 'disloyalty'. In July, Trotsky rejected such accusations, stating in both a letter and an article, that the Opposition stood for the 'unconditional defence' of the USSR. However, he also explained that, if war came and the ruling faction proved unequal to the task of defence, the Opposition would, in the interest of defence, continue to oppose them and would seek to replace them, in order to avoid their young workers' state being defeated by imperialists. In less than conciliatory language, he argued that 'only ignoramuses and scoundrels' could describe the attitude of the Opposition as defeatist, pointing out that 'victory is not obtained from the rubbish heap'.[25]

On 24 July, Trotsky – again encouraged by Zinoviev – moderated his stance at another joint CC/CCC meeting, at which he defended his actions. During that bitter session, he once again referred to Thermidor at length. During it, he made this presciently chilling comment: '…revolution is a serious business. None of us is scared of firing squads. We are old revolutionaries'. Yet again, Stalin failed to win a majority to expel Trotsky. Later, on 8 August, the Opposition released a statement, declaring they would defend the Soviet Union unconditionally: 'To sum up: for the socialist fatherland? Yes! For the Stalinist course? No!' However, on the following day, Trotsky failed to get CC agreement that the statement could include a section which stated his conviction that the situation in the party would only improve if the Opposition got fair coverage and – following the practice 'under Lenin' – could have its rival documents circulated before the Fifteenth Congress. The Politburo then began a fresh campaign attacking Trotsky for Menshevism and anti-Leninism. From then on, Stalin worked even harder to get the Opposition leaders expelled from the CC, thus taking away their right to address the next party congress. In the meantime, he once again delayed the opening date.[26]

In preparation for that Congress, the Opposition sent its *Platform* to the Politburo on 3 September, believing it would be discussed at the Congress, and then circulated amongst ordinary party members. However, on 8 September, Stalin ruled it was a factional paper and therefore couldn't be circulated. Both Trotsky and Zinoviev decided to circulate the *Platform* themselves but, on 12 September – with Trotsky away in the Caucasus – the OGPU seized their printing press. One result was that Preobrazhensky, and two other leaders of the Opposition, were expelled from the party: ominously, for the first time ever, one was also imprisoned for his actions. Then, on 27 September, Trotsky was summoned by Stalin to the Comintern – which itself, along with its national parties, was being purged of Left Opposition supporters – to explain his actions. He also called for Trotsky's expulsion from the ECCI. Trotsky used the opportunity to list twenty-five points where he felt party policy was mistaken; and then made this warning:

> 'You accuse me of transgressing Party discipline. I am quite sure you have your sentence prepared...The Party is under orders to keep silent because Stalin's policy is a policy of bankruptcy...The bureaucratic regime will lead irreversibly to one-man rule.'[27]

After that meeting, Trotsky was expelled from its ECCI. Shortly after, on 15 October, at a procession to mark a special session of the ECCI in Leningrad, Trotsky and Zinoviev stood on a lorry, some distance away from the official stands where the party leaders and ECCI members stood. According to Serge, after passing those stands:

> 'The crowds had eyes only for them [Trotsky and Zinoviev]... the demonstrators made a silent gesture by lingering on the spot, and thousands of hands were outstretched, waving handkerchiefs or caps. It was a dumb acclamation, futile but still overwhelming.'

The police and Stalin's supporters tried, unsuccessfully, to prevent this acclamation of the Oppositionists; in the end, the ECCI officials climbed onto the same lorry as Trotsky and Zinoviev. Although Trotsky and Zinoviev thought this showed the masses were with them, this illusion was quickly shattered. On 21 October, Trotsky sent a letter to the Bureau of Party History, pointing out the historical 'mistakes' and distortions being published, accusing 'the entire official machine' of 'concealing, destroying, or at least distorting every trace' of his role in the November Revolution, and stating it 'would require several volumes' to point out all the 'falsification'.[28]

As they were prevented from presenting their *Platform*, the Opposition organised meetings in Moscow and Leningrad during October and early November – mainly in people's homes – to explain their policies and obtain signatures in support. It's estimated as many as 20,000 people had heard what the *Platform* had to say, and had also heard Lenin's *Testament* read out. One meeting Trotsky addressed was attended by over 300 workers; while, on 4 November, over 2,000 gathered in a lecture hall in Moscow's Polytechnical Institute to hear him; when the authorities cut off the electricity, the meeting continued by candlelight with Trotsky quipping: 'Lenin said that socialism was the *soviets* plus electrification. Stalin has already suppressed the *soviets*, now it's the turn of the electricity!' However, with daily denunciations of their programme as 'subversive', instead of the 20,000–30,000 signatures Zinoviev had hoped for, they got 6,000 at most.[29]

By then, Stalin had finally got his way: on 23 October, a joint CC/CCC meeting agreed Trotsky and Zinoviev, as 'neo-Mensheviks', should be expelled from the CC at the Fifteenth Party Congress. Trotsky, who was present, once again accused Stalin of moving the party 'from left to right', warning about the dangers of 'Thermidor'. This was an exceptionally stormy meeting: as well as shouts and insults, one member tried to pull Trotsky off the platform, while 'books, inkwells, tumblers and other objects' were thrown at him. Rakovsky, who tried to defend Trotsky, was denied the chance to speak. At the end of the meeting, Trotsky: 'collected up his papers and stuffed them into his old briefcase, glanced expressionlessly at the platform and left the hall to the catcalls, hisses and insults of his former colleagues....' This was the last time that Trotsky and Stalin met.[30]

On 7 November, during the tenth anniversary celebrations of the November Revolution, the Opposition marched in towns and cities under their own banners – including ones saying 'Carry Out Lenin's Testament'. However, when they tried to address the crowds, many Opposition members were physically attacked by Stalin's supporters and the security services, and their protests broken up. When Trotsky attempted to speak in Moscow's Red Square, Stalin's supporters shouted out: 'Down with Trotsky, the Jew, the traitor!', and a policeman shot twice at his car, shattering the windscreen. In Leningrad, Zinoviev and Radek were held in 'protective' custody for the duration of the celebrations, to keep them from the crowds. Ironically, as part of the Tenth Anniversary celebrations, the party leaders had intended to show Sergei Eisenstein's new film, *October*. However, at the last moment, they discovered Trotsky was portrayed as the film's hero and central character. The organisers quickly cancelled the screening, ordering Eisenstein to re-edit the film, to drastically reduce Trotsky's role.[31]

That evening, Trotsky – to avoid the indignity of eviction – quietly left their rooms in the Kremlin, moving to a small room in the nearby house of a friend and fellow-Oppositionist, before eventually being allocated a small flat. Sedova – worried as he'd lost so much weight, was suffering from insomnia, headaches and dizzy spells, and was looking hollow-cheeked and sallow – urged him to go to the country, to concentrate on his writing. Deeply depressed by the lies, distortions and threats, at one point Trotsky uttered, after reading that day's newspapers: 'What have they made of the revolution, of the party, of Marxism, of the International!' Nonetheless, determined to carry on the struggle, he refused to leave.

His family, too, now also began to suffer. Lyova – then aged twenty-one – had, since a youth, been inspired by his father's political activities, but now feared for his father's life and increasingly saw himself as bodyguard as well as assistant and fellow-revolutionary. Sergei, at nineteen, had rebelled against his parents and their politics. Unlike Lyova, he didn't join the Komsomol or the party, and didn't get involved with the Opposition. Instead, he loved sport and the arts and, for a time, left home, spending almost two years travelling with a circus girl and her troupe of performers. By 1927, he was back, and displayed real aptitude – like Trotsky – for mathematics and science. Although he avoided politics, he was increasingly outraged by what was being done to his father and his supporters. Meanwhile, Trotsky's two daughters – both active Oppositionists, both married to Trotskyists (who'd lost their jobs, been expelled from the party and were about to be deported to Siberia), and both with two children – were:

'Sunk into poverty, helpless, and tormented by anxiety about children, husbands and parents, both women were ill with consumption, and were marked to be the first victims of a fate which was to destroy all of Trotsky's children.'[32]

The threat of expulsion from the party frightened Zinoviev; thus, at another joint meeting of the CC/CCC, on 14 November, he pushed for the Opposition to declare it would stop organising meetings. Although Trotsky agreed, they were nonetheless expelled from the party, while Kamenev and Rakovsky were expelled from the CC. This was made public the following day. Almost immediately, hundreds of rank and file Oppositionists were expelled. Two days later, Zinoviev, Kamenev and Radek suffered the embarrassing fate Trotsky had avoided, when they were unceremoniously evicted from the Kremlin.

To avoid that fate, on 16 November, Trotsky's friend, Joffe – already seriously ill with tuberculosis, and denied by Stalin the opportunity to seek medical assistance abroad, as recommended by doctors – committed suicide in the Kremlin. Joffe had spoken with Trotsky on the telephone earlier that day, asking Trotsky to visit him; but Trotsky hadn't, as 'some chance prevented me from doing so immediately'. Joffe's political testament, in a letter addressed to Trotsky, was confiscated by the OGPU. However, a photostat copy was eventually given to Rakovsky, who gave it to Trotsky. In it, after expressing his bitter sadness at recent political events, and asking Trotsky to look out for his wife and children, he wrote:

> 'You and I, dear Lev Davidovitch, are bound to each other by decades of joint work, and…personal friendship. This gives me the right to tell you in parting what I think you were mistaken in…you have often abandoned your rightness for the sake of an overvalued agreement, or compromise. This is a mistake.'

The authorities arranged Joffe's funeral on a working day, to discourage crowds. Nonetheless, on 19 November, thousands of Opposition supporters followed the coffin, with Trotsky and Rakovsky – along with I. Smirnov – as chief mourners. Trotsky's speech at the graveside turned out to be his last public appearance in Soviet Russia, his concluding words being: 'The struggle goes on. Everyone remains at his post. Let nobody leave.' Trotsky clearly took Joffe's last words – from one of his few close friends – to heart, because from then on he rejected further compromises, whatever the personal cost.[33]

Although Trotsky had used stirring phrases, to good effect, at critical times during the Civil War, they had little impact now. From 20–27 November, Trotsky met with Zinoviev and Kamenev – both now increasingly concerned to make peace with Stalin – to decide what to do next. They agreed on a statement which said they'd stop factional activity for the sake of party unity. It was to prove their last meeting – and the last time they would ever communicate with each other. Zinoviev, reminding Trotsky that Lenin had warned in his *Testament* the Trotsky–Stalin conflict might cause a split in the party, warned he thus bore a big responsibility. In reply, Trotsky pointed out Lenin had also said in the *Testament*: '…if the divergence of views inside the party coincided with class differences, nothing could save us from a split – capitulation less than anything else!' In Trotsky's opinion, because of the growing influence of the kulaks and NEPmen, such class differences were leading closer and closer to a Thermidorian counter-revolution. However, despite Zinoviev's concerns, the statement did agree Trotsky's position that it was nonetheless impossible for the Opposition leaders to retract or recant their views.[34]

When the Fifteenth Congress finally met, from 7–19 December 1927, there was not a single Opposition member amongst the 1669 delegates. The United Opposition issued a statement signed by 121 of their leading members, asking for the expulsions to be annulled – but this was overwhelmingly rejected, and 'Trotskyism' was unanimously condemned. Zinoviev and Kamenev – partly because of signs that Stalin seemed about to abandon NEP in favour of a programme of industrialisation and the collectivisation of agriculture – announced that, to stop the expulsions, and to prevent the formation of a new party, they would surrender and make no more criticisms. But Stalin wanted more: on 18 December, Zinoviev and Kamenev formally recanted their 'anti-Leninist' views. Thus, the United Opposition was over. Trotsky and his supporters, however, refused to accept the decisions of this Congress and, immediately afterwards, another 1,500 Oppositionists were expelled, soon followed by arrests and imprisonments. In this context, around 2,500 Oppositionists signed statements of recantation: including Pyatakov and Antonov-Ovseenko, two of Trotsky's most important supporters.

Deportation to Alma-Ata

Though Trotsky was more isolated that ever, Stalin – because of growing economic problems – decided to deport Trotsky and his remaining supporters. Initially, Oppositionists were 'offered' minor administrative posts in remote places. Trotsky was given a post in Astrakhan, on the Volga in southern Russia. Trotsky objected on health grounds, because of the area's humid climate. On 17 January 1928, having ignored a summons to report to the OGPU, Trotsky was forcibly deported – under Article 58 of the Criminal Code – to Alma-Ata in Kazakhstan which, near the Chinese border, had a drier climate.

His deportation should have taken place the day before, but thousands of supporters had invaded Kazan railway station and blocked the line. The authorities then said he would be deported on 18 January but, to avoid further protests, brought the deportation forward by a day, using the smaller and deserted Yaroslavl station. When the OGPU arrived to arrest him, Trotsky and his family – along with Sokolovskaya and Joffe's widow – locked themselves in a room, making it clear it wasn't a voluntary departure, thus forcing the police to break down the door. Trotsky then refused to dress, and so was dressed by OGPU agents; he then had to be carried out.

Once at the station, he refused to walk, and had to be dragged into the carriage. According to Sedova – herself feverish with 'flu' –'Leon Davidovitch…was good-humoured and at times even gay. He slept little… While lying down on the seat of the compartment, he suddenly said to me, "I didn't want to die in a bed in the Kremlin…"' Meanwhile, other Oppositionists were deported elsewhere, in an attempt to isolate them from Trotsky. In all, around 8,000 Oppositionists were either arrested, imprisoned or deported during 1928. Nearly thirty years before, Trotsky had first seen Moscow when being transported to Siberia, for his first exile. This was to be his last sight of Moscow – and 1928 would be his last year in the Soviet Union.[35]

Trotsky – still suffering from his malarial infection – initially found it difficult to settle in Alma-Ata, which was extremely backward, suffered from earthquakes and floods, and had few paved streets and fewer houses with running water and electricity. Trotsky described it as 'a realm of horrifying dust'. It was about 250km from the nearest railway, and 4,000km from Moscow. He and Sedova were initially given rooms in the Hotel Dzhetysa. Their elder son, Lyova, opted to accompany them into exile, leaving behind his wife, Anya and their son. When Sedova, too, contracted malaria, Sergei sent them quinine from Moscow.

Eventually, Trotsky was allocated 75 Krasin Street, a modest house close to the police HQ, but with the additional luxury of electricity. Initially, OGPU agents accompanied him on hunting and fishing trips – described by Trotsky as his 'temporary lapse into barbarism'. Trotsky protested and got the supervision relaxed. In the summer, they were even allowed to use a *dacha* in the Tyan-Shan mountains. Surprisingly, the authorities allowed Trotsky's extensive library and archives to be sent on by lorry. He also made use of the local library where he perused a volume of reproductions of murals by the Mexican artist, Diego Rivera; Andrés Nin, a Spanish supporter, also sent him a volume of Rivera's work.

Death of Nina

This exile was similar to his earlier ones, allowing time for reflection and preparation for continuing the struggle. However, on 16 June, whilst holidaying in the *dacha*, he received news from Rakovsky that his younger daughter, Nina, aged only 26 – who had been expelled from the RCP and sacked from her job – had died in Moscow from tuberculosis on 9 June. In a letter that arrived a week later, Rakovsky said: 'You have long been bearing the heavy cross of a revolutionary Marxist, but now for the first time you are experiencing the boundless sorrow of a father. I am with you, with all my heart. I grieve that I am so far from you.'

Though aware that Nina was ill – and that Zina, herself ill, was nursing her – Trotsky hadn't known how seriously ill she was. He'd spent anxious weeks, telegraphing Zina: 'Am grieved that cannot be with Ninuska to help her. Communicate her condition. Kisses for both of you. Papa.' He'd made repeated requests for information, but heard nothing. Nina wrote her father a letter, saying her condition was critical – but the OGPU had held it 'back for seventy-three days', thus Trotsky had had no time to 'apply for permission to see her for the last time'. He was particularly pained by the thought that 'on her death-bed she had waited for his answer in vain'. As an exile, he couldn't return for the funeral, which Sokolovskaya had to attend as the lone parent. By then, Nina's husband – Man Nevelson, also an Oppositionist – had been arrested; at the time, they had two children: Lev and Volina. This was Trotsky's first experience of losing a child – and he took it hard, mourning Nina as 'an ardent revolutionary and member of the Opposition' as well as his daughter. When the news came, he'd been working on an article about the Comintern – he broke off and went into the garden with Sedova, where both of them mourned her, with Trotsky moaning: 'I'm so, so sorry for the girl!'[36]

Zina, his elder daughter – also suffering from tuberculosis – was too ill to join them at Alma-Ata. A letter from her, explaining her own situation, was delayed by forty-three days. She, too, had been expelled from the party and sacked because of her strong support of her father. However, his younger son, Sergei was able to visit them. Sokolovskaya remained in Leningrad, courageously heading a small Trotskyist centre which, just before his deportation, Trotsky had helped form in meetings held in her flat.

Trotsky now accepted commissions from the Marx-Engels Institute in Moscow to translate and edit some of the classics of Marxist literature. He also began research for his autobiography – helped by Sokolovskaya via the post. To relax, he went on occasional duck-shoots – his favourite pastime. Though he was eventually forbidden to go on hunting trips, and was restricted to a 25km radius, Trotsky frequently ignored the ban. However, Trotsky's main focus was establishing clandestine contacts with his supporters in Moscow, in other places of internal exile, and even abroad. In this, he was increasingly helped by Lyova; Sedova, too, helped with the correspondence. Soon, his house was inundated with correspondence. Lyova, acting as 'office manager', kept track of all the correspondence. However, Trotsky did not receive all that was sent; according to Lyova: 'Of the correspondence sent us, we received, in the best months, not more than half.'[37]

Nonetheless, via secret communications, they learned of Stalin's adoption of a new 'Left' economic course, with Stalin's decision to move away from the NEP leading to a rift between the Centre and Right. When, in early 1928, *Pravda* carried articles attacking the *kulaks*, Bukharin and his supporters objected; in April, many Bukharinists – seen as being too 'lenient' with the *kulaks* – were removed from positions of power. This gave Trotsky one last opportunity to limit Stalin's growing power. However, these political developments also presented real problems for Trotsky, as regards maintaining a united front.

Many Oppositionists were gratified to see the adoption of some of the policies they'd advocated – even hoping that, having won the political argument, they'd be readmitted to the party. These included, initially, Rakovsky, who was to remain close to Trotsky longer than almost any other Oppositionist. Trotsky, ever since early 1927, had seen Bukharin's Right faction as more of a danger to the gains of the November Revolution than Stalin's, because it was bigger and more right wing. Thus, he believed Stalin and the Centre should be encouraged to break with the Right, arguing this to fellow-exiles in a letter dated 9 May.

However, several of his supporters had shifted even further; by the middle of May 1928 – when it became clear Stalin was planning a 'second revolution' – some thought they should join him in the struggle against Bukharin and the Right. In May, Preobrazhensky suggested all the exiled Oppositionists should hold a conference to discuss the situation. Trotsky was totally opposed, and the majority supported him. However, in June 1928, Radek – feeling exiled from politics – sent a letter to other Oppositionists, suggesting their chances of being readmitted to the party would be increased if they backed Stalin against Bukharin, before the Sixth Congress of Comintern met in the summer of 1928.

Trotsky's supporters thus began to split into 'conciliators' and 'irreconcilables'. The irreconcilables tended to be younger Oppositionists who, above all, wanted inner-party democracy. The conciliators – generally the older, and who'd been in the party much longer – focussed more on economic issues. The latter were encouraged when, in June 1928, Zinoviev, Kamenev, and around 3,000 other Oppositionists who'd broken with Trotsky, were reinstated in the party. Trotsky believed all the Opposition had to do was stick together to be returned to power. Himself so resolute in opposition, he failed to appreciate the pressures leading many of his supporters to seek readmission to the only legal party. In a letter dated 17 March 1928, Trotsky scathingly described Pyatakov – a consistent Oppositionist from 1923–7 but who, in February 1928, had applied for readmission – as a 'politically finished man' and 'political corpse' who could not be 'relied upon' in 'a serious political matter'.[38]

Then, in July, with the food crisis becoming worse, Bukharin and his faction succeeded in slowing Stalin's 'left turn'. Trotsky – still opposed to allying with Stalin, and not taking his 'leftwards' shift in economic policy seriously – agreed the Opposition should try to push Stalin's Centre to the left: 'With Stalin against Bukharin maybe, but with Bukharin against Stalin never'. However, by August, Stalin's 'leftward' course was resumed, thus confirming his breach with Bukharin. Both the Centre and the Right then turned to Trotsky and the defeated Left Oppositionists for allies. Bukharin, now broken in spirit, was just a shadow of the man who, only nine months previously, had been praised by Stalin at the Fifteenth Congress for 'slaughtering' the leaders of the Opposition 'instead of arguing with them'.[39]

Using Kamenev as a go-between between himself and Trotsky, Bukharin argued the main issue was not economic policy, but freedom of the party and the state, claiming Stalin was creating a police state in order to take total power. Bukharin – aware the OGPU was spying on leading RCP members – was even afraid Stalin would soon resort to physical extermination of his political opponents:

> 'He [Bukharin] arrived at Kamenev's home stealthily, terrified, pale, trembling, looking over his shoulders, and talking in whispers...Without pronouncing Stalin's name he repeated obsessively: "He will slay us". "He is the new Genghiz Khan". "He will strangle us."'[40]

In September 1928, Trotsky resolved his political dilemma, by deciding an alliance with Bukharin, to restore full inner-party and *soviet* democracy, was most important. However, both Trotsky and Bukharin – even though by then Zinoviev, too, had accepted Kamenev's belief that a grand 'anti-Stalin coalition' was needed – faced real problems in concluding such an alliance, as many of their respective supporters were reluctant to cooperate with former political enemies. Those Oppositionists who resisted the idea of an alliance with Bukharin included Radek and Preobrazhensky. Thus, the proposed Trotsky–Bukharin alliance – the only way left to protect themselves from the horrors Stalin was soon to launch against his opponents – collapsed, allowing Stalin to defeat the Right, while Trotsky and the Left remained divided. Bukharin and the Right, fearing expulsion from the party, capitulated.

However, with Stalin adopting some of the Opposition's economic policies, support for Trotsky started to grow in some party cells. Towards the end of 1928, the OGPU imprisoned or deported around 7,000 Left Oppositionists – earlier that year, the total number of Oppositionists was calculated at around 5,000 at most. This sealed Trotsky's fate: Stalin – fearing the emergence of a Left–Right alliance in the future, and suspecting some of his own faction still sympathised with the Opposition – decided Trotsky needed to be expelled entirely from the Soviet Union. From October, as a first step towards further isolating Trotsky, Stalin stopped all letters – including the 'secret' correspondence – from reaching Alma-Ata. Then rumours reached Trotsky he was about to be exiled to an even more remote place. By then, Trotsky's illness had once more flared up.

Nonetheless, during December, Stalin still tried to get Trotsky and his supporters on board. Trotsky – even though only three prominent members of the Opposition were still at liberty – stubbornly insisted they be readmitted to the party, and be allowed to hold their own conference to decide their tactics. So, on 16 December 1928, Trotsky was warned to stop all 'counter-revolutionary' activity, otherwise he'd be forced to move elsewhere. Typically, Trotsky refused point-blank: 'To demand from a revolutionary such a renunciation…would be possible only for a completely depraved officialdom.'[41]

Mistakenly, he assumed he'd be sent somewhere in the Soviet Union, even more remote than Alma-Ata. A month later, on Stalin's orders, he would be expelled from the USSR itself. However, even outside the Soviet Union, he continued to be, in Nietzsche's words: 'A fighter against his times' – fighting for a better future.

Chapter 9

Prophet Without a Home, 1929–36

'I am tired of it all – all of it – do you understand?'[1]

After Trotsky refused, in December 1928, to end his political activity, Stalin urged the Politburo to approve Trotsky's banishment from the Soviet Union. Meanwhile, Trotsky and his household waited in suspense.

Stalin asked several countries to take the legendary revolutionary – but only Turkey proved willing to accept the person Churchill described as 'The Ogre of Europe'. Once exiled, in the remaining eleven years of his life, Trotsky moved from country to country, before leaving Europe for good in 1936 – for Mexico, his final home. In the final chapter of his autobiography, he called this period of political wandering 'The Planet without a Visa'. As well as this rootless existence, those years brought him much personal sadness and loss, and increasing periods of ill health.

However, Trotsky – now a 'prophet outcast' – had no intention of ending his political resistance against the increasing degeneration of the Russian Revolution. During the 1930s, he made perceptive analyses of Stalin's economic policies in the USSR, and of the rise of fascism across Europe. He also worked hard to build a new revolutionary Marxist International.

Leaving the USSR

At a stormy Politburo session on 17 January 1929, during which Bukharin 'screamed, wept and sobbed', Stalin finally obtained a majority for secretly deporting Trotsky. On 20 January, armed guards surrounded Trotsky's Alma-Ata house, and an OGPU official informed him he was being deported 'from the entire territory of the U.S.S.R.' He was given twenty-four hours to get ready, and told he would be notified of his destination en route.[2]

At dawn on 22 January – in one of the severest winters for many decades – Trotsky and his family (and, in an oversight Stalin soon regretted, all his papers and books) were driven to a special train. Trotsky then went on hunger strike, demanding to be informed of his destination; and was finally told it was Istanbul. He protested strongly, as it was a refuge for exiled White Guards – demanding instead to be sent to Germany or another European country. Trotsky also pleaded for Sergei and Zina to be allowed to join him.

The only concession Stalin granted was to allow Sergei – and Anya, Lyova's wife – to join the train; Zina was too ill to travel. The train remained in a small, deserted station for almost two weeks, during which Trotsky read and played chess. Whilst there, he received newspapers which were full of attacks on Trotskyism, and news of the arrests of hundreds of Oppositionists. Finally, Trotsky was informed Germany had refused him an entry permit. The train resumed its journey to Odessa, arriving on the night of 10 February.

There, a ship – ironically called the *Ilyich* – waited to take them to their new home. Sergei – anxious to continue his university course – and Anya left the train and returned to Moscow, entertaining vain hopes for an early reunion. In their final embrace, Trotsky said to Sergei:

> 'Don't be sad, my son. Everything changes in life. Much will change even in Moscow. We'll be back…We'll definitely be back!' This was to be Trotsky's last sight of his younger son. These were also Lyova's last moments with his wife: both Sergei and Anya were later shot on Stalin's orders. Despite a gale and a frozen Black Sea, Stalin ordered the ship to leave immediately. Holding Sedova's hand, Trotsky went aboard, taking the last sight of his homeland.[3]

Turkey 1929–33

Trotsky arrived in Istanbul on 12 February 1929, with a settlement grant of US$1,500, handed to him by his OGPU escort: this was the only money they had. The Turkish government ordered him not to interfere in Turkey's politics, or to publish anything inside the country. Thus began Trotsky's third exile. Although he thought it would be short, Turkey was to be his home until July 1933. Only once in those four and a half years – on a brief trip to Copenhagen in October 1932 – did he leave it.

For the first three weeks, he was provided with two rooms in the Soviet Consulate in Istanbul. Trotsky's friends in Paris – Marguerite and Alfred Rosmer, and Magdeleine and Maurice Paz – informed the world press about his deportation, and he soon began meeting journalists and dashing off articles. He also began to receive offers of help from people like G. B. Shaw and H. G. Wells. Once it became clear Trotsky was determined to continue his opposition to Stalin, they were ordered to leave the Consulate and find alternative accommodation.

In early March, after several moves, they settled in 'Yanaros', a large and dilapidated – but more secure – villa, on Prinkipo (Büyükada), the largest of the Princes' Islands in the Sea of Marmara. The island, one and a half hours from Istanbul, was a summer resort for the rich. Its tiny fishing harbour received one small steamer a day, bringing passengers and post, along with supplies. There, with a small permanent police guard, they received visits from family and friends, and from foreign authors, journalists and publishers, along with a growing international correspondence.[4]

Trotsky described Prinkipo as 'an island of peace and forgetfulness' and 'a fine place to work with a pen'. For him, there was also the distraction of strenuous sea fishing and hunting trips – some of which, despite concerns about the risk of an OGPU attempt on his life – he did on his own. Eastman found such 'relaxation' as 'disagreeable', but Trotsky saw them as diverters of 'sadness and calmer of unquiet thoughts'. Typically, Trotsky didn't use his time in Turkey just for rest and recuperation. He took over most of the second floor as his office, while Lyova ran the secretariat on the ground floor. Despite continuing health problems, Trotsky quickly developed a strict work routine: frequently rising at 4.00 or 5.00am, he spent his days mostly in writing and dictating – in Russian, German or French – correspondence and articles.[5]

Once the settlement grant had been spent, Trotsky and his family initially survived on donations from supporters, such as the Rosmers. For a time, the Rosmers – along with other members of the French Opposition – stayed at the villa. Also spending time there were the Czech Oppositionist, Jan Frankel, and the German Oppositionist, Rudolf Klement. As well as working as Trotsky's secretaries, they acted as armed bodyguards. However, at various times, others staying there were later found to have been OGPU informers. Trotsky, though, was determined to leave, dashing off requests for visas to live in Paris or Berlin. Yet the chances of finding another country to allow him to settle were remote: along with conservatives, most reformist socialists saw Trotsky as more dangerous and extreme than Stalin. Only a year before Trotsky's expulsion, the 1 February 1928 edition of the New York *Nation* had quoted Austen Chamberlain as saying the UK couldn't establish normal diplomatic relations with the USSR until 'Trotsky has been put against the wall'. Not since Napoleon, 'had so many governments proscribed one man or had one man aroused such widespread animosity and alarm'.[6]

Literary Work

Trotsky's plan to publish an International Left Opposition (Bolshevik–Leninist) journal – the *Bulletin of the Opposition* – required more than donations. Fortunately, publishers and newspapers (like the *New York Times*, the *New York Herald Tribune* and even the *Daily Express*) were keen to obtain interviews, articles and books. His earnings soon provided him with the necessary funds – the bulk coming from advances and royalties on *My Life* (his autobiography, completed by October, and which appeared in 1930) and his masterful *History of the Russian Revolution* (1932–33). Extra earnings came from serialisation of parts of his autobiography and commissioned articles.

Trotsky's main motive for writing the *History* was to provide a programme of how to make a revolution, and an overview of the revolutionary movement in 1933, rather than a scholarly history book. Completed in just one year, it has been criticised as being one-sided. Though, in fact, he tended to downplay his own role in comparison to Lenin's; and recent historical research has confirmed most of his account. Trotsky also started gathering materials for books which were completed after he'd left Prinkipo, alongside beginning work on biographies of both Lenin and Stalin. They continued to live modestly – 'Spartanly', according to Eastman – with most of his earnings going towards subsidising the ongoing fight against Stalinist bureaucracy.[7]

The *Bulletin*

By July 1929, Trotsky had established the *Bulletin* – edited by him and, at first, published in Paris, with help from the Rosmers and Raymond Molinier. As much as two-thirds of each issue was written by Trotsky himself, with Lyova responsible for production and distribution. Though it continued until 1940, it never operated at a profit. As well as longer articles on Soviet and international politics, it also printed news of the arrest, imprisonment and exile of Oppositionists. Trotsky saw it as a way of establishing contact with his scattered supporters, both within and outside the USSR. Although distribution in the USSR proved increasingly difficult, copies were often obtained by Soviet officials abroad, and senior party members. Many of these were later imprisoned and, in this way, the *Bulletin* often reached the prisons and work camps – exiled Oppositionists even managed to get their articles to Trotsky for publication in the *Bulletin*.

However, Lyova missed his wife, and his son Lyulik, and was frustrated by lack of news: the OGPU retained or delayed most of the letters between them. In August 1929, he applied for permission to visit them in Moscow – in part, to convey Trotsky's suggestion that the rest of his family should join him in exile. After a delay of over a month, Lyova's request was rejected. Stalin, once informed of the request, is reported to have said: 'For him it's all over. And the same for his family. Reject it.'[8]

Distressed by the little news he received from his wife about their increasingly desperate situation, Lyova nonetheless shared his father's political outlook and commitment, and threw himself into making the *Bulletin* a success. He became his father's pride, though Trotsky was concerned that Lyova was too much in his shadow. Lyova also took charge of his father's security, amidst growing rumours of assassination attempts, either by White Guard émigrés or Stalin's agents. These were genuine fears, based on signs of OGPU surveillance. Consequently, Trotsky hired two more secretaries, and several bodyguards from among his most reliable supporters. One of them, Jean van Heijenoort – a Dutch historian of mathematical logic, and a member of the French Trotskyists – remained with him until just before his assassination in 1940.

Eventually, Lyova decided to go to Berlin, to study physics, maths and engineering at the Technische Höchschule. Trotsky supported this for a number of reasons: with production of the *Bulletin* having already been transferred to Berlin, Lyova could combine his studies with making it the centre of Trotsky's campaign against Stalin, thus increasing the influence of his ILO in Germany. However, there was also the awkward personal situation which arose when Lyova became the lover of Jeanne Martin, married to Raymond Molinier. Thus, in February 1931, Lyova and Martin left for Berlin, to set up an International Secretariat. Under Lyova's management, the *Bulletin* quickly became a rallying point for the ILO's scattered supporters – and a fighting organ against Stalinism and fascism, and for world revolution. Yet, in April 1931, Lyova wrote to his mother to say he was thinking of reapplying for permission to go to Moscow – Sokolovskaya informed Trotsky, who advised Lyova against it: partly because he needed his help in Europe.[9]

Reform or Revolution?

Though Trotsky repeatedly warned of the danger of Thermidor, despite Stalin's 'left turn', he still believed the RCP might remove Stalin, allowing him to return to the USSR. He thus continued to call for reform of the Soviet system, and for the USSR to adopt a revolutionary internationalism. Consequently, he refused to support those urging the formation of new parties and a new International: preaching instead reform, not revolution, in the Soviet Union. However, in April 1929, forty Oppositionists – including Radek and Preobrazhensky – capitulated to Stalin. Trotsky responded by warning that Stalin's left course had only come about because of the Opposition, and that caving in now would allow Stalin to tack back to the centre. Hence the best way to support the left turn was to democratise the party regime.

In August 1929, Rakovsky – his closest supporter, and the main leader of those Oppositionists still resisting capitulation – issued a Declaration which, although saying Trotsky and the others should be allowed to return to the party, called on the Opposition to renounce all factional activity. Trotsky, very reluctantly, co-signed it – hoping it would stop further capitulations. Stalin, however, ignored it, and the capitulations continued. Although Stalin's Five-Year Plans were partly inspired by policies he'd advocated much earlier, Trotsky deplored Stalin's compulsory and harsh methods, and the unrealistic rapidity of this 'revolution from above'. Instead, Trotsky argued for a slower, non-coercive transition from NEP, with improved benefits for industrial workers, and incentives to encourage peasants to join collective farms. He also called for local managers of state enterprises to have the freedom to point out errors without fear of punishment. Essentially, Trotsky and most of his followers still saw the Soviet Union as a workers' state, believing therefore it was the duty of revolutionaries to defend that key gain resulting from the November Revolution.[10]

During 1930, Rakovsky argued for the formation of a 'Coalition CC', comprising the Left, Centre and Right; Trotsky's opinion on this fluctuated. However, at the end of 1931, a German Communist paper published reports that a White Guard group was about to assassinate Trotsky. Fearing this masked Stalin's own plans, Trotsky wrote to the Politburo on 4 January 1932, mentioning Zinoviev and Kamenev's 1926 warnings about Stalin's intentions. Stalin forced those two to deny Trotsky's allegations and, the following month, deprived Trotsky and all members of his family living abroad of Soviet citizenship.[11]

On 1 March 1932, in an *Open Letter to the CC*, as well as protesting at his loss of Soviet citizenship, Trotsky stated it was now necessary to carry out Lenin's recommendations to remove Stalin from power; and that: 'In the work of regenerating the party and Soviet democracy the Left Opposition is ready at all times to take a direct part.' In June 1932, Trotsky once again urged the party to remove Stalin, making it clear the ILO supported the Soviet state:

> 'Today, as on the day when we first raised our voice of warning against the epigonic bureaucracy, we are ready to the last one to place ourselves at the disposal of the Comintern and the Soviet state...We have only one condition: within the framework of the Comintern we must have the right to defend our ideas, that is, the ideas of Marxism, in conformity with the elementary principles of party democracy.'[12]

In September, I. Smirnov – one of Trotsky's oldest supporters, who'd capitulated in July 1929 – sent documents outlining the USSR's mounting economic problems, and a growing conviction amongst party members that the leadership needed changing. These were quickly published in the *Bulletin*. Smirnov advocated the formation of a bloc between the Left Opposition and the Right, with the slogan: 'Down with Stalin!' Though as it also called for the Second Five-Year Plan to be delayed, Trotsky hesitated, as he still saw the Right as more of a Thermidorian threat than Stalin and the Centre. Nonetheless, several communists – including Zinoviev, Kamenev and Bukharin – set up a 'Union of Marxist–Leninists'. However, this was uncovered by the OGPU and, on 9 October, Zinoviev and Kamenev were expelled from the party for trying to revive their faction.

Interlude in Copenhagen

In October 1932, following the request of a student organisation, the Danish government gave Trotsky permission to come to Copenhagen for one week, to give a lecture on the Russian Revolution. Travelling as Mr and Mrs Sedov, he and Sedova left Constantinople on 14 November, hoping for a longer stay. When the ship docked at Athens, they were cheered by onlookers, but weren't allowed to leave the ship. When it docked in Naples, they were only allowed to disembark for one hour under police escort – but managed to visit Pompeii. From Marseille, the French police accompanied them on the train to Paris. They then travelled to Dunkirk, where a ferry took them to Denmark, arriving on 23 November.[13]

Once in Copenhagen, they were housed in a luxurious villa that 'belonged to a *danseuse*' who was on tour, but were placed under constant police surveillance. However, once the press discovered Trotsky's whereabouts, they had to move to a boarding house. Over 2,500 attended his two-hour lecture, in German, at the Copenhagen Stadium, on 27 November – the last time he would address a large public meeting. But it wasn't broadcast on Danish radio, as the Danish royal family objected. So, instead, Trotsky did a broadcast in English for CBS. The Soviet Consul then demanded his immediate expulsion, leading the Danish authorities to insist he leave at the end of his seven-day visa. Nonetheless, before returning to Prinkipo, Trotsky was able to meet Danish supporters, as well as those from Germany, France and Norway. Although they spoke frequently on the phone, Lyova was denied a visa to visit him from Berlin.

On leaving Denmark, they travelled by boat to Antwerp: there, they were forbidden to leave the ship, though Belgian police wanted to interrogate him. He refused to answer questions, as he wasn't on Belgian soil. They then went by train to Paris where, on 6 December, they met Lyova who'd been given permission to join them on the train to Marseille. However, as the next boat to Constantinople wasn't for another nine days, the French authorities quickly put Trotsky on the first train to leave the country. So they parted from Lyova, and journeyed to Venice. On reaching Genoa, Mussolini's police tried to force them onto a cargo boat – but Trotsky refused. In Corinth, they were once more met by supporters who shouted out: 'Long live Trotsky!' By 12 December 1932, the 'escaped lion' was back in his 'cage' on Prinkipo.[14]

On his return, Yelena Eastman – Max Eastman's wife – tried unsuccessfully to get him a visa to visit the US; a request to visit Prague was also refused. Thus, forced to remain in Turkey, Trotsky began putting his papers in order – including Politburo and CC papers, and copies of almost all his correspondence with Lenin and, in Lenin's final months, with his secretary. He did this so he could get on with his planned literary efforts in the most organised and methodical way possible.

Fascism and Comintern

In March 1933, Trotsky once again wrote to the Politburo, offering to assist the new economic turn, in return for an amnesty and the restoration of inner-party democracy – including a genuinely free and open party conference to discuss all these issues. He was prepared to enter secret preliminary talks to do this. As he still believed in his theory of 'Permanent Revolution', he continued to argue that, even with the right approach to economic planning, the Soviet Union wouldn't be able to achieve full socialism without the help of new revolutionary regimes in Europe. Unsurprisingly, Stalin ignored his offers.

For Trotsky, the Great Depression of the 1930s showed capitalism was in crisis and that, therefore, revolution was once more on the agenda – hence the importance of Comintern having the right policies. However, he was also acutely aware that, if the workers' movement failed to defend its own interests, fascism would 'solve' the economic crisis in capitalism's favour. As early as April 1931, following the fall of the monarchy in Spain, he'd urged the Spanish Communist Party to form a united front with socialists and anarchists: warning that not doing so would lead to the rise to power of a Mussolini-style fascism.

Nowhere was the struggle against fascism more acute than in Germany – which had the largest and most organised working class movement. As early as November 1930, Trotsky – stuck on the margins in Turkey – called for a United Front of all German Communists, Socialists and trade unionists to oppose the emerging Nazi Party. He continued calling for this in article after article and, initially, was encouraged as many rank and file members of both parties began constructing an anti-fascist united front from below. However, the Communist and SDP leaderships prevented such collaboration, fighting each other instead.

Thus, in December 1931, Trotsky wrote:

> 'The key to the international situation is found in Germany. The climax is coming: the prerevolutionary situation will turn into revolution or counter-revolution…The destiny of Europe and of the entire world, for many years to come, will hinge on its outcome…The victory of German fascism will inevitably drag the U.S.S.R. into a war…We must unite the working class.'

The following month, his pamphlet, *What Next?* reiterated his concerns about the fascist threat: 'When a state turns fascist…it means, primarily and above all, that the workers' organizations are annihilated; that the proletariat is reduced to an amorphous state…Therein precisely is the gist of fascism.'[15]

Yet he still refused to support calls for new parties and a new International. Instead, he sought to pressure the official Communist movement to reform itself and adopt what he saw as the right policies. As he pointed out to those wanting a clean break, merely raising a new banner wouldn't lead to success, if the political context was unfavourable. For him, the Soviet Union – despite Stalin's actions – remained a workers' state, albeit one that was now 'bureaucratically deformed'.

In March 1933, with Hitler now in power, the *Bulletin* was banned: Lyova and Martin had to escape across the border; and the International Secretariat and the *Bulletin* relocated to Paris. Trotsky and Sedova meanwhile became increasingly worried about Lyova. As well as his work on the *Bulletin*, he was also central to the running of the International Secretariat, whilst also writing brilliant articles and pamphlets. But it became increasingly clear he was being followed by agents of Stalin's secret police.

Losing Zina

During this period of political uncertainty, a family tragedy had also been unfolding. Once exiled, Trotsky maintained contact with his family in the USSR by telegram and letter – especially with Zina and Sergei – and sent money when he could. Zina had been devastated by Nina's death – and by the arrest, in 1929, of her husband, an outspoken Trotskyist, who'd then been deported. In October 1930, because of growing concerns over Zina's health, Trotsky advised her to ask permission to join him and Sedova. In January 1931, Zina – who herself had been detained twice because of her involvement with the Left Opposition – finally got permission to visit him in Turkey.

However, by then, Zina was already suffering from depression and anxiety. This was exacerbated by her illness; the poor health of her son, Seva; and by the fact that the Soviet authorities had only allowed her to bring one of her two children – thus leaving behind her daughter with Sokolovskaya, who was also looking after Nina's two children. Zina – who stayed with Trotsky for ten months – was excited to be reunited with her father, later writing to Sokolovskaya: 'In the first period of my stay, he was so soft and attentive to me that I cannot even describe it....' Very like Trotsky in appearance and temperament, and highly intelligent, they cried together over Nina. While Trotsky – for the first time – was able to enjoy being a grandfather with Seva. Zina also got on well with Sedova, who'd often spent time with Trotsky's daughters during his absences.[16]

At first, Zina's health improved; she revelled in reading his articles and manuscripts, and was keen to help. Trotsky, however – in order not to tax her health, or compromise her return to the USSR and her daughter – restricted her political involvement. Thus, he only allowed her to provide limited help. Zina's lung condition then worsened, requiring several operations; while her mental health problems became more apparent: becoming increasingly resentful of Sedova's ties to her father. Tragically, as her outbursts increased, Trotsky withdrew into himself – thus distressing Zina even more.

As her mental health deteriorated, Trotsky advised her to seek treatment in Berlin. She left in October 1931, leaving Seva behind on Prinkipo. What would be Trotsky's last spoken words to her, were: 'You are an astonishing person. I have never met anyone like you.' Despite meeting up with Lyova in Berlin, her mental health deteriorated, with her becoming jealous of Lyova's relationship with Trotsky; she was eventually diagnosed with schizophrenia. When Stalin's government, on 20 February 1932, deprived all Trotsky's family living abroad of Soviet citizenship, Zina's depression increased, as it meant she could no longer go back to her daughter.[17]

In June 1932, Lyova advised her to go to Vienna, believing its calmer political atmosphere and doctors would be better for her. She refused and, unable to manage her monthly allowance, ended up in a low-grade boarding house. In October, she sent a postcard to Trotsky, blaming him for her nervous attacks. By then, Trotsky and Sedova were having regular phone conversations with Lyova over Zina's increasingly confused behaviour. Lyova himself was under more pressure: there were tensions with Martin, and he received letters from his wife, detailing the problems and unhappiness she and their son were facing, and even mentioning suicide. But all Lyova could do was send her money. His situation was made worse by Trotsky suggesting he wasn't supporting Zina enough.

Despite Seva eventually joining her in Berlin in December 1932, Zina felt increasingly alone, and hated seeing Hitler's Brownshirts take control of the streets. She was also distressed by the infrequent letters from Trotsky – Lyova pointed this out in a letter to him, saying her doctor said she needed 'more tenderness', and how it was 'very important for you to write to her'. Zina, desperate now to be back with her father, suggested returning to Prinkipo, to help his work. But Trotsky instead urged her to take her doctor's advice and seek medical help in a Russian resort first – even saying if she didn't follow medical advice, 'he would effect "a complete and final break" with her'. On one occasion, Zina confided to Lyova that, because of what she'd 'done to Papa, he'll never write to me'. It appears Trotsky only belatedly realised just how serious her mental state was. In her last letters to Sokolovskaya, written during a deep depression, Zina seemed to blame her mother for not being able to keep the family together, yet also saying: 'It is sad that I can no longer return to Papa. You know how I have adored and worshipped him from my earliest days. And now we are in utter discord. This has been at the bottom of my illness.'[18]

A week after Seva arrived, the Soviet Embassy got the German authorities to order her and her son to leave Berlin. With no passport for herself or Seva, and short of money, on the morning of 5 January 1933, Zina left Seva with some neighbours. She then phoned Lyova, asking him to see her – but he was busy that morning and so suggested meeting later that day. She agreed, but then barricaded her door and turned on the gas in her apartment. After her suicide, Lyova informed Trotsky by telegram, and managed to get through to Sergei in Moscow – in what turned out to be their last communication. Sergei then related the sad news to Sokolovskaya. Two days after learning of Zina's death, Trotsky wrote to her, saying: 'Zinushka is no longer alive. I turned to wood.' Sokovolskaya later wrote back to Trotsky, saying 'Our children were doomed'; initially, Lyova and Martin assumed care of Seva. In less than eight years, Trotsky had lost both his daughters – aware they'd both been deeply affected by separation from him, and by his fall from power. Zina's death increased Trotsky and Sedova's concerns for Lyova and Sergei.[19]

Towards a New International

After Hitler became Chancellor in January 1933, Trotsky's view about forming a new International shifted. In the *Bulletin,* he wrote that if the German Communist Party (KPD) still refused to form a united front, then: '...the working class will have to make its way towards a Fourth International; and it will have to make it through mountains of corpses and years of unbearable sufferings and calamities'. In March 1933, in his *The Tragedy of the German Proletariat*, he bitterly condemned the Stalinists for rejecting 'the united front' and for sabotaging 'the slightest initiative for the united front for local defense....' Trotsky thus called for the KPD to ignore control from Moscow and, instead, hold an open party conference to elect new independent leaders. In preparation for such a conference, he called for genuine party democracy – including the KPD opening its journals to the ILO.[20]

The general view of Trotsky's writings on fascism in Germany is that he was mostly correct. Deutscher saw Trotsky's attempts to get German workers to adopt the right tactics as his 'greatest political deed in exile'; while more recently released eyewitness accounts and KPD documents confirm Trotsky's analysis was essentially sound, and that if his call for a genuine united front had been successful, Germany – and the world – would almost certainly have been spared the horrors of Nazism and the Second World War. Others, however, doubt whether Trotsky's policies would have been sufficient to prevent Hitler's rise to power.[21]

Regardless of how correct Trotsky's analysis may have been, the triumph of fascism in Germany finally decided him that the Communist Parties and the Third International were beyond reform from within – in the same way that the Second International's attitude to the First World War had necessitated the formation of the Third International. For Trotsky, who'd played such a big role in setting up the Comintern, this was very hard. Despite recognising the time was hardly propitious, he saw the formation of a new communist International and national parties as essential. Though he also insisted the new International must critically defend the USSR against capitalist imperialism – predicting that if Hitler were not opposed, there would be a world war in five to ten years.

He was now desperate to escape his relative isolation in Turkey and, instead, move to mainland Europe. He tried several countries, but all to no avail – partly because Stalin claimed Trotsky had left the USSR in order to foment revolution in Europe! After the Nazi takeover in Germany, Trotsky saw France as the country to be in: he felt if he could help a successful socialist revolution take place there, it would be possible to roll back the tides of fascism and undermine Stalinism's influence on the international workers' movement. His supporters in western Europe eventually secured him a French visa, even though his 1916 expulsion order was still in effect. Yet – despite Zina's suicide – his time on Prinkipo would prove to be the 'calmest, the most creative, and the least unhappy time of his exile'.[22]

France 1933–35

Thus, with high revolutionary hopes, Trotsky (again travelling as Mr Sedov) – accompanied by van Heijenoort and Klement, and US Oppositionists Sara Weber and Max Schachtman – left Turkey on 17 July 1933, on board an old Italian steamer called the *Bulgaria*. They arrived off Marseille on 24 July, where a crowd of reporters waited to interview him. Instead, Lyova and Raymond Molinier came alongside in a motor launch, landing them at nearby Cassis, where Trotsky was given a document revoking the 1916 expulsion order. However, he was ordered to live in southern departments; not to stay outside any main city, including Paris; and to live *incognito*, initially as part of an American couple.

Trotsky hoped the move to France would enable him to meet more easily with his European supporters. Frustratingly, however, he was unable to exert the influence on France's political scene he'd hoped for during his two-year stay. Much of his time was taken up with frequent changes of address: staying, in all, in a dozen different houses – occasionally shaving off his beard, to avoid recognition. These moves were dictated by too much public attention; fears of attacks by French fascist groups; and growing awareness of Soviet agents following them. Consequently, his secretaries – Klement, van Heijenoort, and Weber – tightened security measures, including providing two Alsatian guard dogs, Benno and Stella. Although these constant moves were time-consuming, and poor health often dogged him, Trotsky still managed to maintain most of his work routines.

At first, Trotsky and Sedova settled at St Palais, near Royan on the Atlantic coast, where the Moliniers had rented them a villa, called 'Les Embruns' ('Sea Spray'). During the voyage, Trotsky had become bedridden with an attack of lumbago, followed by an outbreak of fevers that kept him in bed until the end of September. Nonetheless, he received some fifty visitors – including the French novelist, André Malraux.

The International Communist League

The construction of new communist parties and a new International became his main goal during his final years, believing only a new revolutionary International would be able to save 'the Russian Revolution from Stalinist degeneration, and humanity from fascism and war'. Just three days after arriving in France, on 27 July, he published *For New Communist Parties and the New International*, a short article in which he declared:

> 'The idea of reform [of the Comintern and existing communist parties] is to be rejected, nationally and internationally…
>
> 'What does this turn mean in its essence? We cease to be a faction; we are no longer the Left Opposition; we become embryos of new parties.'

However, given the serious defeats suffered by the international working class at the hands of fascism, he argued it was not yet time for 'proclaiming the split', as the Opposition didn't yet 'have sufficient forces'. Instead, he urged the small disparate groups of Trotskyists to orient themselves to the left wing currents emerging within the various socialist parties.[23]

At the end of July 1933, the ILO became the International Communist League (Bolshevik–Leninist) [ICL-B–L], which Trotsky reluctantly concluded would have to operate within the USSR as a separate party. In August 1933, his supporters organised a conference in Paris, as the first step towards establishing this new revolutionary International. In all, fourteen socialist and communist organisations took part. Though too ill to attend, Trotsky drafted its 'Theses' and resolutions. At its conclusion, Lyova – representing the Russian section – along with delegates from the German Socialist Workers' Party, and the Revolutionary Socialist Party and Independent Socialist Party of the Netherlands, signed a declaration outlining the basic principles of the new International. Though disappointed at the small numbers involved, Trotsky saw it as akin to the 1916 Zimmerwald Conference, which had eventually led to the Third International; and hoped this 'firm nucleus' would be the first 'open step in the direction of the building of a new International on the principled foundations of Marx and Lenin'. He was convinced that, with the political bankruptcy of 'Stalinism' finally exposed, his correct political assessments would soon see genuinely revolutionary communists and workers gather round the standard of this emerging Trotskyist International.[24]

At this point, Sedova had to go to Paris for medical treatment. Trotsky – disappointed by the August Conference, and now increasingly dependent on her to sustain his morale – wrote despairingly to her, commenting how he'd gone into 'your room and touched your things', and later saying: 'Dearest, dearest mine…Already the recent past seems better than it was. Yet we looked forward with so much hope to our stay in France.' Sedova replied: 'How sad you are. You have never been like that….' On 1 October, they moved temporarily to a refuge in Bagnères-de-Bigorre in the Hautes-Pyrénées, for a rest cure.[25]

With the *Bulletin* back in Paris, the NKVD (OGPU's replacement) began paying more attention to Lyova's activities and, in the summer of 1934, they managed to get an agent – Mark Zborowski (referred to by various codenames, including 'Max') – onto Lyova's staff. 'Etienne' – as he was known to Lyova – was completely trusted by Trotsky, resulting in many of his plans and writings being quickly relayed to the Soviet authorities – sometimes even before articles had been published: 'As reported, the source 'Max' has begun working in the Trotskyists' 'International secretariat'… this alone is evidence that your orders to infiltrate the source into Trotsky's entourage has been carried out.'

'Etienne' even attempted to distort the meanings of some of Trotsky's articles – however, this proved unsuccessful, largely because of excellent proofreading by Lilia Estrin, a relation of the Menshevik leader, Fedor Dan. Despite Dan's best efforts to dissuade her, she'd become a Trotskyist, working as Lyova's secretary. She later accompanied Trotsky to Mexico.[26]

Defence of the Soviet Union

The October issue of the *Bulletin* – in which all the articles were written by Trotsky – was devoted to the need to form his new International. His article *The Class Nature of the Soviet State* set out his definitive attitude to the Soviet Union. He rejected those who argued Thermidor had taken place, and that what existed in the USSR now was a form of 'state capitalism', with the Soviet bureaucracy as a new ruling class. Instead, Trotsky adamantly proclaimed the USSR remained a workers' state, albeit a degenerated one, in which the bureaucracy acted as a parasitic and privileged caste. Trotsky argued that, by defeating the Right, Stalin and the Centre were protecting the main social gains of the Russian Revolution. As he saw it, the Stalinist bureaucracy's fate was bound up with that of the working class – any capitalist restoration would see the end of the bureaucracy's power. Thus it was still the duty of revolutionaries to defend the Soviet Union – via critical support – against any internal or external attempts at capitalist restoration, even while also irreconcilably working to end bureaucratic rule and restore *soviet* democracy:

> 'The new International will offer the Stalinist bureaucracy a united front against the common foe...
>
> 'The problem of the world revolution as well as the problem of the Soviet Union may be summed up in one and the same brief formula: The Fourth International.'[27]

This remained the distinctive feature of Trotsky's Fourth International: calls for a political revolution in the Soviet Union (and, later, in the deformed workers' states of Eastern Europe and Asia), and for social and economic revolutions in the capitalist states. In many ways, this was a logical continuation of his 'Permanent Revolution' theory – with the victory of socialist revolutions in developed European countries paving the way for restoring *soviet* democracy in the USSR, and then assisting the leftward course of the Russian Revolution.

On 1 November, the police allowed him to move to Barbizon, on the edge of Fontainebleau Forest and Paris. While there, in February 1934, the Seventeenth Party Congress – the first since 1930 – took place in the USSR, during which Kirov emerged as the 'human face of Stalinism'. Earlier, Bukharin and other leading Rightists had been restored to important positions; while Stalin had made a final appeal to all Left Oppositionists to capitulate – the NKVD even 'briefed' party activists that Trotsky was about to apply for permission to return to the USSR. A serious setback for Trotsky was Rakovsky finally capitulating, because the latter felt 'the victorious offensive of fascism requires the unity of all forces in the defence of Soviet power'. Deeply saddened by this, Trotsky wrote in his diary:

> 'One great revolutionary less...Rakovsky was virtually my last contact with the old revolutionary generation. After his capitulation there is nobody left....'[28]

Developments in the USSR

Trotsky resumed his work routine, gathering more materials for Lenin's biography. He was pleased Ruth Fischer supported his new International, but disappointed when Nin broke away to form the POUM in Catalonia. However, after six months, his presence at Barbizon was discovered, reporters soon gathered, and the police said they could no longer guarantee his safety. Trotsky's writings on the prospects of revolution in France made him a potential source of trouble at a time when French politics – as in most of Europe – was moving to the extremes. As his permission to stay in France had included a commitment to abstain from political activity, France's right wing government considered expelling him. However, since no other state was prepared to accept him, he was ordered to move at least 300km from Paris.

On 17 April 1934, they quickly left for Paris – staying briefly with Lyova and Martin, in a small run-down house they'd rented – before moving to other refuges, including a stay at Chamonix, near the Swiss border. But each time – after only short stays – Trotsky's presence was discovered. In late June 1934 – pursued by the press – they fled to Domène, a small village near Grenoble. It was to be their final residence in France, living there in complete isolation for the next eleven months. His health was again poor – and he spent much of the time in bed, or writing his diary; it was the longest relapse since the mid-1920s. Unusually for him, despite having signed contracts, he was unable to complete his book on Lenin. Sedova also fell ill – and was surprised by Trotsky's apparent 'lack of a steely will to fight back'.[29]

As well as frequent changes of address, a lot of Trotsky's time in France was spent trying to settle disputes between his various followers. His pre-1933 warnings about the rise of fascism had begun to gain a wide audience in France, and hundreds of mainly young people were attracted to these Trotskyist groups. When members of the Socialist and Communist parties formed an unofficial united front against French fascists in July 1934, Trotsky urged the French Trotskyists to join the Socialists, to try to shift them to support revolutionary positions and the Fourth International – such as calling for the formation of *soviets*. However, the different views and rivalries amongst some of his French supporters made this difficult.

While at Domène, in December 1934, Trotsky learned of the assassination of Kirov, by someone linked to the NKVD. At the Seventeenth Party Congress, Kirov – the Leningrad chief – had been elected to the CC with votes from almost all the 1,225 delegates, whereas about 300 hadn't voted for Stalin. Apparently, some leading officials had asked him to replace Stalin. At this stage, Trotsky still didn't think Stalin would resort to physically eliminating his rivals, maintaining the assassination hadn't been ordered by Stalin, but was merely a symptom of growing pressures. However, he predicted Stalin would use the assassination to remove opponents from office, and to crack down on the remnants of the Left Opposition, to consolidate his power. He also warned this would be followed by trials against former Oppositionists, in which Zinoviev and Kamenev would denounce him as the leader of a terroristic plot against the USSR.

In February 1935, his article – *The Workers' State, Thermidor and Bonapartism* – formally abandoned his 'Thermidor' concept, which he argued had been essentially correct up to around 1928. However, by way of 'self-criticism' of a 'partial, even though an important error', he now argued: 'today we can and must admit that the analogy of Thermidor served to becloud rather than clarify the question' of developments in the USSR. He went further, stating recent developments showed the Soviet 'Thermidor' was already far behind, and that what now existed was a Stalinist Bonapartism, within a degenerated workers' state. He saw this revision of his ideas as a strength, not a weakness: 'Our tendency never laid claim to infallibility. We do not receive ready-made truths as a revelation, like the high priests of Stalinism.'[30]

Further Family Tragedies

In early 1935, he learned that, soon after Kirov's assassination, Sokolovskaya had been arrested and exiled, and that, consequently, the grandchildren had been sent to an older sister in the Ukraine. In his diary,

Trotsky wrote: 'Alexandra Lvovna Sokolovskaya, my first wife, who was living in Leningrad with my grandchildren, has been deported to Siberia.' At first, Trotsky was able to communicate with her by letter, and to send her money orders; but then the authorities stopped all communications. In addition, Trotsky also found out his two sons-in-law, Volkov and Nevelson, had also been arrested and sent to prison camps – where both would perish. Around the same time, he also learned Sergei was at risk. Since 1929, Sergei had only written to his mother, to avoid association with his father. In December 1934, Sergei – in what proved to be his last letter – wrote how the 'general situation is proving extremely difficult, much more difficult than you can imagine', and that his situation was becoming 'very grave'. Sergei's letters then stopped, plunging Trotsky into anxiety and depression – even considering suicide should his physical strength to continue the struggle give out. As Deutscher remarked: 'He was now at his nadir' and even began to sense that maybe his 'Fourth International was stillborn'. Trotsky reckoned he needed at least five more years to make it a viable International – in the end, that was all he would have.[31]

In May 1935, they received news that Sergei – then aged twenty-seven and a professor in the Institute of Technology – had been arrested on 4 March. By then, his first marriage to Olga Greber had ended, and he was married to Genrieta Rubinstein – Yulia, his daughter from that second relationship, was born after his arrest. On 1 June, Trotsky wrote in his diary: 'Poor boy...And my poor, poor Natasha....' Trotsky and Sedova (who, at first, seemed more concerned about Sokolovskaya's fate) lodged a formal protest, which was ignored. Then, after a few weeks, an international money order they'd sent to Sergei's wife, was returned, marked 'no forwarding address': she, too, had been arrested. They tried hard to find out more about what had happened to Sergei, but with no luck. Trotsky and Sedova entertained the hope their son was in a prison camp, but without permission to write.[32]

Although Trotsky was encouraged by signs of left unity in France, and believed his supporters' entry into the French Socialist Party was about to bear fruit, he was also impatient to end his political isolation in France – later noting that he'd been more isolated there than he'd been on Prinkipo Island. When the French government informed him he was no longer *persona grata*, he turned to Norway. On 9 June 1935, he was informed Norway had granted him a visa; the following day, he and Sedova – accompanied by van Heijenoort and Frankel – travelled to Paris, where they had a brief meeting with Lyova and Seva (they hadn't seen their grandson for three years), and with some French Trotskyists.

Norway 1935–36

After some administrative hitches, they left for Antwerp, where they caught a ferry, entering their new country of exile on 18 June. They arrived in Oslo with virtually no money, and a visa valid for only six months. Norway's Labour government welcomed him – on condition he refrained from political activity, which Trotsky assumed meant not getting involved in Norway's political life. He looked forward to concentrating on writing and correspondence, and his friends found them a small hotel, but there was much hostility to his stay, and many were unwilling to rent them a house. 'Etienne' quickly passed on his Norway addresses to the NKVD, who resumed their watching and following.

For the next eighteen months, they lived in two rooms with Konrad Knudsen, a painter, left wing publisher and journalist, and Labour Party politician, at his large house in Vexhall, just outside the small city of Hønefoss, thirty miles north of Oslo. They occasionally went with the Knudsens to the local cinema, and Trotsky felt secure enough to go for walks on his own in the woods. During the winter, they went with the Knudsens to a mountain hut, on skis. Despite hoping the move from France would assist his attempts to influence European politics, if anything the move to Norway weakened them. The only way of communicating with Trotsky was via the offices of the Labour Party's newspaper in Hønefoss.

Health Problems

In July 1935, the Seventh Congress of the Third International – the first one since 1928 and, as it turned out, the last – adopted what Trotsky saw as an opportunistic policy of forming Popular Fronts with bourgeois parties in the struggle against fascism. This confirmed him in his call for a new International, and he now saw the USSR as a 'contradictory society halfway between capitalism and socialism', with a Soviet Bonapartist regime. He was further depressed to learn his French followers had ended their entry into the Socialist Party and had, instead, broken up into several small sects. This impacted his health, causing him, in September, to spend a few expensive weeks in Oslo's hospital, followed by periods of being bedridden by insomnia and fever. An entry in his diary shows just how much he appreciated Sedova, and the support she gave him – especially at critical times:

> 'Natalya and I have been together for thirty-three years (a third of a century!), and always in tragic moments I am amazed by her reserves of character. I can say one thing: Natalya has never "reproached" me, not in the most difficult times; she doesn't reproach me now, either, in the worst days of our life, when everyone has ganged up against us....'[33]

On 27 December, he was so exhausted and disappointed that he experienced a low moment – asking Lyova for a month's leave of absence as regards dealing with the various Trotskyist groups. According to Sedova, Trotsky – frustrated at not being able to demand proof of his 'crimes' – was 'like a man in a delirium during those days, as if plunged into an insane nightmare'. During a winter walk that year, Sedova relates how: 'One day, well before all this bloodthirsty madness [the Show Trials and Purges] had started, he said to me as we stood in the winter snow, "I am tired of it all – all of it – do you understand?" This was no lapse or weakness, but revolutionaries, too, are only human.'[34]

The Revolution Betrayed

One of Trotsky's main concerns was to expose Stalin's betrayal of the November Revolution, and his crimes against fellow communists. His major effort to that end was *The Revolution Betrayed*, a book that – despite three months of ill health – was completed by the beginning of August 1936, and was published the following year, by which time he was in Mexico. It was also the last major book he wrote – a classical indictment of bureaucracy, and something of a rather pessimistic and complex political testament, combining 'all the weakness and the strength of his thought'. It was also an outline of the political revolution needed in the USSR, and, as such, was adopted by subsequent Trotskyist groups. As well sending a manuscript to his publishers, Trotsky also sent a copy to Lyova, asking him to publish extracts in the *Bulletin*. As a result, 'Etienne' was able to send a copy to the NKVD well before the book appeared in print.

The Revolution Betrayed was his most comprehensive analysis of the Soviet Union. In it, he set out the many ways in which he felt Stalin and his supporters had betrayed the ideals of the Bolshevik programme of 1917. His conclusion was that, while the USSR was still a workers' state, it was a 'transitional state', somewhere between capitalism and the very earliest stages of socialism. He used the analogy of a person who'd started crossing a bridge to the other side of a river, but had stopped in the middle: pointing out this was untenable and that, sooner or later, the person would either have to continue their journey, or turn around and go back where they'd come from. As Trotsky saw it, only his ICL – and successful socialist revolutions in Europe – could prevent Russia returning to capitalism and instead guide it across to construct socialism. Many of these ideas had been advocated in earlier copies of the *Bulletin*. Later research has confirmed most, though not all, of Trotsky's analyses and claims.

Having completed it, he resumed work on his book on Lenin. However, his secure asylum was shattered on 5 August 1936 when, the day after the manuscript of *The Revolution Betrayed* had been sent off to the publishers, members of Quisling's fascist party broke into Knudsen's house and stole some correspondence. They were seen off by Knudsen's daughter, Hjørdis who by then had fallen in love with Erwin Wolf, one of Trotsky's secretaries. This event unsettled the Norwegian government, which – increasingly under pressure from the USSR, and concerned about visits from leaders of various Trotskyist groups – expelled one of his secretaries. To avoid trouble, Trotsky asked his supporters to remove his name from the International Executive of the ICL, and published any articles to do with it under the pen name of 'Crux'.[35]

The First Show Trial

Because of its timing, *The Revolution Betrayed* didn't cover the first of the great 'Show Trials' of Stalin's opponents. Beginning on 19 August, sixteen 'Old Bolsheviks' – including Zinoviev and Kamenev – were charged with belonging to a 'Trotskyist–Zinovievist Terrorist Centre,' part of a 'counter-revolutionary fascist plot' against the Soviet state and its leaders. Trotsky first learned of the trial whilst on a fishing trip with Knudsen. They rushed back to the house, reading Russian newspapers that mentioned a large number of arrests. Fourteen of the accused admitted their 'guilt', and, by the end of August, all had been shot. Trotsky and Lyova were condemned as the two main organisers of this 'terrorism'. This 'Trial of the Sixteen' began what became known as the 'Great Purge' and the 'Great Terror'. Trotsky poured over newspaper reports of the trial, 'armed with red, blue and black pencils', jotting down notes and pointing out inconsistencies. He also received journalists and gave interviews, and immediately began a press campaign to disprove the allegations. All he needed, he thought, was the freedom to refute Stalin's lies.

However, Trotsky's outspoken criticisms of Stalin's Show Trial and the subsequent executions, led Norway's Minister of Justice to judge he'd broken the terms of his permit, thus demanding he cease commenting on any political matters, and insisting he agree to having all correspondence inspected. Trotsky refused; so his secretaries, including Wolf, were expelled. On 29 August 1936, a Note from the Soviet Embassy was delivered to the Norwegian government, saying Trotsky's continued presence in Norway risked impairing relations between the two countries, and threatening economic sanctions.

Consequently, the government asked Trotsky to sign a declaration not to make even indirect attempts to interfere in the politics of any country. He refused and, on 2 September, Trotsky was evicted from Vexhall, to a farm at Sundby, near Hurum, on the edge of a fjord. There, Trotsky and Sedova were placed under house arrest, ordered to stay inside the house for twenty-two hours a day, and forbidden visitors. They were given the first floor, with fifteen police officers on the ground floor; one of the police in charge of his house arrest described Trotsky as calm, dignified and self-disciplined, though always protesting, politely, at each infringement of his rights. While there, he began to reread Ibsen.

All Trotsky's refutations of the Stalinist lies were held back by the censor – a supporter of Quisling's fascist party! Thus the task fell to Lyova, who now became the public face of Trotskyist opposition. Like his father, he was shocked by the humiliating 'confessions' from 'Old Bolsheviks' whom, as a boy, he'd known. But he allowed for the 'exceptional times' and pressures put upon them. In the October 1936 issue of the *Bulletin*, Lyova published his first piece on the Show Trial – *The Red Book* – which was later published as a book. Trotsky and Lyova were accused of having met with one of the 'plotters' at the Hotel Bristol, during his trip to Copenhagen in October 1932. There, they'd allegedly given instructions for the assassination of Kirov, Stalin and other Soviet leaders. Lyova proved the hotel had been demolished in 1917! Trotsky was proud of his son's writing – calling it 'an inestimable gift', and referring to him as 'Our brave dear Lyova' – and both he and Sedova were kept informed by Lyova about the campaign he was conducting against the purges. Trotsky later said that all he'd written since 1928 should also have Lyova's name on it, as he'd helped so much with research and production.[36]

172

However, Lyova's efforts on his father's behalf made him a high-profile target, and he became increasingly aware of being watched, and having his post intercepted – even fearing possible kidnap. Cut off from his parents, he relied for support on 'Etienne' and the small group of French Trotskyists. In October 1936, worried by the Show Trials and signs of increased surveillance, Trotsky asked Lyova to deposit a large section of his archives with the Paris Institute of Historical Research: as well as wanting to protect them from the NKVD, he needed the money. Ironically, the bulk of his documents and correspondence were being kept 'securely' by 'Etienne'! On 6 November 1936, a few days after Lyova – accompanied by 'Etienne' – had deposited the archives, there was a break-in, and parts were stolen. Other than the curator, only Trotsky, Lyova and 'Etienne' had known the archives had been deposited there. Lyova assured the French police that 'Etienne' was above suspicion. It was at this point that Lyova came to feel increasingly anxious about being watched and followed.

Leaving Norway

The never-ending fabrications coming out of Moscow, reports of arrests, deportations and executions – and Radek and even Rakovsky reportedly joining in demands for the blood of 'that super-bandit Trotsky' – led to another breakdown in Trotsky's health, news of which was duly passed on by 'Etienne' to Moscow: '...the "Old Man" is very sick...he is sweating profusely which weakens him drastically. He should be in a sanatorium, but the Norwegian authorities are making his position more difficult.' Although Trotsky bounced back, Stalin put increasing pressure on the Norwegian government to expel him.[37]

When Stalin announced the new Soviet Constitution on 5 December 1936 – which Stalin described as the 'most democratic in the world' – Trotsky dashed off an article on the Stalinist reality, urging those who wanted genuine democracy to join his ICL. When the Minister of Justice visited in December 1936 to tell Trotsky he'd be moved to the remote north of the country, Trotsky replied by quoting from Ibsen's *An Enemy of the People*: 'We shall yet see whether meanness and cowardice are strong enough to close the mouth of a free and honest man.' He then informed the Minister that his friends were already making approaches to Mexico, where he'd rather go; when the Minister left, Trotsky refused to shake hands with him. A week later, Mexico – one of the few countries to support the beleaguered Spanish Republic – granted him asylum. Trotsky gratefully accepted – although he'd hoped for the US, this was categorically refused.[38]

On 19 December 1936, Trotsky and Sedova – with only twenty-four hours' notice – were hastily deported on the Norwegian oil tanker, *Ruth*, as it was considered too dangerous to risk sailing on a normal cruise ship. They had to leave without even being allowed to say farewell to the Knudsens. Trotsky and Sedova – without Lyova or secretaries – thus bade farewell to Europe. Fearing possible assassination, Trotsky hastily wrote Lyova a letter, entitled *Shame!* – a sort of last testament, informing Lyova he had no money to leave him and Sergei other than incomes from future royalties. He also stated his intention to give a full exposé in Mexico 'if ever I arrive there'. It was his last letter from Europe – and it was almost exactly twenty years since Trotsky had last sailed from Europe. Then, he returned within five months – this time, it proved to be forever. Three days later, Lyova received a telegram informing him of his father's expulsion and destination. Though disappointed they'd not be passing through Paris, where he'd hoped for a reunion, Lyova immediately sent van Heijenoort and Jan Frankel to Mexico, as reliable bodyguards.

In rough seas, Trotsky began making notes on Zinoviev and Kamenev, which formed the basis for his *Stalin's Crimes*. However, despite everything, Trotsky had clearly enjoyed some aspects of his time in Norway:

> 'All this nothwithstanding, we carried away with us warm remembrances of the marvelous land of forests and fjords, of the snow beneath the January sun, of skis and sleighs…and of the slightly morose and slow-moving but serious and honest people. Norway, goodbye!'[39]

Chapter 10

Love and Death in Mexico, 1937–40

'For forty-three years of my conscious life I have remained
a revolutionist; for forty-two of them I have fought under
the banner of Marxism. If I had to begin all over again
I would of course try to avoid this or that mistake, but the
main course of my life would remain unchanged. I shall die
a proletarian revolutionist, a Marxist, a dialectical materialist
and, consequently, an irreconcilable atheist.'[1]

This extract from Trotsky's *Testament* was written in Mexico on 27 Feb
1940 – six months before his death – at a time when he was concerned about
his health and increasingly expected to be assassinated. Three years before,
on 9 January 1937, Trotsky and Sedova had arrived, almost penniless, in
Mexico's oil port of Tampico. Mexico would be Trotsky's final country of
exile. In the time left to him, his main political tasks were to refute Stalin's
charges of terrorism and to establish the Fourth International (FI).

To pay for those political campaigns – and for living expenses – he
needed to earn money: in particular, by completing his biographies of Lenin
and Stalin. With the former, he intended to 'purge the teachings of Lenin of
the poisonous distortions and falsifications of the Soviet bureaucracy'. In
the end, his political campaigns meant he finished neither. As well as writing
books, he wrote articles, and gave seminars and newspaper interviews. He
also sold copies of his political correspondence from 1918–22 to the Institute
of Social History in Amsterdam. On a personal level, he and Sedova were
to suffer more family tragedies – made worse by the brief affair he had with
Frida Kahlo, the renowned Mexican artist.[2]

Final Exile

When they arrived in Mexico, they were met by a group of supporters,
including Max Shachtman, George Novak and Frida Kahlo. Mexico's
radical president, Lázaro Cárdenas, provided his special train to take them

to Mexico City, where they were met by Diego Rivera, Kahlo's husband and a famed painter and muralist, whose work Trotsky had long admired. A key founder of the Mexican Communist Party, Rivera had become disillusioned after witnessing the street attacks on the Opposition in Moscow in November 1927; by 1937, both he and Kahlo were supporters of Trotsky.

Rivera and Kahlo took them to 'La Casa Azul', Kahlo's house on Avienda Londres in Coyoacán, a western suburb of Mexico City: this was to be Trotsky's home until May 1939. As before, Trotsky relaxed by going on fishing trips in the Gulf of Mexico; while he and Sedova enjoyed the scenery and the exotic flora and fauna of the surrounding countryside.

The Second Show Trial

On 23 January, two weeks after arriving in Mexico, Trotsky's writing plans were disrupted by the start of the Second Show Trial – the 'Trial of the Seventeen' – in the Soviet Union. By then, the CC had agreed on the need to 'destroy' the 'Trotskyist Conspiracy'. Those accused included former Oppositionists such as Pyatakov and Radek. Once again, Trotsky and Lyova were accused of directing an 'Anti-Soviet Centre' – in alliance with Nazi Germany and Japan – to defeat the USSR via terrorism, sabotage and espionage.

As Sedova recorded, Trotsky – 'With pencil in hand…over-tense, overworked, often feverish, yet tireless, made a note of all the forgeries and lies…' – tried hard to refute these allegations, sending telegrams to the court asking for exact dates and times of alleged meetings. He also challenged Stalin once again to demand his extradition, so he could defend himself in Moscow; and informed the League of Nations he was prepared to submit his case to their Commission on Political Terrorism. Both remained silent.[3]

As before, this new Show Trial witnessed courtroom 'confessions': including Pyatakov saying he'd flown from Berlin to meet Trotsky in Oslo in December 1935, to discuss sabotage methods. With more freedom to refute the 'evidence' than he'd had in Norway, Trotsky – with little money and minimal help – nonetheless set to work over the next few months. This Oslo 'evidence' was quickly disproved when the Norwegian authorities stated no plane from Berlin had arrived that December. After the 'confessions', thirteen were executed, including Pyatakov; Radek was sent to a prison camp, as he'd agreed to implicate Bukharin; he was shot later.

Meanwhile, Trotsky and Sedova found out that Sergei, their younger son – who'd been sent to a prison camp in Siberia in 1935, and then drafted to work as an engineer in a factory – had been rearrested, charged with trying to poison the factory workers on his father's orders. Trotsky assumed that, in order to get him to incriminate his father and older brother, 'The GPU will not hesitate to drive Sergei to insanity and then they will shoot him'. However, the non-political Sergei had been politicised by his earlier arrest and imprisonment: his refusal to betray his father the first time had led to a five-year sentence of exile in Siberia. Then, at some point in 1936, he was placed in a prison camp. Whilst there, he'd met Trotskyists and, after the first Show Trial, had joined them in a widespread hunger strike lasting over four months. In early 1937, he was brought back to Moscow for interrogation – but, once again, refused to betray his father. It is not known exactly what happened to him, though it seems he was executed in late October 1937.

All Trotsky and Sedova could do, once they learned he'd been rearrested, was worry about his fate. The news depressed Trotsky 'beyond measure', leading him to say to Sedova 'Perhaps my death would have saved Sergey'. However, Trotsky only shared such dark thoughts with Sedova – when he heard that Angelica Balabanova had become deeply depressed by the trials, he wrote to her on 3 February 1937: '…I will not believe that you have succumbed to pessimism…History must be taken as she is; and when she allows herself such extraordinary and filthy outrages, one must fight her back with one's fists.'[4]

Refuting Stalin's Charges

Even before landing in Mexico, Trotsky had begun work on disproving Stalin's allegations. During the journey from Norway to Mexico, he'd written several articles, warning that further show trials were likely. He'd also completed a book, published later in 1937 as *Stalin's Crimes*. He argued that the trials and purges were more to do with the Bonapartist bureaucracy wishing to preserve their power and privileges than with Stalin's personal quest for complete dominance, seeing them instead as a symptom of a crisis revealing just how unpopular the bureaucracy's policies were. His *The Revolution Betrayed* – completed before the first Show Trial, but published in 1937 – calling for a political revolution, specifically rejected terrorism:

> 'In themselves, terrorist acts are least of all capable of overthrowing a Bonapartist oligarchy…Individual terror is a weapon of impatient or despairing individuals….'[5]

Around 6,500 attended a meeting at which Trotsky talked about the Second Show Trial – plans to transmit his speech, by telephone, to New York, where thwarted by technical difficulties, so someone in New York read out the speech. In it, Trotsky guaranteed, if a public and impartial Commission of Inquiry found him 'guilty in the slightest degree' of the crimes he was accused of, he'd return to the USSR for punishment.[6]

Once established in Mexico, Trotsky and his supporters decided to organise a 'counter-trial' so he could defend himself in public, rather than just via the printed word. In preparation, he wrote scores of letters and articles, while 'Committees For The Defence Of Trotsky' were established in several countries. These included people opposed to communism, but who saw the Show Trials as a travesty of justice. In March 1937, several Committees came together, and the US Committee began arranging a quasi-legal 'trial'. Trotsky initially hoped the Second International would be involved, along with the International Federation of Trade Unions. Lyova was given a heavy workload in relation to this, specifically instructed to gather together a range of relevant documents, along with witness statements. Yet Trotsky often hurt Lyova by his frequent irritation if materials didn't arrive from Paris as promptly or as completely as he'd expected. At times, Lyova wrote to Sedova, expressing how unjust he felt his father was being, and complaining of being a 'beast of burden' – he also wrote to Trotsky saying his reproaches were unfair.[7]

The distinguished US liberal philosopher, Dr John Dewey, agreed to chair an international Joint Commission of Inquiry, soon known as the Dewey Commission. From the beginning, the Commission invited representatives of the Soviet government and Comintern to present any evidence they had. The only member of this Commission who'd had any links with Trotsky was Alfred Rosmer – several of the members were political opponents. Thus Trotsky obtained a hearing which had both 'objectivity and authority' for his attempt at 'clearing his name'.[8]

Unable to get a visa to travel to the US, Trotsky's deposition was taken in Mexico. The 'trial' itself lasted from 10–17 April, with both press and interested public associations present. In 'Casa Azul', Trotsky was rigorously cross-examined in English – over thirteen sessions lasting a total of forty-one hours – by the counsel for the Commission, and was defended by his own lawyer. The two defence witnesses were Jan Frankel (one of Trotsky's secretaries in Turkey and Norway) and Trotsky himself. Trotsky also allowed unrestricted examination of his archives. He was questioned not just about his alleged 'anti-Soviet' conspiracy, but also his political activities pre-1917 and post-1929. He replied fully to all questions, stating, in his final plea: 'In the very fact of your Commission's formation…I see a new and truly magnificent reinforcement of the revolutionary optimism which constitutes the fundamental element of my life.' Dewey, who'd intended to sum up, was so impressed, he merely said: 'Anything I can say will be an anti-climax.'[9]

The Dewey Commission also took a mountain of evidence in many cities, including New York, Paris and Prague. On 21 September 1937, the Commission categorically concluded that the trials were frame-ups and that both Trotsky and Lyova were 'not guilty' on all charges of terrorism and working with fascist governments. However, its verdict, and the verbatim report of the hearings – which ran to over 600 pages – were not made public until 13 December, in the book *The Case of Leon Trotsky*. That day, Trotsky gave a press conference, during which he quoted Émile Zola's comment on the notorious Dreyfus Case: 'Truth is on the march and nothing can stop it.'

However, although the verdict was welcomed by Trotsky and his supporters, it had little impact. Exhausted by his efforts, Trotsky and Sedova were lent a villa in Taxco by a US lecturer, where they rested before returning to Coyoacán.[10]

Affair With Frida Kahlo

Whilst preparing for the Dewey Commission, Trotsky embarked on a brief affair with Kahlo. When they first met, she was twenty-nine, and Trotsky was twenty-eight years older. Kahlo and Rivera's marriage was stormy – both had had extra-marital liaisons before Trotsky arrived. But tensions were particularly high in 1937, after Kahlo discovered Rivera, aged fifty, was having an affair with her younger sister. Kahlo was, in addition, excited by her close connections to such a famous revolutionary as Trotsky.

Sometime in mid-April, a sexual relationship between Trotsky – who even Deutscher stated was a bit of flirt – and Kahlo began. Over the months, they exchanged love notes concealed in books, and frequently held brief conversations in English – a language Sedova didn't speak. By the summer of 1937, the two lovers were meeting in Kahlo's sister's flat. Sedova became increasingly suspicious and the tensions between her and Trotsky reached such a pitch it was agreed Trotsky should move out for a while – Rivera suggested a ranch in the countryside around the village of Gomez Landero. On 7 July, Trotsky set out, accompanied by bodyguards. Once there, he wrote – and relaxed by riding and fishing. However, Kahlo turned up just a day later.

Sedova found out, and wrote to Trotsky demanding to know what was going on. Trotsky replied, detailing his 'shame and self-hatred', and urging her 'to stop competing with a woman who means so little'. He also suggested that, in 1918, she'd had an affair with a younger man who was infatuated with her, but Sedova insisted she'd not reciprocated. Deutscher suggests the letters from this time indicate this was the only time Sedova had cause to be jealous and hurt. Trotsky also wrote a special diary whilst away, meant only for her eyes. He resolved to end the affair, and his last note to Kahlo, at the end of July 1937, was distant: 'Natasha and I wish you the best of health and real artistic success and I embrace you as our good and sincere friend.' He also asked her to return all his love letters to her, so he could burn them. It seems Kahlo, too, was tiring of the affair. However, Trotsky and Kahlo remained on good terms: she dedicated a self-portrait, 'Between the Curtains', to him on his fifty-eighth birthday. In the painting, she is holding a document that says: 'To Trotsky with great affection, I dedicate this painting November 7, 1937. Frida Kahlo, in San Angel, Mexico.'[11]

Despite speculation about affairs with Reissner and Sheridan, Swain too believes this affair was the only one during Trotsky's thirty-seven year relationship with Sedova. Certainly, his very sexually explicit letters to Sedova whilst he was away – saying he felt 'abashed at putting such words on paper for the first time in my life' and 'behaving just like a young cadet officer' – show he and Sedova still maintained a full and passionate love life together: 'Since I arrived here my poor prick has not once got hard… But I myself – all of me…am thinking with tenderness about your sweet old cunt. I want to stuff it, to push my tongue right into its depths. Natalochhka, sweetest, I'm going to fuck you hard with my tongue and my prick.' Three years later, in February 1940, when drafting his will, he wrote this about Sedova: 'Fate gave me the happiness of being her husband; during the almost 40 years of our life together she remained an inexhaustible source of love, magnanimity and tenderness.'

Service, however, claims that, despite repairing his relations with Sedova, Trotsky almost immediately on his return became attracted to a young Mexican woman who lived nearby, but was dissuaded from embarking on another affair by van Heijenoort – who himself had just begun an affair with Kahlo.[12]

Marxism, Philosophy and Art

Trotsky was determined to make clear that Stalin's actions and policies were not what revolutionary Marxism was all about. In particular, for all those who wanted a better world than that created by capitalism, he was at pains to refute those bourgeois philosophers – including Dewey – who argued that Marxism, as a philosophy, was bound to end in dictatorship. For Trotsky, Stalinism grew, not out of Marxism, but out of Russia's low cultural level and the hostile interventions of internal and external supporters of capitalism. He believed the crucial factors were the class struggle and its aims, not necessarily the means used: 'Moral evaluations, along with political ones, flow from the inner needs of struggle.' For him, it was only the Trotskyists – or 'Bolsheviks', as he often termed them – who'd properly understood the needs and possibilities of the class struggle, and the ebb and flow of historical periods. The book which emerged was *Their Morals and Ours*, completed in February 1938.

Also in February 1938, Trotsky was visited by André Breton, the French Surrealist poet and one of Trotsky's long-time admirers. Following intense discussions with him and Rivera, the result was the *Manifesto: Towards A Free Revolutionary Art*, which appeared later that year. Although only Breton and Rivera's names appeared on the book, it was almost entirely written by Trotsky, who was generally supportive of the Surrealist movement. In many ways, it was a continuation of ideas he'd expressed in *Literature and Revolution*. The *Manifesto* summarised its aims thus: 'The independence of art – for the revolution. The revolution – for the complete liberation of art!'[13]

Death of Lyova

In *Their Morals and Ours*, Trotsky had argued that his followers, as well as understanding 'the rhythm of history' and 'the dialectics of the class struggle', had 'also learned...not to fall into despair over the fact that the laws of history do not depend on their individual tastes....' Poignantly, he'd also reiterated that '... the Fourth International wages a life and death struggle against Stalinism'. When writing this, he was unaware how death was once more about to strike his family as a direct result of that struggle.[14]

A year before, on 4 September 1937, Ignaz Reiss – a former NKVD agent – was murdered near Lausanne, after having declared, on 18 July, in a letter to the CC, his support for Trotsky and his plans to establish a new International. Reiss had also warned Lyova that Stalin was determined to liquidate Trotskyism both within and without the USSR, by any means. Reiss's body, riddled with bullets, had been found on a roadside. During the investigations, it emerged how the NKVD had detailed inside knowledge of meetings, and how Lyova himself had been under close observation by its agents in France, who'd even made plans to kidnap or kill him. It was also revealed that one of Reiss's assassins had applied for a Mexican visa and had obtained detailed plans of Mexico City. Lyova immediately informed Trotsky; yet, despite warnings, he and Trotsky refused to believe 'Etienne' was the 'leak'.

Towards the end of 1937, Lyova – still editing the *Bulletin* and mainly responsible for establishing the Fourth International – began to show increased signs of exhaustion and poor health. He was also deeply depressed by the 'ludicrous confessions' made by revolutionaries he'd known as a boy. He'd worked flat out for years, and was occasionally urged by Trotsky to allow himself extra expenses instead of living so frugally. Lyova's personal life was also increasingly difficult, as Martin supported a rival Trotskyist group, formed by her ex-husband Molinier, with whom Trotsky had broken in 1935. In part, this had led Lyova into an affair with Hélène Savanier. On 5 November 1937, Rudolf Klement, one of Lyova's comrades, wrote to Trotsky and Sedova, begging them to get Lyova to go to Mexico for recuperation and safety reasons. Trotsky however agreed with Lyova that this wouldn't be useful – or even safer, as Mexico City seemed to be crawling with NKVD agents.

Lyova had had increasing stomach pains, but had delayed an operation for suspected appendicitis. Instead, he worked hard for the *Bulletin* to carry the verdict of the Dewey Commission – in early February, he wrote to Trotsky to say the proofs were ready, outlining future plans. But he said nothing about his poor health. It was to be his last letter to his father. Then, on 8 February 1938, Lyova suffered extreme stomach pains; leading him to give a sealed letter to Martin, saying she was only to open it if an 'accident' happened to him. The following day, 'Etienne' – instead of taking him to the main hospital – arranged for him to go into a private clinic, run by Russian émigrés, ensuring only he and Martin would know Lyova's whereabouts or be allowed to visit him.

Lyova was operated on that evening for acute appendicitis, and was making a good recovery, and talking about future work. Then, on the night of 13–14 February, he suffered a serious and unexplained relapse. His doctor was so surprised that he wondered if Lyova had tried to commit suicide. He was operated on again on 15 February but, after hours of excruciating pain, died the following day. An open verdict was recorded but, in the weeks that followed, speculation grew that he'd been poisoned – his only visitors had been Martin and 'Etienne'. Twenty years later, 'Etienne' admitted he'd been an NKVD agent, and had immediately informed them which hospital Lyova was in. Depriving Trotsky of such a key worker was a huge blow – especially when, as expected, 'Etienne', who took his place, then did what he could to undermine those who, like Serge, suspected him; he also blocked a second inquest into Lyova's death.[15]

Trotsky had earlier been sent by Rivera – alarmed by suspicious movements outside Casa Azul – to a house at Chapultepec Park. It was there Rivera broke the news of Lyova's death. Trotsky returned immediately to inform Sedova, who'd been sorting through family photographs. According to Sedova, 'He came in, more bent than he had ever been before, and his face was ash-grey; he seemed to have turned into an old man overnight.' They were both grief-stricken, and spent days locked in their bedroom. Trotsky's usual tidy appearance, and punctiliousness in dealing with correspondence, fell apart for several months, while Sedova was prone to tears for even longer.[16]

On 16 February, the day Lyova died, Trotsky had finished the main section of *Their Morals and Ours*. Once informed of Lyova's death, he wrote the following dedication:

'IN MEMORY OF LEON SEDOV
1906–1938'

and added this postscript:

'I wrote these lines during those days when my son struggled, unknown to me, with death. I dedicate to his memory this small work...Leon Sedov was a genuine revolutionist....'

On 18 February, Trotsky released a statement, saying: 'He [Lyova] was not only my son but my best friend.' Two days later, he wrote what is acknowledged as his most emotional and moving work: *Leon Sedov – Son, Friend, Fighter*. It concluded:

'He was part of both of us, our young part...Together with our boy has died everything that still remained young within us. Goodbye, Leon, good-bye dear and incomparable friend.'[17]

In it, he regretted his recent harsh rebukes – resulting from his own 'pedantic habits of work' and his inclination to demand the utmost of everyone – and his advice that it was safer for Lyova to remain in Paris. Alexander Orlov, an NKVD agent who'd defected in 1938, stated in 1953 that Lyova had been murdered by the NKVD; he'd also sent a letter, warning Trotsky of a possible assassination attempt on his own life, and informing him that 'Mark', one of his closest associates, was an NKVD agent. Trotsky assumed it was a hoax and dismissed the warnings.

A month after Lyova's death, the Third Show Trials began in Moscow – the final and bloodiest of all. This 'Trial of the Twenty-One', from 2–13 March 1938, focussed on Bukharin and his associates – with the usual accusations against Trotsky as the main conspirator. Although many of the accused 'confessed', Bukharin refused; he along, with seventeen others, was shot. As the 'Great Terror' grew in the Soviet Union – intended to wipe out all Trotskyists and other Oppositionists – Trotsky resumed his campaign to expose this 'greatest frame-up in history'. However, he was also more determined than ever to get his new International established.[18]

The Fourth International

The Comintern's response to the rise of Nazism in Germany had decided Trotsky, in 1933, that reforming the official Communist movement was now impossible, and that establishing a new International was vital. Trotsky saw building the Fourth International as the most important part of his life's work. A small preliminary meeting of revolutionary youth organisations had taken place in Brussels on 28 February 1934; but there was opposition to Trotsky's call for a new International.

The decision to replace the 'Stalinised' Third International with a new revolutionary Marxist one was confirmed – in his eyes – by the role played by the Communist Party during the Spanish Civil War. There, as part of the Comintern's new 'Popular Front' policy, the Spanish Communist Party stamped out revolutionary developments. After May 1937, the Spanish Communists – aided by NKVD agents – began arresting, executing and assassinating members of the semi-Trotskyist POUM and anarcho-syndicalist groups. One victim was Erwin Wolf, Trotsky's former secretary, who disappeared in late July; another was Andrés Nin, leader of the POUM. George Orwell, the novelist – who'd volunteered to fight against fascism – had been sent to Barcelona where the POUM was strong, and may well have been executed if he'd not managed to return to England.[19]

While even sympathisers sometimes thought Trotsky was overly optimistic about chances for revolutionary victories, it's certainly true that the conflicts within the ranks of the Republicans didn't help the struggle against Franco and his fascist backers. Trotsky believed, if Republican forces were denied the chance to make a revolution, fascism would win in Spain, making a new world war inevitable – which he thought would probably begin in 1940–41, though August 1939 was possible. On 17 December 1937 – almost two years *before* Franco's victory – Trotsky wrote, in *The Lessons of Spain – The Final Warning*, that: '[Stalin] placed the technique of Bolshevism at the service of bourgeois property…But the commissars of private property proved capable of only guaranteeing defeat'. As he saw it, the only hope for a successful revolutionary struggle was the planned new International, under whose banner 'revolutionary cadres' were already gathering: 'Born amidst the roar of defeats, the Fourth International will lead the toilers to victory.' Hence he placed great urgency on launching 'a world offensive against Stalinism' and getting the Fourth International established.[20]

One significant problem was the small number of supporters. In July 1936, a confidential report on membership listed 2,500 in the Netherlands, 1,000 in the US and only 150 in Germany – which Trotsky had seen as the most important country. The French section – once the biggest – was split into various factions, as were the British Trotskyists. In an interview given in March 1937, Trotsky had spoken of having 'tens of thousands' of supporters – seen by Volkogonov as 'a considerable exaggeration'. In addition, many of the groups were riven by factional disagreements which sometimes led to splits. In some instances, these were the result of NKVD infiltrators and provocateurs.[21]

Another problem was that not all his supporters felt the time was right, given that, since 1933, counter-revolution rather than revolution appeared ascendant. One such supporter was Deutscher, a Polish Trotskyist who broke with him on this. Another was his long-time supporter, Victor Serge. Nonetheless, Trotsky remained highly optimistic regarding the imminent success of his project, as he felt both capitalism and Stalinism were in such deep crises that, if the masses wanted to change things for the better, they'd have to turn to the FI, as the only political body with a truly revolutionary programme. Similar to Luxemburg's dictum of 'Socialism or barbarism', he believed if revolution failed, the alternative was capitalism's inequalities and wars.

In April 1938, he wrote the pamphlet *The Death Agony of Capitalism and the Tasks of the Fourth International* – this quickly became known as *The Transitional Programme*. While acknowledging the relatively small number of supporters – and the opposition and hostility it faced from 'Stalinists, Social Democrats, bourgeois liberals, and fascists' – Trotsky was confident the FI, which he termed the 'World Party of Socialist Revolution', would soon attract greater support, as it was the only 'revolutionary current on this planet meriting the name', pointing out that it was 'strong in doctrine, program, tradition, in the incomparable tempering of its cadres'. He believed, after the coming war, there'd be 'a revolutionary aftermath similar to that which had followed' the First World War, 'but larger in scope and force'. This pamphlet also made clear the Fourth International's positions and aims:

> 'It uncompromisingly gives battle to all political groupings tied to the apron-strings of the bourgeoisie. Its task – the abolition of capitalism's domination. Its aim – socialism. Its method – the proletarian revolution.'

This pamphlet became the basis for a pre-Conference discussion, lasting from April to September 1938, by supporters in the Movement of the Fourth International (MFI) in various countries.[22]

Trotsky's endeavour was further hampered by his insistence that, despite Stalinist degeneration, the USSR remained a workers' state and that, therefore, it was the duty of revolutionary Marxists to support it in the coming world war, against both fascist and capitalist states. He made it clear such defence of the Soviet Union:

> 'means not only the supreme struggle against imperialism, but a preparation for the overthrow of the Bonapartist bureaucracy'.[23]

However, a more serious blow to his plans came in the summer of 1938, when Rudolf Klement, who was to have been its Secretary, was assassinated. Following Lyova's unexpected death, Klement – then Secretary of the Fourth International's Bureau in Paris – had finally been asked by Trotsky to investigate 'Etienne', after he'd received information from several sources that the latter might be a NKVD agent. By 13 July, it appears Klement had put together a file which he intended to take to Brussels the following day. But he never arrived, as he was kidnapped from his room. Instead, Trotsky received a typewritten letter, purporting to come from Klement, stating he'd broken with Trotsky because of his 'fascist connections'. About a week later, Klement's headless body – identified by its distinguishing marks – was found floating in the Seine. Walter Krivitsky, an NKVD agent, later told Trotsky that both Lyova and Klement had been murdered by the NKVD – thus confirming Orlov's statement.

The delayed Foundation Congress of the FI finally took place – with Shachtman presiding – on 3 September 1938, in the Rosmers' home, on the outskirts of Paris. There were twenty-one delegates, representing eleven countries, with a combined membership of around 10,000 members. Trotsky was unable to obtain a visa, so was not present: in his absence, 'Etienne' represented the Russian section – immediately passing on all the participants' names to Moscow, along with documents he'd photographed. This Congress formally adopted *The Transitional Programme*, as slightly amended during the pre-Congress discussions. It then elected an Executive Committee – with Trotsky elected as a 'secret' Honorary Member. The only section represented which voted against declaring the Fourth International was the Polish delegation, which presented arguments drafted by Deutscher.[24]

However, a year later, in September 1939 – following the Nazi–Soviet Non-Aggression Pact – a serious dispute broke out within the new International amongst Trotskyists in the US Socialist Workers' Party, over the class-nature of the USSR. With around 2,500 members, this was then the largest group of Trotskyists. On 25 September, in *The USSR in War*, Trotsky criticised their view that the USSR had become a state capitalist society – pointing out that if the proletariat ultimately failed to take control, then: '… nothing else would remain except only to recognize that the socialist program, based on the internal contradictions of capitalist society, ended as a Utopia'. Trotsky, however, rejected such pessimism – as a lifelong revolutionary, he stated even if they were not 'on the side' of historical developments, Marxists must remain on the side of the exploited and oppressed: in the *Bulletin* of August–October 1939, he maintained: 'The defence of the USSR coincides for us with the preparation of world revolution.'[25]

When, after the Soviet occupation of eastern Poland, Stalin imposed a top-down social revolution regarding land and industry ownership, Trotsky argued this showed the USSR was still a workers' state, not a capitalist one. However, after the Soviet attack on Finland in November 1939 – and months of argument and counter-argument – in May 1940, Shachtman and a minority of US Trotskyists split from the Fourth International. In copious correspondence, Trotsky maintained there was a fundamental difference between capitalist and Stalinist imperialism – the class nature of the Soviet state. Although urging Shachtman, who'd been a supporter since 1929, to visit him in Mexico to discuss the issues, no visit took place.

Death Approaches

Meanwhile, Rivera pushed himself forward as the main force amongst Trotsky's Mexican supporters, wanting to be their secretary. Trotsky, however, didn't think he was efficient enough for the role. Rivera then accused Cárdenas of being Stalin's accomplice – bizarrely backing the right wing candidate in the presidential elections, thereby threatening to undermine Trotsky's promise to stay out of Mexican politics. After a bitter argument, Rivera stormed out and, on 12 January 1939, broke with Trotsky and the Fourth International.

Consequently, in March 1939, Trotsky and Sedova moved to a large but dilapidated – and expensive – house on Avienda Viena, not far from where they'd been staying. Initially, Trotsky was forced to borrow from supporters, but realised he needed to increase his earnings as an author. But his delays over *Stalin* and *Lenin* now meant publishers were holding back advances, and it was becoming difficult to get articles commissioned. To help pay for its purchase (to stop a rumoured NKVD purchase) and so making them secure, he sold his archives to Harvard University, though only for $15,000. It was a relatively isolated house, surrounded by a shady garden. There, Trotsky developed a new passion: collecting different types of cacti. Accompanied by guards – and often with Sedova – he went on early morning trips, hiding in a car, to the countryside. By then, Trotsky was experiencing high blood pressure, in addition to other longstanding problems. However, despite his age and health, he was able to outpace his younger guards as they strode up mountain slopes.[26]

In July 1939, they were joined by their grandson, Seva. Immediately following Lyova's death, Trotsky had written to Martin, inviting her and Seva to Mexico. However, she declined, and also initially refused to hand over Trotsky's archives. There then followed a long and bitter custody case – with the courts twice ruling in Trotsky's favour. Martin – whose mental state had been weakened by Lyova's death – however refused to be parted from the boy but, eventually, Seva was secured by the Rosmers, who brought him to Mexico, where Trotsky and Sedova formally took charge of him. Ironically, it was to be partly through the Rosmers that Trotsky's assassin would gain admittance to his new home.

Although Trotsky still rose early and, after feeding his rabbits and chickens, maintained a punishing work schedule, he was increasingly feeling the strain – according to Sedova: 'On his sixtieth birthday, Leon Davidovitch felt alone, the last survivor of an annihilated legion.' By then, it became increasingly obvious the house was being observed, and his bodyguards were concerned about his willingness to accept visits from relative strangers. At times, Sedova overheard him, whilst working in his study, heaving a 'deep sigh' and saying to himself: 'I am tired, so tired. I can't take anymore.' When they were alone, he'd sometimes speak the names of former friends and political comrades who'd 'confessed' and been executed or imprisoned – Sedova noting: 'Even the wide-open spaces of Mexico did little to relieve his pain.' But he never admitted it openly, and:

> 'He still bore himself as of old; his head was held high, his gait sprightly and his gestures were animated; he seemed not to have aged, though his unruly locks had become grey.'

However – believing either his high blood pressure or a successful assassination attempt would result in death – on 27 February (with a postscript added on 3 March 1940) he wrote his last *Testament*, bequeathing his literary rights to Sedova.[27]

In March 1939, Stalin – concerned by reports of the influence the small Trotskyist International was having amongst several Communist Parties – had finally ordered Trotsky's assassination. As a first step, the Mexican Communist Party was ordered to step up its campaign for the expulsion of 'the traitor sheltering at Coyoacán'. However, detailed planning didn't begin until September 1939 – with the transfer of several experienced NKVD agents from Spain to Mexico.

The main organiser was Naum Eitingon, who'd been deputy chief of the NKVD in Spain during the Civil War. Whilst there, he'd met Ramón Mercader, and his mother, Caridad. In 1937, Mercader – a lieutenant and political commissar in the Civil War – had been wounded and sent to the USSR, where he was trained in espionage, acquainted with the NKVD files on Trotsky, and given a false passport. Eitingon was then appointed as the NKVD boss in Mexico, recruiting both Mercarder and his mother to help.[28]

In June 1938, in Paris, NKVD agents had introduced Mercader to Sylvia Agelof, a US Trotskyist; posing as 'Frank Jacson', a businessman uninterested in politics, he soon became Agelof's lover. In September 1938, she helped organise the Foundation Congress of the FI and, by January 1940, had become one of Trotsky's secretaries. At first, Mercader made himself useful to the Rosmers, running them in his Buick to the shops, on picnics with Seva, and sometimes bringing sweets for Sedova and toys for Seva. In late April 1940, he first gained access to the garden by helping the Rosmers carry shopping from the car. Trotsky's guards soon became used to him. He then passed on information, to assist an assassination attempt.

On 1 May, 20,000 uniformed communists had marched through Mexico City, with the slogan 'Out with Trotsky' on their banners. Stalinist newspapers also attacked the presence of the 'arch-traitor' in Mexico – leading Trotsky to comment: 'People write like this only when they are ready to change the pen for the machine-gun.' At 4.00am, on 24 May, twenty-five would-be assassins, pretending to be police, overpowered Trotsky's guards and then, over twenty minutes, fired around 200 bullets into his study and other rooms, including 73 bullets into Trotsky and Sedova's bedroom. Incendiary grenades – and a powerful bomb that failed to explode – were also used. Trotsky had taken a sleeping pill, so his initial reactions were slow, with Sedova pushing him to the ground and shielding his body – both he and Sedova, and Seva, were slightly injured by flying glass and ricocheting bullets.[29]

After this failed attempt, the would-be assassins escaped by stealing Trotsky's two cars, taking with them Robert Sheldon Harte, the inexperienced US guard on duty that night. On 25 June, Harte's body was discovered buried, in a lime pit near a farm close to Mexico City. When he came to view the body, the chief of Mexico's secret police noted that Trotsky 'wept in silence'. Trotsky erected a small plaque in his garden, commemorating Harte, as having been 'murdered by Stalin'. In *Stalin Seeks My Death*, an article published in early June, Trotsky made clear his determination to carry on his struggle:

> 'In a reactionary epoch such as ours, a revolutionist is compelled to swim against the stream. I am doing this to the best of my ability.'

It later emerged the attack had been organised by Mexican Stalinists, led by David Sequeiros, the Mexican painter. On the night of the attack – acting on NKVD instructions – he'd posed as an army major. Two women, linked to the Communist Party, had struck up close friendships with a couple of the policemen, who were overpowered and tied up. The farm near where Harte's body had been found, had been rented by the two brothers of Sequeiros's wife. Sequeiros was arrested on 4 October, and released on bail in April 1941: he then fled to Chile.[30]

The Assassination

After the failed attack, security measures were tightened: the number of guards was tripled, while new alarms and electronically-controlled gates were installed. Trotsky's bodyguards pleaded to be allowed to search visitors for concealed weapons; suggested he wore a bulletproof vest; and even advised him to go underground. Trotsky, however, was tired of running, and ignored their advice: he was determined to endure, as normally as possible, the Learesque 'hell-black night' to the end. Each morning, he would rise and say to Sedova: 'You see, they did not kill us last night', or: 'You see, Natasha, we have had a reprieve.'[31]

Mercader was now ordered to carry out the assassination himself. On 28 May 1940, the Rosmers left Mexico, with Mercader taking them in his car to their ship in Vera Cruz – this was the first time he met Trotsky, who was feeding his pet rabbits when he arrived early in the morning. On 12 June, he said he needed to go to New York, where it appears he was given final instructions. He returned on 29 July, though in a clearly agitated state. Soon after, he was invited to have tea with Agelof and Sedova, and the number of visits increased. Though he only met Trotsky on a couple of occasions, it appears even Trotsky – generally the last to be suspicious – was beginning to have doubts about him. Sedova, too, questioned the lack of detailed information about his business activities. Nonetheless, Trotsky dismissed suggestions by one of his guards that Mercader should be searched.

To gain access to Trotsky, Mercader pretended he'd lately become interested in politics, supporting Trotsky's position in the dispute with some of his US followers – although Agelof supported the minority faction. On 17 August, Mercader arrived unannounced, with a raincoat over his arm – under which he'd concealed a mountaineer's ice axe – asking Trotsky to read an article he'd just drafted on the dispute amongst US Trotskyists. Trotsky reluctantly agreed, took him into his study and suggested some changes. This was the first time Mercader had been alone with Trotsky – who afterwards confided in Sedova that Mercader's behaviour unsettled him and he no longer wished to see him, suggesting they should try to find out more about him; he also mentioned his disquiet to Joe Hansen, one of his bodyguards.

However, before any steps were taken, Mercader returned on Tuesday 20 August, at around 5.00pm, with his amended article, asking Trotsky to check it through, as he planned to return to New York the next day. Outside, in a parked car, his mother and Eitingon were waiting to whisk him away as soon as he'd killed Trotsky. That morning, Trotsky – who'd again taken sleeping pills the night before – had said to Sedova on rising: 'It is a long time since I felt so well.' When Mercarder arrived, he seemed nervous and unwell. Trotsky, who'd been feeding his pet rabbits, reluctantly agreed to reread the article – commenting that Mercader, who was wearing a raincoat on what was a warm day, must be hot. They then went into Trotsky's study – where he'd been working on a new article, and on his delayed biography of Stalin. Trotsky sat at his desk, with Mercader standing over him.

As Trotsky read, Mercader took out the ice axe, and struck Trotsky's head. The blow didn't kill him – though Mercader said he issued a 'cry that I shall never forget. It was a long "Aaaa", endlessly long'. Instead, Trotsky rose, threw assorted items at his assassin, and prevented Mercader from striking a second blow by wrenching the ice axe from him. In the end, it was Mercader's screams, rather than Trotsky's cry, that brought bodyguards into the study – Trotsky had bitten Mercader's thumb! Trotsky, with blood streaming down his face, then stumbled out of his study, muttering 'See what they have done to me!' Sedova rushed to him and flung her arms around him, crying 'What happened? What happened?' Trotsky quietly said 'Jacson', took a few steps, and then collapsed on the floor.[32]

As he lay waiting for the ambulance, still conscious – but with his left arm and leg already paralysed – he said, in Russian: 'Natasha, I love you', and pleaded for Seva to be kept out; in English, to the bodyguards, he said: 'Take care of Natasha, she has been with me many, many years.' Trotsky was then rushed to hospital; in the ambulance, he tried to dictate a final political message to Hansen, saying: 'I am sure...of victory...of Fourth International...go forward.' On arrival, he was prepared for an operation. His final conscious moments were recorded by Sedova:

> 'The nurses began to cut his clothes. Suddenly he said to me distinctly but very sadly and gravely, "I don't want them to undress me...I want you to do it....." These were his last words to me. I undressed him, and pressed my lips to his. He returned the kiss, once, twice and again.'

He then lost consciousness at about 7.30pm, and was operated on. But, the following day, 21 August 1940, at 7.25pm, he died, without ever having regained consciousness. The autopsy showed a brain of 'extraordinary dimensions', and 'the heart too was very large'.[33]

After Trotsky's death, President Cárdenas and his wife paid Sedova a visit of condolence, and on 22 August, large crowds followed or watched the funeral procession – with Trotsky's coffin covered with the flag of the Fourth International – as it wound its way from the funeral parlour to the Pantheon, via Mexico City's working class districts. After speeches, Trotsky's body lay in state for five days, with around 300,000 people filing past. On 27 August, his body was cremated, and his ashes buried in the grounds of the house on Avienda Viena. Later, his US supporters arranged for the erection of an obelisk on the grave – engraved on it were a hammer and sickle, and the words: 'Leon Trotsky.' A flagpole was later added, with a red flag hung at half-mast. Whilst Sedova was alive, fresh flowers surrounded the grave. In May 1946, it was turned into a museum. [34]

Pravda announced that Trotsky had been killed by a 'disillusioned follower', but no doubt Stalin was displeased by the obituary that appeared in the London *Times*. This described Trotsky as Lenin's 'chief associate'; referred to his leading roles in both the November Revolution and the Civil War; noted that he 'remained a name' around whom communists opposed to Stalin gathered; and ended by mentioning his 'outstanding literary abilities'. It was articles like this that led Deutscher to comment that Trotsky achieved some kind of 'victory' in death.

The final paragraph of Trotsky's *Testament* had ended on a hopeful note: 'Life is beautiful. Let the future generations cleanse it of all evil, oppression, and violence and enjoy it to the full.' Despite all that had happened to him and his families, he remained a passionate optimist – and a passionate revolutionary:

> 'My faith in the communist future of mankind is no less ardent, indeed it is firmer today, than it was in the days of my youth.' [35]

Conclusion

Legacy

'Please tell my friends that I am sure of the victory of the
Fourth International...Go forward!'[1]

This was the last political message dictated by the 'Old Man'. Trotsky had
dedicated decades to the revolutionary cause for one reason, and one only:
because he passionately believed if global capitalism wasn't overthrown,
humanity would be forced to endure the poverty and wars it led to. For him, it
was the simple choice that Rosa Luxemburg had posed in 1915: socialism or
barbarism. Like Antonio Gramsci – destined to die in Mussolini's prisons –
despite political setbacks and personal tragedies, Trotsky always followed
Gramsci's maxim 'Pessimism of the intellect, but optimism of the will'.[2]

Yet, long before the twenty-first century, it was clear Trotsky's
confidence in the victory of his Fourth International was misplaced.
In addition, everything else he fought for – upholding the gains of the
November Revolution, defeating the bureaucratic degeneration of the
Soviet Union, preventing the rise of fascism, and the victory of a world
socialist revolution – turned to ashes in the decades that followed his death.

Trotsky and Marxism

Although some historians question Trotsky's contribution to Marxist thought,
it's important to note that the theory most associated with him – 'Permanent
Revolution' – allowed him to predict it would be socialism, not liberal
capitalism, that would replace Tsarism in Russia. His view that socialism in
backward Russia would ultimately fail, if unaided by revolutions in Europe's
economically developed countries, also proved ultimately correct. Although
his argument that Stalinism would soon collapse – because it was impossible
for the USSR to remain as a 'transitional society' – seemed invalidated by
Stalinism not only surviving the war, but growing stronger after it (even
becoming a regional superpower), that, too, ultimately proved correct: 'The
causes of the collapse of the USSR in 1991 can easily be found in Trotsky's

writings on the Russian Revolution produced as early as 1905.' In addition, his writings on bureaucratic degeneration and on fascism continue to have much relevance. He also believed a United States of Europe – albeit a socialist one – was necessary for both prosperity and peace. As Thatcher states, it may turn out that the European Union 'eventually adopts a more socialist direction'.

Not surprisingly, Trotsky's contribution to Marxism and to an understanding of history since 1900 is viewed much more positively by academics more sympathetic to Trotskyist politics:

> 'Of all the important socialists of the twentieth century, it was Trotsky who recognized most clearly the main tendencies of development and the principal contradictions of the epoch, and it was Trotsky also who gave the clearest formulation to the appropriate emancipatory strategy for the international labour movement.'[3]

The Fourth International After 1940

Although Trotsky saw the creation of the Fourth International as his most important work, it has failed to live up to his expectations.

Deutscher was one of several followers who believed Trotsky was wrong to form it at such a politically unfavourable time. Yet, if Trotsky hadn't persisted, it's likely the relatively small number of revolutionary Marxists who supported him would have been blown to the winds and cut off from each other by WW2. The wisdom of Trotsky's decision, and his practical importance to the embryonic Fourth International, is perhaps shown by the fact that the *Bulletin* ceased publication after August 1941. After some time, Sedova got re-involved with Fourth International affairs but, after 1951, sided with those who, against Trotsky, had argued the USSR was no longer a workers' state.

After 1933, Trotsky had been encouraged by the political crises in France and Spain – and had initially been pleased by the results of the 'entryism' tactic he encouraged those sections to adopt. It was partly the early fruits of this tactic that had led to his determination to launch the Fourth International. Yet, by 1940, the Spanish Revolution had been defeated; while French politics had settled down, without significant numbers joining the French section.

Nonetheless, during the war, Trotskyists were often to the forefront in combatting fascism in Germany, Italy and occupied Europe. In Belgium,

Ernest Mandel – who became one of the main leaders of the post-war Fourth International – joined the Belgian Trotskyist organisation whilst still a teenager, after the German occupation, and was active in the resistance movement. He escaped twice after being arrested, and survived imprisonment in the Mittelbau-Dora concentration camp in Germany.

After the war, in 1946, the Fourth International held an International Congress and, in 1948, its Second World Congress took place. Despite suffering significant losses as a result of Stalinist and then fascist persecution before and during the war, sizeable Trotskyist groups developed in Bolivia and, especially, in Sri Lanka. Elsewhere, the entryist tactic was adopted. However, the Trotskyist movement continued to be plagued by factionalism – something that had been apparent even whilst Trotsky was alive – and a serious split took place in 1953. Eventually, in 1963, a large majority of Trotskyist sections agreed to form a reunified Fourth International. This allowed it to play leading roles within the anti-Vietnam War movement and the wider student revolutions in Europe and North America during the late 1960s. That upsurge had subsided by the late 1970s; though, in the late 1980s, the emergence of Gorbachev – and his rehabilitation of Stalin's victims – led to a brief upsurge of interest in Trotskyism within the USSR itself. Although the Fourth International continues to the present day, it remains a tiny minority movement.

Why Did He Lose?

Trotsky wasn't much of a team player, and was often politically isolated: he 'always lacked...the intuition to sustain a factional group under his leadership'. Consequently, although always surrounded by loyal assistants, he found it difficult to build up personal alliances with equals, or the power base necessary for a successful political career. This may have been linked to his early years when – unlike most Bolsheviks – he'd had to rely for funds on his earnings as a journalist, while his pre-1917 activities had been very much his own affairs. Furthermore, during the Civil War, he'd been away at the various fronts, running things his way.

As Swain notes: 'Trotsky was simply not easy to work with'; Deutscher, too, noted he 'did not possess the habits of free and easy teamwork which makes the strength of a real leader of men'. Trotsky himself admitted he'd little time for fools, and was usually convinced that, in most important political matters, he was right. It was this that had led Lenin, in his *Testament*, to refer to Trotsky's 'too far-reaching self-confidence'. Even his one-time ally, Lunacharsky, noted:

> 'His colossal arrogance and an inability or unwillingness to show any human kindness or to be attentive to people, the absence of that charm which always surrounded Lenin, condemned Trotsky to a certain loneliness.'

His isolation was also the result of a lack of sociability outside work – his supporter, Pyatakov, advised him in 1926 to be 'more sociable'. Trotsky himself later referred to how his reluctance to take 'part in the amusements that were becoming more and more common' amongst leading Bolsheviks after the revolution was a factor in his eventual loss of power.[4]

More significant was his total dedication to, and passionate self-identification with, the revolutionary cause – a weakness that made him 'the prisoner of the Communist idea'. This often led him to take positions not shared by his revolutionary comrades, and to behave in ways that often appeared arrogant. For example, his initial conviction that Stalin was the embodiment of a bureaucratic Thermidorian counter-revolution meant he refused to see Stalin's industrialisation campaign as serious – an attitude that perplexed many of his supporters. As Swain commented, Trotsky's dedication meant he was often 'blinded by passion'.[5]

Trotsky himself commented on these weaknesses after he'd been exiled. In considering the enemies he made within the ranks of the Bolsheviks during the Civil War, he wrote:

> 'It is no wonder that my military work created so many enemies for me. I did not look to the side; I elbowed away those who interfered with military success, or in the haste of the work trod on the toes of the unheeding and was too busy even to apologize. Some people remember such things. The dissatisfied and those whose feelings had been hurt found their way to Stalin or Zinoviev, for these two also nourished hurts.'

This was not a serious weakness whilst Lenin was alive, as he 'respected' that Trotsky had his 'own ways of working' and his 'own methods of carrying out a decision once it had been adopted'. However, it proved fatal once Lenin had died. Especially as, unlike most of his comrades after 1917, Trotsky hadn't been a Bolshevik from the beginning – and, for a period, had been associated with the Mensheviks, their bitter political opponents.[6]

Other factors include his unwillingness to 'fight dirty' – in the early days of the Left Opposition, he ignored Max Eastman, his supporter, who rebuked him for refusing to respond to Stalin's personal attacks on him. Of greater significance, was that 'he lacked the overwhelming desire to become the leader' once Lenin had died. Ultimately, he was 'a perpetual revolutionary, never a full-time politician'. As Service notes: 'He felt better as a battered contender than as a fighter consumed by ambition to be champion. He did not want paramount authority badly enough.'[7]

There is also the argument that perhaps the Bolshevik Revolution had come 'before its time' – or, at the very least, had occurred in the wrong country. As early as the Brest-Litovsk peace negotiations in 1918, Trotsky had made the remark – described by Deutscher as 'hinting at a most ominous contingency' – that it might be their duty to declare: '…we have come before our time'. Much earlier, Marx and Engels had both written about the tragic fate of revolutionaries who 'come before their time'. According to Deutscher: 'This was his strongest intimation so far that the Russian Revolution might have been a false spring.'[8]

Trotsky had always argued that backward Russia, on its own, couldn't become a fully socialist country without successful workers' revolutions in the economically developed countries of Europe. Until Lenin's death, all Marxist revolutionaries had held this position – that was why he'd opposed Stalin's idea of 'Socialism in One Country'. No one was more convinced than Trotsky that such European revolutions would come. Consequently, despite revolutionary setbacks in the 1920s and 1930s, he remained confident in his theory of 'Permanent Revolution'. Just before his assassination, he predicted the Second World War would result in victorious revolutions led by sections of the young Fourth International. History appears to have given a resoundingly negative verdict on the hopes of Trotsky and his followers.

The Spectre of Trotskyism?

The opening words of Marx and Engels' *The Communist Manifesto* are: 'A spectre is haunting Europe – the spectre of communism.' After 1917, Trotsky – perhaps more than anyone – appeared to be the embodiment of that 'spectre'. Yet, between 1989 and 1991, all the 'communist' regimes in Eastern Europe, and then the Soviet Union itself, collapsed. There followed a rapid 'retreat from Marxism' and the imposition of unregulated capitalism in all of those states. Apart from China (which also soon started applying capitalist economic policies), the only other states to retain 'communism' as their official ideology were North Korea, Cuba and Vietnam – of these, the latter two (once Soviet aid had ceased) also began moving towards market-based economic reforms.[9]

Thus, as early as 1992, Francis Fukuyama, a US official, had announced these developments heralded the 'end of history'. By this, he meant the final victory of 'liberal' capitalism over Marxism and all communist movements based on that philosophy. By 2000, history's verdict on communism seemed to be that it had conspicuously failed, and that the 'spectre of communism' had been defeated. However, the 2008 financial crash, austerity and the global economic crisis of 2011; continuing world poverty; ecological destruction and the worsening Climate Crisis; and the increased risks of global pandemics from zoonotic viruses, all suggest that Fukuyama's claim that capitalism was secure and that Marxism had been permanently consigned to the 'dustbin of history' may prove to be a rather premature judgement. Indeed, historians like Eric Hobsbawm have argued the events of 1989–1991 and afterwards didn't necessarily mark the end of Marxism:

'The risk of a sharp shift of politics to a nationalist or confessional demagogic right is probably greatest in the formerly communist European countries...

'Economic and political liberalism, singly or in combination, cannot provide the solution to the problems of the twenty-first century. Once again the time has come to take Marx seriously.'[10]

Some commentators have suggested a more libertarian version of communism might emerge which will increasingly challenge neoliberal capitalist globalisation, Chinese 'capitalism' and Stalinist versions of 'communism'. Tariq Ali – for several years after the mid-1960s, one of the main leaders of the British section of the Fourth International (then the International Marxist Group, now Socialist Resistance) – argues it's important to 'take the long view of the historical process':

'For as long as contemporary capitalism, a system based on exploitation and inequality and recurring crises, not to mention its impact on the fragile ecology of the planet, continues to exist, the possibility of anti-capitalist movements taking power cannot be ruled out.'[11]

The modern Trotskyist Fourth International claims to be just such an 'anti-capitalist movement'. As has been seen, from the mid-1920s, Trotsky had been one of many – though the most determined – who'd warned the ideals of communism were being 'betrayed' in the Soviet Union. Consequently, for Trotskyists, what failed in those countries was not communism *per se*, but a bureaucratically deformed 'Stalinised' version of Marxism. Whilst keeping alive much of what Trotsky wrote, today's Fourth International has – given that Marxism is an ongoing method of analysis, and not dogma written in stone – adapted his views, and those of Marxism more generally, to take note of developments in the twenty-first century.

In particular, in 2001, Michael Löwy – a leading member of the Fourth International – co-authored the *International Ecosocialist Manifesto*. This declared that ecosocialism had to be international and universal, and that: 'The crises of our time can and must be seen as revolutionary opportunities.' Ecosocialism didn't really develop until the mid-1970s, when it was often called 'Red-Green socialism'; by the end of the 1980s, the term 'ecosocialism' was in general use. In 2010, the Fourth International officially declared itself to be an explicitly ecosocialist movement. This has had particular resonance amongst younger generations increasingly alarmed about Climate Breakdown.[12]

Yet, today, the Fourth International – that Trotsky made so much effort to establish – remains not much bigger or more influential than when it was established in 1938. Deutscher disagreed with Trotsky over forming a new International, and over his belief that reform within the Soviet Union – leading to the replacement of Stalinism with a democratic communism – was impossible. Yet, like Trotsky, he remained convinced about the need for socialism replacing capitalism:

> 'Humanity needs unity for its sheer survival; where can it find it if not in socialism?...
>
> 'In this sense the Russian revolution still confronts the West with a grave and challenging *tua res agitur*.'[13]

Deutscher also wrote about the 'Great Contest' that began with the Bolshevik Revolution of November 1917. Until the collapse of the Soviet Union in 1991, this was a contest between two opposed social and economic systems: capitalism v communism. While one of those 'systems' disappeared after 1991, it can be argued that the 'Great Contest' continues on ideological and political levels. Although, at present, Trotsky's Fourth International only operates on the political margins, it nonetheless is still occasionally described as a threat to capitalism. As Thatcher comments: 'no one knows what the future holds'.[14]

Bibliography/Further Reading

Trotsky's Writings

Trotsky, L., 1975, *My Life: An Attempt at an Autobiography*, Harmondsworth, Penguin Books.

Trotsky, L., 1973, *1905*, Harmondsworth, Penguin Books.

Trotsky, L., 1967, *History of the Russian Revolution*, Vols 1, 2, & 3, London, Sphere Books.

Trotsky, L., 1974, *The Young Lenin*, Harmondsworth, Penguin Books.

Trotsky, L., 1974, *Military Writings*, New York, Pathfinder Press.

Trotsky, L., 1972, *The Stalin School of Falsification*, New York, Pathfinder Press.

Trotsky, L., 1972, *The Revolution Betrayed: What Is the Soviet Union And Where Is It Going?*, New York, Pathfinder Press.

Trotsky, L., 1977, *The Transitional Program For Socialist Revolution*, New York, Pathfinder Press.

Trotsky, L., 1973-76, *Writings of Leon Trotsky*, [12 volumes, covering 1929-1940], New York, Pathfinder Press.

Biographies on Trotsky

Deutscher, I., 1954, *The Prophet Armed: Trotsky 1879-1921*, New York, OUP.

Deutscher, I., 1959, *The Prophet Unarmed: Trotsky 1921-1929*, Oxford, OUP.

Deutscher, I., 1970, *The Prophet Outcast: Trotsky 1929-1940*, Oxford, OUP.

Eastman, M., 1926, *Leon Trotsky: the Portrait of Youth*, London, Faber & Gwyer.

Thatcher, I. D., 2003, *Trotsky*, Abingdon, Routledge.

Serge, V. & Trotsky, N. S., *The Life and Death of Leon Trotsky*, 2015, Chicago, Haymarket Books.

Service, R., 2010, *Trotsky: A Biography*, London, Pan Books.

Swain, G., 2006, *Trotsky*, Harlow, Pearson/Longman.

Swain, G., '*Trotsky and the Russian Civil War*', in Thatcher, I. D., (ed.), 2006, *Reinterpreting Revolutionary Russia*, London, Palgrave/Macmillan.

Volkogonov, D., 1997, *Trotsky: The Eternal Revolutionary*, London, HarperCollins.

Wyndham, F. and King, D., 1972, *Trotsky: a documentary*, Harmondsworth.

Trotskyism

Bensaid, D., 2009, *Strategies of Resistance: Who are the Trotskyists?*, London, Resistance Books.

Callinicos, A., 1990, *Trotskyism*, Buckingham, Open University Press.

Frank, P., 1979, *The Fourth International: The Long March of the Trotskyists,* London, Ink Links.

Maitan, L., 2019, *Memoirs of a critical communist: Towards a History of the Fourth International*, Dagenham, Merlin Press.

Mandel, E., 1995, *Trotsky as Alternative*, London Verso.

Endnotes

Introduction

1. Serge, V. & Sedova Trotsky, N., 1973, *The Life and Death of Leon Trotsky*, Chicago, Haymarket Books, p.268.
2. Deutscher, I., 1970, *The Prophet Unarmed: Trotsky 1921-1929*, London, OUP, p.27.
3. Service, R., 2010, *Trotsky: A Biography*, London, Pan Books, p.319.; Trotsky, L., 1975, *My Life*, Harmondsworth, Penguin Books, p.354.
4. Swain, G., 2006, *Trotsky*, Harlow, Pearson/Longman, p.6.
5. Deutscher, I., 1970, *The Prophet Outcast: Trotsky 1929-1940*, London, OUP, p.384.
6. Volkogonov, D., 1997, *Trotsky: The Eternal Revolutionary*, London, HarperCollins, p.xxxi.
7. Deutscher, I., *The Prophet Unarmed: Trotsky 1921-1929*, p.ix.; Swain, G.,*Trotsky*, p.1.
8. Service, R., *Trotsky: A Biography*, p.xxi., p.4.; *Evening Standard*, 23/10/09.
9. Swain, G.,*Trotsky*, p.3.; Thatcher, I., 2003, *Trotsky*, Abingdon, Routledge, pp.1-2.
10. The Russian TV series, *Trotsky* – with English subtitles – is freely available on: https://www.youtube.com/watch?v=N_MIaWG76gM&list=PL6J1OzLHamQ9_SJbYXxzAZcJN7-Ngihnk The Joseph Losey film can be watched, also free, on: https://www.youtube.com/watch?v=AeKHthb-YMM While *Frida* is available to rent or buy on: https://www.youtube.com/watch?v=nm9ySB81UPY
11. Deutscher, I. (ed.), 1964, *The Age of Permanent Revolution: A Trotsky Anthology*, New York, Dell Publishing, pp.40-41. [emphasis added]
12. Deutscher, I., *The Prophet Armed: Trotsky 1879-1921*, p.35.; Trotsky, L., *My Life*, p.353.
13. Trotsky, L., *My Life*, pp.604-05.

Chapter 1

1. Trotsky, L., 1975, *My Life*, Harmondsworth, Penguin Books, p.67.
2. Trotsky, L., *My Life*, pp.18-19.
3. Trotsky, L., *My Life*, p.1.
4. Service, R., 2010, *Trotsky: A Biography*, London, Pan Books, pp.21, 28.
5. Deutscher, I., 1954, *The Prophet Armed: Trotsky 1879-1921*, New York, OUP, p.10.
6. Trotsky, L., *My Life*, pp.40-41.
7. Trotsky, L., *My Life*, p.93.
8. Deutscher, I., *The Prophet Armed*, p.14.; Eastman, M., 1926, *Leon Trotsky: The Portrait of a Youth*, London, Faber & Gwyer, p.17.; Service, R., *Trotsky: A Biography*, p.32.
9. Eastman, M., *Leon Trotsky: The Portrait of a Youth,* p.19.
10. Vera went on to become the famous Soviet poet and writer, Vera Inber (1890-1972); Service, R., *Trotsky: A Biography*, p.33.
11. Service, R., *Trotsky: A Biography*, p.35.
12. Trotsky, L., *My Life*, p.67.
13. Trotsky, L., *My Life*, pp.45, 63.
14. Trotsky, L., *My Life*, pp.66-67.; Deutscher, I., *The Prophet Armed*, p.17.
15. Trotsky, L., *My Life*, p.82.
16. Swain, G., 2006, *Trotsky*, Harlow, Pearson/Longman, p.9.; Trotsky, L., *My Life*, p.101.
17. Trotsky, L., *My Life*, p.99.
18. Deutscher, I., *The Prophet Armed*, pp.22-23.
19. Thatcher, I., 2003, *Trotsky*, Abingdon, Routledge, p.23.; Trotsky, L., *My Life*, p.102.
20. Ziv returned to Kiev at various points during 1896-97, to complete his studies, returning during the holidays to continue working with the group. This, however, earned Trotsky's scorn; eventually, Ziv moved away politically from his erstwhile comrades, becoming critical of Trotsky's actions.
21. Trotsky, L., 1975, *My Life*, p.101.
22. Trotsky, L., 1975, *My Life*, p.102.
23. Volkogonov, D., 1997, *Trotsky: The Eternal Revolutionary*, London, HarperCollins pp.7-8.
24. Wyndham, F. & King, D., 1972, *Trotsky: a documentary*, Harmondsworth, Penguin Books, p.14.

25. Deutscher, I., *The Prophet Armed*, pp.26-27.; Volkogonov, D.,*Trotsky: The Eternal Revolutionary*, p.8.
26. Deutscher, I., *The Prophet Armed*, pp.27-28.
27. Deutscher, I., *The Prophet Armed*, p.27.; Service, R., *Trotsky: A Biography*, p.45.
28. Service, R., *Trotsky: A Biography*, p.46.
29. Deutscher, I., *The Prophet Armed*, p.28.

Chapter 2

1. Volkogonov, D., 1997, *Trotsky: The Eternal Revolutionary*, London, HarperCollins, p.11. 'Shurochka' and 'Sashenka' are diminutives of 'Aleksandra'.
2. Deutscher, I., 1954, *The Prophet Armed: Trotsky 1879-1921*, New York, OUP, p.32.
3. Trotsky, L., 1975, *My Life*, Harmondsworth, Penguin Books, p.105.
4. Trotsky, L., *My Life*, p.114.
5. Deutscher, I., *The Prophet Armed*, p.32.
6. Deutscher, I., *The Prophet Armed*, p.34.
7. Though Labriola was convinced by Marx's dialectical materialism regarding the philosophy of History, he didn't fully embrace the revolutionary *political* implications of Marxism.
8. Trotsky, L., *My Life*, pp.123, 126-7.
9. Trotsky, L., *My Life*, p.127.
10. Trotsky, L., *My Life*, p.128.
11. Volkogonov, D., *Trotsky: The Eternal Revolutionary*, p.11.
12. Trotsky, L., *My Life*, p.128.
13. Swain, G., 2006,*Trotsky*, Harlow, Pearson/Longman, p.13.
14. Deutscher, I., *The Prophet Armed*, p.49., quoted from Trotsky, L., *Sochineya*, vol. xx, p.20.; Thatcher, I., 2003, *Trotsky*, Abingdon, Routledge, p.25.
15. Deutscher, I., *The Prophet Armed*, Footnote 1, p.46.
16. Deutscher, I., *The Prophet Armed*, pp.45-46.
17. Trotsky, L., *My Life*, p.137.
18. Volkgonov, D., *Trotsky: The Eternal Revolutionary*, pp.12-13.; Service, R., *Trotsky: A Biography*, p.67.; Swain, G.,*Trotsky*, p.14.
19. Service, R., *Trotsky: A Biography*, pp.51-2.; Volkogonov, D.,*Trotsky: The Eternal Revolutionary*, p.15.

20. Serge, V., and Trotsky, N. S., 2015, *The Life and Death of Leon Trotsky*, Chicago, Haymarket Books, p.11.; Volkogonov, D., *Trotsky: The Eternal Revolutionary*, p.16.

Chapter 3

1. Swain, G., 2006, *Trotsky*, Harlow, Pearson/Longman, p.200.
2. Trotsky, L., 1975, *My Life*, Harmondsworth, Penguin Books, pp.136, 138.
3. The generally accepted view is that Trotsky decided to use the name of one of his jailors in Nikolaev or Odessa; but other suggestions are that the name was already on the passport, or that it was the name of a Polish town where Trotsky's ancestors had lived.
4. Deutscher, I., 1954, *The Prophet Armed: Trotsky 1879-1921*, New York, OUP, p.56.
5. Deutscher, I., *The Prophet Armed*, p.57.
6. Deutscher, I., *The Prophet Armed*, p.61.
7. Deutscher, I, *The Prophet Armed*, p.62.
8. Deutscher, I., *The Prophet Armed*, pp.63, 67.
9. Deutscher, I., *The Prophet Armed*, p.70.
10. Trotsky, L., *My Life*, p.152.; Service, R., 2010, *Trotsky: A Biography*, London, Pan Books, p.72.
11. Deutscher, I., *The Prophet Armed*, p.79.
12. Deutscher, I., *The Prophet Armed*, pp.83-84.
13. Swain, G.,*Trotsky*, p.18.; Service, R., *Trotsky: A Biography*, p.79.
14. Deutscher, I., *The Prophet Armed*, pp.89-90.
15. Service, R., *Trotsky: A Biography*, p.88.
16. Service, R., *Trotsky: A Biography*, p.84.
17. Deutscher, I., *The Prophet Armed*, pp.110-111.
18. Deutscher, I., *The Prophet Armed*, p.114.
19. Deutscher, I., *The Prophet Armed*, pp.118-119.
20. Swain, G,*Trotsky*, p.30.
21. Deutscher, I., *The Prophet Armed*, p.132.
22. Volkogonov, D.,*Trotsky: The Eternal Revolutionary*, p.39.
23. Deutscher, I., *The Prophet Armed*, p.136.
24. Deutscher, I., *The Prophet Armed*, p.137.
25. A government's right to repudiate illegitimate debts is now enshrined in international law: http://www.cadtm.org/Russia-Repudiation-of-debt-at-the (Accessed 10/10/20)

26. Deutscher, I., *The Prophet Armed*, p.143.
27. Trotsky, L., *My Life*, p.191.
28. In *'Address of the Central Committee to the Communist League'*, March 1850, Marx wrote that their future task was *'to make the revolution permanent'*, and ended with the battle cry: *'The Permanent Revolution.'* Marx, K., 1973, *The Revolutions of 1848*, Hardmondsworth, Penguin Books, pp. 323, 330.
29. Deutscher, I., *The Prophet Armed*, p.158.
30. Deutscher, I., *The Prophet Armed*, p.146.
31. Service, R., *Trotsky: A Biography*, p. 98.; Deutscher, I., *The Prophet Armed*, p.146.
32. Trotsky, L., 1973, *1905*, Harmondsworth, Penguin Books, p. 410.

Chapter 4

1. Trotsky, L., 1973, *'There...and Back'*, in *1905*, Harmondsworth, Penguin Books, pp. 430, 490.
2. Deutscher, I., 1954, *The Prophet Armed: Trotsky 1879-1921*, New York, OUP, pp.176-177.
3. Trotsky, L., *'There...and Back'*, in*1905*, pp. 450-451.
4. Trotsky, L., 1975, *My Life*, Harmondsworth, Penguin Books, p.205.; Serge, V. & Sedova Trotsky, N., 1973, *The Life and Death of Leon Trotsky*, Chicago, Haymarket Books, pp.21-22.
5. Volkogonov, D., 1997, *Trotsky: The Eternal Revolutionary*, London, HarperCollins, pp.50-51.
6. Trotsky, L., *My Life*, p.210.
7. Amongst those Bolsheviks involved in these raids was Stalin (Joseph Djugashvili, known as 'Koba' at the time), who was present at that Congress, though Trotsky didn't recall seeing him. Their paths first crossed, very briefly, in Vienna in 1913.
8. They eventually broke with the reformist leaders of the German SPD and set up the German KPD.
9. Deutscher, I., *The Prophet Armed: Trotsky 1879-1921*, p.184.
10. This paper is usually referred to as the Vienna *Pravda*, to distinguish it from the much later Bolshevik paper, which – much to Trotsky's anger – 'stole' the name. Joffe helped Trotsky see that Marx and Freud had more in common than most Marxists believed; he later committed suicide in 1927, in despair and protest at Trotsky's expulsion from the Russian Communist Party

11. Service, R., 2010, *Trotsky: A Biography*, London, Pan Books, p.112.
12. Some in both factions wondered if his independence was part of an ambition to lead a united RSDWP.
13. Trotsky, L., *My Life*, p.230.
14. Deutscher, I., *The Prophet Armed: Trotsky 1879-1921*, p.196.
15. At this time, Stalin supported reunification.
16. Trotsky, L., *My Life*, p.225.
17. Trotsky, L., *My Life*, p.232.
18. Trotsky, L., *My Life*, p.232.
19. Serge, V. & Sedova Trotsky, N., *The Life and Death of Leon Trotsky*, p.27.; Deutscher, I., *The Prophet Armed*, p.202.
20. Volkogonov, D.,*Trotsky: The Eternal Revolutionary*, p.54.
21. Thatcher, I., 2003, *Trotsky*, Abingdon, Routledge, p.64.
22. Volkogonov, D.,*Trotsky: The Eternal Revolutionary*, pp.52-53.
23. Trotsky, L., *My Life*, p.227.
24. Marx, K., 'Eighteenth Brumaire of Louis Napoleon', in Fernbach, D, ed.,1973, *Surveys from Exile: Political Writings, Vol. 2*, Harmondsworth, Penguin Books, pp.236-237. In the late 1960s, this term was often used by revolutionary student newspapers: Harvard students published *'Old Mole'* in 1969; and, in 1970, the International Marxist Group (IMG) – the British Section of the Fourth International – brought out *'The Red Mole.'* Although not agreeing with everything he said, the IDO – made up of Bolsheviks and Mensheviks – generally supported Trotsky and, as will be seen in Chapter 5, eventually joined the Bolsheviks.
25. Swain, G., 2006, *Trotsky*, Harlow, Pearson/Longman, p.49.; Thatcher, I., *Trotsky*, pp.68-69.; Trotsky, L., *My Life*, pp.231-232.

Chapter 5

1. Trotsky, L., 1975, *My Life*, Harmondsworth, Penguin Books, p.241.
2. Service, R., 2010, *Trotsky: A Biography*, London, Pan Books, p.136.
3. Deutscher, I., 1954, *The Prophet Armed: Trotsky 1879-1921*, New York, OUP, p.214.
4. This was almost four years before US President Woodrow Wilson issued his Fourteen Points. According to Deutscher, the US edition of Trotsky's pamphlet directly influenced Wilson.
5. Trotsky, L., *My Life*, p.253.
6. Lenin, *Sochineya*, vol. xxi, p.21.; quoted in Deutscher, I., *The Prophet Armed: Trotsky 1879-1921*, p.216.

7. Deutscher, I., *The Prophet Armed: Trotsky 1879-1921*, p.217.

8. Serge, V. & Sedova Trotsky, N., *The Life and Death of Leon Trotsky*, 1973, Chicago, Haymarket Books, p.28.

9. For more on the history of this bookshop, see: https://leftinparis.org/places/96-quai-de-jemmapes/(Accessed 15/10/20)

10. During the interwar years, the Café Rotonde became renowned as the meeting place of artists and writers such as Matisse, Picasso, Hemingway and Beckett.

11. Swain, G., 2006, *Trotsky*, Harlow, Pearson/Longman, p.49.; Thatcher, I., 2003, *Trotsky*, Abingdon, Routledge, p.51.

12. Volkogonov, D., 1997, *Trotsky: The Eternal Revolutionary*, London, HarperCollins, p.62.; Deutscher, I., *The Prophet Armed: Trotsky 1879-1921*, pp.225-226.

13. Deutscher, I., 1964, *The Age of Permanent Revolution: A Trotsky Anthology*, Dell Publishing, New York, p.83.

14. Service, R., *Trotsky: A Biography*, p. 146.

15. Deutscher, I., *The Prophet Armed: Trotsky 1879-1921*, pp.232-233.

16. Swain, G.,*Trotsky*, p.52.

17. Both Lenin and Trotsky agreed that, because of Russia's economic backwardness, a revolution in Russia couldn't develop full socialism without assistance from more developed economies. Stalin later argued the opposite – though only after Lenin's death.

18. Quoted in Service, R., *Trotsky: A Biography*, p.146.

19. Thatcher, I., 2003, *Trotsky*, Abingdon, Routledge, p.79.

20. Deutscher, I., *The Prophet Armed: Trotsky 1879-1921*, p.241.

Chapter 6

1. Wyndham, F. & King, D., 1972, *Trotsky: a documentary*, Harmondsworth, Penguin Books, p.35.

2. Deutscher, I., 1954, *The Prophet Armed: Trotsky 1879-1921*, New York, OUP, p.244.

3. Deutscher, I., *The Prophet Armed: Trotsky 1879-1921*, pp.243-245.

4. Serge, V. & Sedova Trotsky, N., 1973, *The Life and Death of Leon Trotsky*, Chicago, Haymarket Books, p.33.

5. The full text of Order No. 1 can be seen at: https://www.marxists.org/history/ussr/government/1917/03/01.htm (Accessed 20/11/20)

6. Trotsky, L., 1965, *The History of the Russian Revolution, Vol.1,* London, Sphere Books, pp.340-341.

7. Deutscher, I., *The Prophet Armed: Trotsky 1879-1921*, p.258.
8. Service, R., 2010, *Trotsky: A Biography*, London, Pan Books, pp.166-167.
9. Deutscher, I., *The Prophet Armed: Trotsky 1879-1921*, p.261.
10. Trotsky, *The History of the Russian Revolution, Vol.2*, London, Sphere Books, p.296.
11. Deutscher, I., 1954, *The Prophet Armed: Trotsky 1879-1921*, New York, OUP, p.273.
12. Trotsky, L., 1975, *My Life*, Harmondsworth, Penguin Books, p.330.
13. Trotsky, L., *My Life*, pp.328-329.
14. Service, R., *Trotsky: A Biography*, pp.177, 190.
15. Swain, G., 2006, *Trotsky*, Harlow, Pearson/Longman, pp.65-66.
16. Deutscher, I., 1954, *The Prophet Armed: Trotsky 1879-1921*, New York, OUP, p.284.
17. Thatcher, I., 2003, *Trotsky*, Abingdon, Routledge, p.91.
18. Trotsky, *The History of the Russian Revolution, Vol.3*, pp.102-103.
19. Volkogonov, D., 1997, *Trotsky: The Eternal Revolutionary*, London, HarperCollins, pp.84-85.; Serge, V. & Sedova Trotsky, N., 1973, *The Life and Death of Leon Trotsky*, Chicago, Haymarket Books, p.53.; Trotsky, L., *My Life*, p.306.
20. Wyndham, F. & King, D., *Trotsky: a documentary*, p.46.; Swain, G., *Trotsky*, p.71.
21. Deutscher, I., 1954, *The Prophet Armed: Trotsky 1879-1921*, New York, OUP, p.310.
22. Service, R., *Trotsky: A Biography*, p.187.; Trotsky, L., *My Life*, p.337.; Serge, V. & Sedova Trotsky, N., *The Life and Death of Leon Trotsky*, p.65.
23. Wyndham, F. & King, D., *Trotsky: a documentary*, p.46.
24. Trotsky, L, *The History of the Russian Revolution, Vol.3*, p.289. Most books give either 'dustbin' or 'dustheap' instead of 'rubbish-can'.
25. Service, R., *Trotsky: A Biography*, p.194.
26. Trotsky, L., *My Life*, pp.353-354.
27. Service, R., *Trotsky: A Biography*, p.195.
28. Service, R., *Trotsky: A Biography*, p.197.
29. Volkogonov, D., *Trotsky: The Eternal Revolutionary*, p.127.; Thatcher, I., *Trotsky*, p.158.
30. Deutscher, I., 1954, *The Prophet Armed: Trotsky 1879-1921*, New York, OUP, pp.407-408.
31. Service, R., *Trotsky: A Biography*, p.229; Trotsky, L, *My Life*, p.427.

32. Service, R., *Trotsky: A Biography*, p.230; Thatcher, I., *Trotsky*, p.101.
33. Trotsky, L., *My Life*, p.432.; Serge, V. & Sedova Trotsky, N., *The Life and Death of Leon Trotsky*, p.86.
34. Serge, V. & Sedova Trotsky, N., *The Life and Death of Leon Trotsky*, pp.91-92.; Swain, G., *Trotsky*, p.104.
35. Trotsky, L., *My Life*, pp.425-426.; Reissner, L., *Svyazhsk*, https://www. icl-fi.org/english/esp/63/reissner.html (Accessed 09/11/20); Service, R., *Trotsky: A Biography*, p.342.
36. Service, R., *Trotsky: A Biography*, p.239.
37. Trotsky, L., *My Life*, p.446.
38. Quoted in Service, R., *Trotsky: A Biography*, p.230.
39. Service, R., *Trotsky: A Biography*, p.250.; Trotsky, L., 1972, *The First 5 years of the Communist International, Vol. 1*, New York, Monad Press, pp.30, 34.

Chapter 7

1. Trotsky, L., 1975, *My Life*, Harmondsworth, Penguin Books, pp.491-492.
2. Deutscher, I., 1954, *The Prophet Armed: Trotsky 1879-1921*, New York, OUP, p.486.; Volkogonov, D., *Trotsky: The Eternal Revolutionary*, p.250.; Trotsky, L., *My Life*, p.525.
3. Quoted in Deutscher, I., *The Prophet Armed: Trotsky 1879-1921*, p.493.
4. Wyndham, F. & King, D., 1972, *Trotsky: a documentary*, Harmondsworth, Penguin Books, p.78.
5. Swain, G., *Trotsky*, p.125.; Wyndham, F. & King, D., *Trotsky: a documentary*, p.78.; Deutscher, I., *The Prophet Armed: Trotsky 1879-1921*, p.498.
6. Swain, G., *Trotsky*, p.126.
7. The Treaty of Riga, of March 1921, which ended the war, saw Poland extend its borders beyond the Curzon Line – but not as far eastwards as their army had reached in 1920.
8. https://spartacus-educational.com/Clare_Sheridan.htm (Accessed 10/12/20); Service, R., 2010, *Trotsky: A Biography*, London, Pan Books, pp.264-266. Simon Sebag Montefiore's review in the *Telegraph*, 24 Jan 2009, of Service's debunking book, was entitled: '*Trotsky: the eccentric ladies' man*'

9. Trotsky, L., *My Life*, p.480.
10. Trotsky, L., *My Life*, p.484.
11. Wyndham, F. & King, D., *Trotsky: a documentary*, p.84.
12. Deutscher, I., *The Prophet Armed: Trotsky 1879-1921*, p.504.
13. Trotsky, L., 1976, *Writings of Leon Trotsky: 1937-38*, New York, Pathfinder Press, pp.491-92.; Thatcher, I., 2003, *Trotsky*, Abingdon, Routledge, p.115.
14. Swain, G., *Trotsky*, p.133.; Thatcher, I., *Trotsky*, p.110.
15. Deutscher, I., *The Prophet Armed: Trotsky 1879-1921*, pp.508-509.
16. Deutscher, I., *The Prophet Armed: Trotsky 1879-1921*, p.521.
17. Serge, V. & Sedova Trotsky, N., *The Life and Death of Leon Trotsky*, p.84.
18. Deutscher, I., 1970, *The Prophet Unarmed: Trotsky 1921-1929*, London, OUP, p.26.
19. Swain, G., *Trotsky*, p.134.
20. Swain, G., *Trotsky*, pp.135-136.
21. Volkogonov, D., 1997, *Trotsky: The Eternal Revolutionary*, London, HarperCollins, p.219.
22. Service, R., *Trotsky: A Biography*, p.296.
23. Deutscher, I., *The Prophet Unarmed: Trotsky 1921-1929*, pp.51-53.
24. Service, R., *Trotsky: A Biography*, p.298.
25. Trotsky, L., *My Life*, p.499; Thatcher, I, *Trotsky*, p.123.
26. Wyndham, F. & King, D., *Trotsky: a documentary*, p.96.
27. Service, R., *Trotsky: A Biography*, p.300.
28. Trotsky, L., *My Life*, pp.502-504.; Deutscher, I., *The Prophet Unarmed: Trotsky 1921-1929*, p.90.
29. Deutscher, I., *The Prophet Unarmed: Trotsky 1921-1929*, p.93.; Trotsky, L., *My Life*, p.511.
30. Deutscher, I., *The Prophet Unarmed: Trotsky 1921-1929*, pp.100-103.
31. Deutscher, I., *The Prophet Unarmed: Trotsky 1921-1929*, pp.103-104.
32. In February 1922, after the Ninth Congress of Soviets, the GPU had replaced the Cheka; in November 1923, it became the OGPU, and remained so until 1934, when it became the NKVD.
33. Volkogonov, D., *Trotsky: The Eternal Revolutionary*, p.246.
34. Deutscher, I., *The Prophet Unarmed: Trotsky 1921-1929*, p.113. The full Letter can be found at: https://www.marxists.org/history/etol/document/ilo/1923-lo/ch02.htm (Accessed 22/12/20)
35. Volkogonov, D., *Trotsky: The Eternal Revolutionary*, p.249.
36. Thatcher, I., *Trotsky*, p.127.
37. Trotsky, L., *My Life*, p.520.

38. Trotsky, L., 'The New Course', in Trotsky, L., ed., Allen, N., 1975, *The Challenge of the Left Opposition, 1923-25*, New York, Pathfinder Press, p.125.
39. Deutscher, I., *The Prophet Unarmed: Trotsky 1921-1929*, p.125.
40. Swain, G., *Trotsky*, pp. 154-155.

Chapter 8

1. Trotsky, L., 1975, *My Life*, Harmondsworth, Penguin Books, p.554.
2. Serge, V. & Sedova Trotsky, N., 1973, *The Life and Death of Leon Trotsky*, Chicago, Haymarket Books, pp.123-124.
3. Wyndham, F. & King, D., 1972, *Trotsky: a documentary*, Harmondsworth, Penguin Books, p.101.
4. Volkogonov, D., 1997, *Trotsky: The Eternal Revolutionary*, London, HarperCollins, p.21.; Service, R., 2010, *Trotsky: A Biography*, London, Pan Books, pp.310-311.
5. Trotsky, L., 1975, *My Life*, Harmondsworth, Penguin Books, p.531.
6. Wyndham, F. & King, D., *Trotsky: a documentary*, p.100.
7. Deutscher, I., 1970, *The Prophet Unarmed: Trotsky 1921-1929*, London, OUP, pp.139-40.; Trotsky, L., ed., Allen, N., 1975, *The Challenge of the Left Opposition, 1923-25*, New York, Pathfinder Press, p.161.; Thatcher, I., 2003, *Trotsky*, Abingdon, Routledge, p.127.
8. Deutscher, I., *The Prophet Unarmed: Trotsky 1921-1929*, p.140.
9. Swain, G., 2006, *Trotsky*, Harlow, Pearson/Longman, p.158.; Deutscher, I., *The Prophet Unarmed: Trotsky 1921-1929*, p.151.
10. Volkogonov, D., *Trotsky: The Eternal Revolutionary*, p.258.; Trotsky, L., *My Life*, pp.536-537.
11. Trotsky, L., *My Life*, p.540.
12. Deutscher, I., *The Prophet Unarmed: Trotsky 1921-1929*, p.201.
13. Deutscher, I., 1975, *The Unfinished Revolution: Russia 1917-67*, New York, OUP, p.66.
14. Trotsky, L., *My Life*, p.534.
15. Deutscher, I., *The Prophet Unarmed: Trotsky 1921-1929*, p.249.
16. Deutscher, I., *The Prophet Unarmed: Trotsky 1921-1929*, pp.253-258.
17. Trotsky, L., *My Life*, p.546.
18. Serge, V. & Sedova Trotsky, N., *The Life and Death of Leon Trotsky*, p.139.; Wyndham, F. & King, D., *Trotsky: a documentary*, p.109.
19. Swain, G., *Trotsky*, p.167.
20. Deutscher, I., *The Prophet Unarmed: Trotsky 1921-1929*, p.296.

21. Deutscher, I., *The Prophet Unarmed: Trotsky 1921-1929*, pp.297-299.
22. Deutscher, I., *The Prophet Unarmed: Trotsky 1921-1929*, pp.299-303.; Swain, G., *Trotsky*, p.169.
23. Trotsky, L., *My Life*, pp.553-554.
24. Trotsky, L., 1976, *Leon Trotsky on China*, eds. Evans, L. & Block, R., New York, Monad Press, pp.216-218.
25. Deutscher, I., *The Prophet Unarmed: Trotsky 1921-1929*, p.349.
26. Deutscher, I., *The Prophet Unarmed: Trotsky 1921-1929*, p.344, p.353.
27. Volkogonov, D., *Trotsky: The Eternal Revolutionary*, pp.291-292.
28. Wyndham, F. & King, D., *Trotsky: a documentary*, p.110.; Trotsky, L., 1972, *The Stalin School of Falsification*, New York, Pathfinder Press, p.1.
29. Service, R., *Trotsky: A Biography*, p.362.
30. Volkogonov, D., *Trotsky: The Eternal Revolutionary*, pp.295 & 299.
31. Wyndham, F. & King, D., *Trotsky: a documentary*, p.111.
32. Deutscher, I., *The Prophet Unarmed: Trotsky 1921-1929*, pp.370-72.
33. Wyndham, F. & King, D., *Trotsky: a documentary*, p.113.; Deutscher, I, *The Prophet Unarmed: Trotsky 1921-1929*, p.384.
34. Trotsky, L., 1978, eds., Allen N. & Breitman, G., *Writings of Leon Trotsky 1936-37*, New York, Pathfinder Press, p.65.
35. Serge, V. & Sedova Trotsky, N., *The Life and Death of Leon Trotsky*, pp.156-157.
36. Trotsky, L., *My Life*, p.575 & p.583.; Serge, V. & Sedova Trotsky, N., *The Life and Death of Leon Trotsky*, p.160.; Service, R., *Trotsky: A Biography*, pp.371-72.; Deutscher, I., *The Prophet Unarmed: Trotsky 1921-1929*, p.429.
37. Volkogonov, D., *Trotsky: The Eternal Revolutionary*, pp.309-310.
38. Trotsky, L., ed., Allen, N. & Saunders, G., 1981, *The Challenge of the Left Opposition, 1928-29*, New York, Pathfinder Press, pp.64-65.
39. Swain, G., *Trotsky*, p.185.
40. Deutscher, I., *The Prophet Unarmed: Trotsky 1921-1929*, p.441.
41. Trotsky, L., *My Life*, pp.581-584; Swain, G., *Trotsky*, p.186.

Chapter 9

1. Serge, V. & Sedova Trotsky, N., 1973, *The Life and Death of Leon Trotsky*, Chicago, Haymarket Books, p.206.
2. Deutscher, I., 1970, *The Prophet Unarmed: Trotsky 1921-1929*, London, OUP, pp.468-69.

3. Volkogonov, D., *Trotsky: The Eternal Revolutionary*, p.258.; Trotsky, L, *My Life*, p.317.

4. There is a short video of the area on: https://www.youtube.com/watch?v=UJ2AkpnxBaU (Accessed 06/03/21)

5. Trotsky, L., 1972, *Writings of Leon Trotsky, 1932-33*, New York, Pathfinder Press, p.312.; Deutscher, I., *The Prophet Outcast: Trotsky 1929-1940*, p.24.

6. Serge, V. & Sedova Trotsky, N., *The Life and Death of Leon Trotsky*, p.169.; Deutscher, I., *The Prophet Outcast: Trotsky 1929-1940*, p.19.

7. Thatcher, I., *Trotsky*, pp.184-185.

8. Volkogonov, D., *Trotsky: The Eternal Revolutionary*, p.325.

9. Service, R., 2010, *Trotsky: A Biography*, London, Pan Books, pp.383-384.

10. Trotsky, L., 1975, *Writings of Leon Trotsky, 1929*, New York, Pathfinder Press, pp. 340 & 358.; Thatcher, I., 2003, *Trotsky*, Abingdon, Routledge, p.173.

11. Swain, G., 2006, *Trotsky*, Harlow, Pearson/Longman, pp.190-91.

12. Trotsky, L., 1973, *Writings of Leon Trotsky, 1932*, New York, Pathfinder Press, pp. 69-71. & pp.125-126.

13. There is footage of the Pompeii tour on YouTube: https://www.youtube.com/watch?v=qhRBfKqBRZg (Accessed 06/03/21)

14. Deutscher, I., *The Prophet Outcast: Trotsky 1929-1940*, p.193.; part of his talk and interview can be seen on: https://www.youtube.com/watch?v=WiK_8YD6ob8 (Accessed 06/03/21) https://www.youtube.com/watch?v=kBLnTNL5ZPQ&list=PLxqj63x4QU6EPr5nIfW_UcSc4_9Irs_LB (Accessed 06/03/21)

15. Serge, V. & Sedova Trotsky, N., *The Life and Death of Leon Trotsky*, p.184.; Trotsky, L., 1971, *The Struggle Against Fascism in Germany*, New York, Pathfinder Press, pp. 155-156.

16. Deutscher, I., *The Prophet Outcast: Trotsky 1929-1940*, p.146.

17. Wyndham, F. & King, D., 1972, *Trotsky: a documentary*, Harmondsworth, Penguin Books, p.138.

18. Service, R., *Trotsky: A Biography*, p.387.; Wyndham, F. & King, D., *Trotsky: a documentary*, p.138.

19. Volkogonov, D., *Trotsky: The Eternal Revolutionary*, p.351.; Service, R., *Trotsky: A Biography*, p.387.

20. Wyndham, F. & King, D., *Trotsky: a documentary*, pp.132-33.; Trotsky, L., *The Struggle Against Fascism in Germany*, p.376.

21. Thatcher, I., *Trotsky*, pp.179-180.

22. Deutscher, I., *The Prophet Outcast: Trotsky 1929-1940*, p.217.

23. Thatcher, I., *Trotsky*, p.190.; Trotsky, L., 1975, *Writings of Leon Trotsky, 1933-34,* New York, Pathfinder Press, p.27.
24. Trotsky, L., *Writings of Leon Trotsky, 1933-34,* p.63.
25. Deutscher, I., *The Prophet Outcast: Trotsky 1929-1940*, p.265.
26. Volkogonov, D., *Trotsky: The Eternal Revolutionary*, pp.335-336.
27. Trotsky, L., *Writings of Leon Trotsky, 1933-34,* p.122.
28. Swain, G., *Trotsky*, p.196; Wyndham, F. & King, D., *Trotsky: a documentary*, p.137.
29. Serge, V. & Sedova Trotsky, N., *The Life and Death of Leon Trotsky*, p.193; Service, R., *Trotsky: A Biography*, p.422.
30. Trotsky, L., 1974, *Writings of Leon Trotsky, 1934-35,* New York, Pathfinder Press, pp.166-184.
31. Wyndham, F. & King, D., *Trotsky: a documentary*, p.138.; Deutscher, I., *The Prophet Outcast: Trotsky 1929-1940*, pp.284-85.
32. Wyndham, F. & King, D., *Trotsky: a documentary*, p.139.
33. Volkogonov, D., *Trotsky: The Eternal Revolutionary*, p.367.
34. Serge, V. & Sedova Trotsky, N., *The Life and Death of Leon Trotsky*, pp.202-206.
35. Deutscher, I., *The Prophet Outcast: Trotsky 1929-1940*, p. 298.; After Wolf was expelled from Norway, Hjørdis joined him in Paris, from where they went to fight with the semi-Trotskyist POUM in the Spanish Civil War – she managed to leave before being arrested by the NKVD, but Wolf disappeared after his arrest in Barcelona.
36. Deutscher, I., *The Prophet Outcast: Trotsky 1929-1940*, pp.346-47.
37. Serge, V. & Sedova Trotsky, N., *The Life and Death of Leon Trotsky*, pp.206-209.; Volkogonov, D., *Trotsky: The Eternal Revolutionary*, p.372.
38. Deutscher, I., *The Prophet Outcast: Trotsky 1929-1940*, p.352.
39. Deutscher, I., *The Prophet Outcast: Trotsky 1929-1940*, pp.353-55.; Trotsky, L., 1978, *Writings of Leon Trotsky, 1936-37,* New York, Pathfinder Press, p.41.

Chapter 10

1. Trotsky, L., 1973, *Writings of Leon Trotsky, 1939-40*, New York, Pathfinder Press, p.158.
2. Service, R., 2010, *Trotsky: A Biography*, London, Pan Books, p.429.; Wyndham, F. & King, D., 1972, *Trotsky: a documentary*, Harmondsworth, Penguin Books, p.144.

3. Serge, V. & Sedova Trotsky, N., 1973, *The Life and Death of Leon Trotsky*, Chicago, Haymarket Books, p.212.; Deutscher, I., 1970, *The Prophet Outcast: Trotsky 1929-1940*, London, OUP, pp.361-62.

4. Wyndham, F. & King, D., *Trotsky: a documentary*, pp.144-145.; Serge, V. & Sedova Trotsky, N., *The Life and Death of Leon Trotsky*, p.219.; Deutscher, I., *The Prophet Outcast: Trotsky 1929-1940*, p.363.

5. Trotsky, L., 1972, *The Revolution Betrayed*, New York, Pathfinder Press, pp.286-87.

6. Serge, V. & Sedova Trotsky, N., *The Life and Death of Leon Trotsky*, p.217.

7. Volkogonov, D., 1996, *Trotsky: The Eternal Revolutionary*, London, Harper Collins, p.387.; Deutscher, I., *The Prophet Outcast: Trotsky 1929-1940*, p.366.

8. Thatcher, I., 2003, *Trotsky*, Abingdon, Routledge, p.196.; see also Trotsky's press release at: https://www.youtube.com/watch?v=_Eyjyceo3vU (Accessed 06/03/21)

9. Wyndham, F. & King, D., *Trotsky: a documentary*, p.151.

10. Trotsky, L., 1976, *Writings of Leon Trotsky, 1937-38*, New York, Pathfinder Press, p.125.; Thatcher, I., *Trotsky*, pp.197-98.

11. Deutscher, I., *The Prophet Outcast: Trotsky 1929-1940*, pp.384-86.; Volkogonov, D., *Trotsky: The Eternal Revolutionary*, p.395.; https://dangerousminds.net/comments/frida_kahlos_secret_revenge_affair_with_leon_trotsky (Accessed 06/03/21)

12. These letters – along with Trotsky's correspondence with members and supporters of the Fourth International – lay in the Closed Section of the Trotsky Archives; before 1980, only Deutscher had been granted access. Deutscher, I., *The Prophet Outcast: Trotsky 1929-1940*, p.385.; Swain, G., 2006, *Trotsky*, Harlow, Pearson/Longman, pp.200-01.; Service, R., *Trotsky: A Biography*, pp.450-51.

13. Trotsky, L., 1973, *Their Morals and Ours*, New York, Pathfinder Press, p.51.; Wyndham, F. & King, D., *Trotsky: a documentary*, p.152.

14. Trotsky, L., *Their Morals and Ours*, pp.51-52.

15. Deutscher, I., *The Prophet Outcast: Trotsky 1929-1940*, pp.396-97.

16. Serge, V. & Sedova Trotsky, N., *The Life and Death of Leon Trotsky*, p.228.; Service, R., *Trotsky: A Biography*, p.437.

17. Trotsky, L., *Their Morals and Ours*, p.52.; Trotsky, L., *Writings of Leon Trotsky, 1937-38*, p.230.

18. Volkogonov, D., *Trotsky: The Eternal Revolutionary*, p.381.

19. Orwell's experiences during the Spanish Civil War are recorded in his book, *Homage to Catalonia*.

20. Trotsky, L., 1973, *The Spanish Revolution 1936-39*, New York, Pathfinder Press, pp. 322, 326.
21. Volkogonov, D., *Trotsky: The Eternal Revolutionary*, p.399.
22. Deutscher, I., *The Prophet Outcast: Trotsky 1929-1940*, p.427.; Trotsky, L., 1977, *The Transitional Program for Socialist Revolution*, New York, Pathfinder Press, p.152.
23. Trotsky, L., *Writings of Leon Trotsky, 1937-38*, p.88.
24. See Trotsky's message to US supporters on the FI's foundation: https://www.youtube.com/watch?v=6TFEnnh_7Ec (Accessed 06/03/21)
25. Trotsky, L., 1973, *In Defense of Marxism*, New York, Pathfinder Press, p.9.; Deutscher, I., *The Prophet Outcast: Trotsky 1929-1940*, pp.468.; Service, R., *Trotsky: A Biography*, p.477.
26. Views of this house and garden can be found on: https://www.youtube.com/watch?v=aGvXg7JfZgQ   https://www.youtube.com/watch?v=WI82XRYBLTQ   https://www.youtube.com/watch?v=nef9br5-hg4 (Accessed 06/03/21)
27. Serge, V. & Sedova Trotsky, N., *The Life and Death of Leon Trotsky*, pp.251-56.
28. Volkogonov, D., *Trotsky: The Eternal Revolutionary*, pp.458-61.
29. Deutscher, I., *The Prophet Outcast: Trotsky 1929-1940*, p.486.; See Seva (Esteban Volkov)'s account of this raid given to the *Guardian* in 2012: https://www.youtube.com/watch?v=pI-arymQl94 (Accessed 06/03/21)
30. Deutscher, I., *The Prophet Outcast: Trotsky 1929-1940*, p.494.; Trotsky, L., *Writings of Leon Trotsky, 1939-40*, pp.233-34, 250.
31. Deutscher, I., *The Prophet Outcast: Trotsky 1929-1940*, p.493.
32. Volkogonov, D., *Trotsky: The Eternal Revolutionary*, pp.465-66.; Wyndham, F. & King, D., *Trotsky: a documentary*, pp.171-173.
33. Deutscher, I., *The Prophet Outcast: Trotsky 1929-1940*, pp.507-08.; Serge, V. & Sedova Trotsky, N., *The Life and Death of Leon Trotsky*, p.268.
34. Deutscher, I., *The Prophet Outcast: Trotsky 1929-1940*, pp.508-09.; Volkogonov, D.,*Trotsky: The Eternal Revolutionary*, p.469. Sedova – and Seva, who was fourteen when his grandfather was assassinated – remained in that house. Seva, who changed his name to Esteban Volkov, eventually married and had four children. In 1960, Sedova moved to Paris, where she died two years later, aged seventy-nine. Her ashes were brought back to the house, where Seva and his family had remained living. Trotsky's study was kept as it had been during his life. Footage of the funeral can be seen via these links: https://www.youtube.com/watch?v=DnbMaeN5y-o   https://www.youtube.com/watch?v=84_FnYLE1tQ (Accessed 06/03/21)
35. Trotsky, L., *Writings of Leon Trotsky, 1939-40*, pp.158-159.

Conclusion

1. Serge, V. & Sedova Trotsky, N., 1973, *The Life and Death of Leon Trotsky*, Chicago, Haymarket Books, p.271.
2. Gramsci, A., 1971, *Selections from the Prison Notebooks*, London, Lawrence & Wishart, p.175.
3. Thatcher, I., 2003, *Trotsky*, Abingdon, Routledge, pp.216-17.; Mandel, E., 1995, *Trotsky as Alternative*, London, Verso, p.1.
4. Swain, G., 2006, *Trotsky*, Harlow, Pearson/Longman, pp.211-13.; Service, R., 2010, *Trotsky: A Biography*, London, Pan Books, p.336.; Deutscher, I., 1954, *The Prophet Armed: Trotsky 1879-1921*, New York, OUP, p.396.; Trotsky, L., 1975, *My Life*, Harmondsworth, Penguin Books, p.525.
5. Volkogonov, D., 1997, *Trotsky: The Eternal Revolutionary*, London, HarperCollins, p.484.; Swain, G., *Trotsky*, p.216.
6. Trotsky, L., *My Life*, pp.463-64, 497.
7. Service, R., *Trotsky: A Biography*, pp.339, 498.
8. Deutscher, I., *The Prophet Armed: Trotsky 1879-1921*, p.396.
9. Marx, K. & Engels, F., 1967, *The Communist Manifesto*, Harmondsworth, Penguin Book, p.78.
10. Hobsbawm, E., 2009, *How to Change the World: Tales of Marx and Marxism*, London, Little, Brown, pp.417-19.
11. Ali, T., 2009, *The Idea of Communism*, London, Seagull Books, pp.112-13.
12. Löwy, M., 2015, *Ecosocialism: A Radical Alternative to Capitalist Catastrophe*, Chicago, Haymarket Books, p.82.
13. Deutscher, I., 1967, *The Unfinished Revolution: Russia 1917-1967*, London, OUP, pp.114-15.
14. Thatcher, I., *Trotsky*, p.216.

Index

Adler, Alfred, 60
Adler, Victor, 34, 42, 70
Agelof, Sylvia, 189, 191
Alexander III, 5, 10
All-Russian Congress of Soviets,
    vii, 87-8, 91-5, 98, 106, 110-11
Antonov-Ovseenko, Vladimir, 75,
    100, 121-2, 130, 132, 144
armoured train, 99-100
atheism, 23
August Bloc, 64-5, 67, 74
Axelrod, Paul, 34, 35, 38-40, 74, 77

Balabanova, Angelica, 75, 177
Balkan Wars, 65-7, 78
Bernstein, Edouard, 24
Black Hundreds, 55
Bolsheviks, viii, 38, 40-1, 43, 50,
    55-6, 63, 67, 77, 88-9, 91, 98-9
Bonapartism, 167
Bonch-Bruevich, Gen. M. D., 98,
    100, 102
Bor'ba (The Struggle), 68
Boycotters, 57-8, 62
Brest-Litovsk Treaty (1918), 96-8
Breton, André, 181
Bronstein, Anna, 1-4, 50, 65
Bronstein, Alexander, 1, 6
Bronstein, David, 2, 14, 114
Bronstein, Leon D., (see Trotsky),
Bronstein, Olga, 1, 14, 62, 85, 109
Bronstein, Yelizaveta, 65

Bukharin, Nikolai, 71, 82, 97, 112,
    119-120, 128, 130-1, 133, 138,
    147-50, 156, 165, 176, 184
Bulletin of the Opposition, 153-4,
    156, 159, 161, 164-5, 170-2,
    182, 187, 195
bureaucracy, 134, 156, 165, 170,
    175, 177, 186

Cárdenas, Lázaro, 175, 188, 192
Central Committee (CC), 38, 40,
    42, 44, 55-6, 62, 86, 90-3, 95,
    102-3, 106-7, 110, 112-14,
    116-18, 120-2, 124, 127-30,
    132-43, 155, 157, 167, 176, 181
Central Control Commission
    (CCC), 120, 130, 134, 139,
    141-2
Central Executive Committee
    (CEC), 87-9, 91-2, 95, 98
Chamberlain, Austen, 152
Cheka (secret police - see also GPU,
    OGPU, NKVD), ix, xi, 212
Chernov, Victor, 88
Chicherin, Georgy, 75
China crisis, 138-9
Chinese Communist Party (CCP),
    138
Chkheidze, Nikolay S., 79
Cirque Moderne, 87
Coalition Government (Bolsheviks
    & Left SRs), 87-8

Committees for the Defence of Trotsky, 178
collectivisation, 106, 144
Communist (Kommunist), 76
Communist International (Comintern), 74, 78, 103-4, 115, 129, 132, 136, 138, 140, 147, 156-8, 162-4, 169, 178, 184
Communist Manifesto (1848), 15, 198
Communist Youth (Komsomol), 122, 142
Congress of Soviets, Northern Region (CSNR), 92-3
Constituent Assembly, 87, 90, 95, 98
Constitutional Democratic Party (Kadets), 46, 56, 85, 98
Council of People's Commissars (Sovnarkom), 95-6, 98
Curzon Line, 108, 211
Czechoslovak Legion, 99

Dan, Fedor, 164
Darwin, Charles, 23
Declaration of the Eighty-four, 138-9
Declaration of the Thirteen, 135
Democratic Centralists (Decemists), 107, 111, 113, 116, 121-2, 135
Democratic Conference, 90
Denikin, General A. I., 102
Dewey Commission, 178-9, 182
Dual Power, 85
Dumas, 43, 57-8, 61, 64, 79
Dzerzhinsky, Felix, 109, 121, 135

Eastern Review (Vostochnoye Obozreniye), 27, 30
Eastman, Max, 6, 132, 136, 152-3, 198

Eastman, Yelena, 157
Ecosocialism, 200
Eitingon, Naum, 189, 191
Engels, Friedrich, 15, 35, 198
Estrin, Lilia, 164

fascism, 150, 154, 157-8, 161-3, 166, 169, 184-5, 194-5
First World War, 68-70, 80, 83, 96, 104, 162, 186
Fischer, Ruth, 166
Five-Year Plans, 155-6
foreign trade, 116
Forverts (Forwards), 82
Forward (Vperëd), 87
Fourth International, 161, 165, 167-8, 175, 181-2, 184-8, 192, 194-6, 198-200
Frankel, Jan, 152, 168, 174, 178
French Communist Party, 78, 129

Georgian Affair, 118-19
German Communist Party (KPD), 129, 158, 161
German Social Democratic Party (SPD), 24, 40, 58-60, 62-4, 70, 72, 75, 158
Goldman, Emma, 83
Gorky, Maxim, 28, 57, 60, 87, 92
Gosplan Controversy, 113-14, 116-17, 119, 122-5, 128
GPU, ix, 121, 177
Gramsci, Antonio, 194
Greben, Ivan, 3
Greber, Olga, 168
Gromokla, 4
gulags, 32
Guomindang (GMD), 138

Hansen, Joseph, 191-2
Harte, Robert S., 190
Hitler, Adolf, 159-162

Ibsen, H., 28, 172-3
Inter-District Organisation
   (Mezhraionka), 68, 80, 86-90, 124
International Communist League
   (Bolshevik-Leninist) (ICL-B-L),
   163, 171
International Left Opposition,
   153,163
International Marxist Group,
   199, 208
Irkutsk, 25-7, 30, 33-4
Iskra (*The Spark*), 30, 34-9, 41, 43
Izvestya (Tidings), 44-5

Jacson, Frank (see Mercader,
   Ramón)
Joffe, Adolfe, 60, 87, 90, 94, 96,
   107, 124, 130. 143, 145
July Days, 88-9

Kahlo, Frida, xiv, 175-6, 179-80
Kamenev, Lev, 62, 84-6, 89-96,
   109, 111, 113, 115, 117-20,
   128-34, 136-7, 142-4, 147-8,
   155-6, 167, 171, 174
Kamenev, Sergei (C-in-C), 100, 102
Kautsky, Karl, 58
Kazan, 102, 144
Kerensky, Alexander, 85,
   87-90, 93-4
Kherson, 1, 22, 67
Khrustalev-Nosar, P. A., 50
Kienthal Conference, 80
Kievan Thought (Kievskaya Mysi),
   59, 65, 73, 78
Kirov, Sergei, 165, 167, 172

Klement, Rudolf, 152, 162-3,
   182, 186
Knudsen, Konrad, 169, 171, 174
Knudsen, Hjørdis, 171
Kolchak, Admiral A., 101-2
Kollontai, Alexandra, 75, 82, 107
Kornilov, Gen. L., 90
Krasin, Leonid, 42-4
Kresty Prison, 89
Krestinsky, Nikolai, 124
Krivitsky, Walter, 186
Kronstadt Rebellion (1921), 110-12
Kronstadt sailors, 46, 87-8, 90
Krupskaya, Nadezhda, 34, 117-18,
   122, 127-8, 132-4, 137-8
Krylenko, Nikolai, 96
Krzhizhanovsky-Clair, Gleb, 34
kulaks, 9, 124, 144, 147

labour armies/battalions, 106, 110
Labriola, Arturo, 23
Larin, Yu, 137
Lashevich, Mikhail, 133-5
Lassalle, Ferdinand, 19-20
League of Nations, 176
Left Opposition, 120, 127, 129,
   131-2, 134, 140, 148-9, 155-6,
   159, 163, 165, 167, 198
Left Social Revolutionaries, 92,
   94-5, 97-9
Lenin, Vladimir I., xv, 10, 13, 24,
   28, 30, 34-5, 37-40, 42-4, 46,
   48-9, 54-8, 61-4, 70-4, 76-7,
   79-81, 86-7, 89-97, 99, 102-13,
   115-20, 122, 125-33, 136, 139,
   141, 143, 153, 155, 157, 197-8
Lenin Levy, 128
Lenin's *Political Testament,* 117,
   126, 133, 136, 141, 143,
   155, 196

Leninism, 127, 140, 144, 175, 198
Letter of the 46, 122-4, 127
Liebknecht, Karl, 58, 64, 72, 76, 85
Liquidators, 57, 62, 64, 67, 73
Löwy, Michael, 200
Lunacharsky, Anatoly, 44, 46, 68, 75, 87-9, 103, 197
Luxemburg, Rosa, 58, 72, 76

Machine Gun Regiment (Petrograd), 88
Mandel, Ernest, 196
March Revolution (1917), 60, 84-6, 94
Martin, Jeanne, 154, 159-61, 166, 182, 188
Martov, Julius, 30, 35, 37-43, 45-6, 50, 54, 56-8, 62, 64, 69, 73-6, 80, 87, 94
Marx, Karl, 10, 15, 17, 19, 49, 68, 164, 198-9, 205, 207
Marxism, xvii, 10, 12-13, 15-19, 21-4, 26-7, 29, 36, 49, 71, 83, 142, 156, 175, 180-1, 194-5, 198-200
Mensheviks, 30, 38-41, 43-7, 49-50, 55-7, 62-5, 67, 69, 73-5, 77, 84-8, 91-2, 94-5, 98-9, 110, 124, 130, 141, 197, 208
Mercarder, Ramón, 189, 191-2
Military Revolutionary Committee (MRC), 91-4, 130
Miliukov, Pavel, 43, 46, 61
Molinier, Raymond, 153-4, 162-3, 182
Molotov, Vyacheslav, 135
Muralov, Nikolai, 132, 136

Nachalo (The Beginning), 45
Narodniks, 10-17, 19-20, 29, 36, 57

Narodnaya Volya (People's Will), 10
Nasha Revolutsia (Our Revolution), 48
Nashe Delo (Our Cause), 20
Nashe Slovo (Our Word), 74
Nazi Party, 158, 161, 184
Nazi-Soviet Non-Aggression Pact, 187
NEPmen, 144
'Neither Peace Nor War', 95-8
Nevelson, Man, 146, 168
New Economic Policy (1921-28), 107, 112-14, 121, 124, 128, 131-2, 144, 147, 155
New York, 82-3
New World, 82-3
Nicholas II, 11, 29, 41, 43-4, 47, 55, 57, 62, 73, 84, 89
Nikolaev, 4, 10-14, 16, 18, 20-2, 50
NKVD, ix, 164-5, 167, 169-70, 173, 181-6, 188-90
Novaya Zhizn (New Life), 44
Novy Mir (Our World), 73, 84
Novak, George, 175
November Revolution (1917), vii, xv, 60, 75, 91-5, 105, 109, 111, 126, 129-30, 141, 147, 155, 170, 193-4

October Manifesto (1905), 43-5, 47, 50
Octobrist Party, 58
Odessa, 1, 4-8, 10, 14-5, 19-20, 23, 25, 60, 136, 151, 206
Odesskie Novosti (Odessa News), 59
OGPU, ix, 136, 140, 143-6, 148-52, 154, 156
Okhrana, ix, 19, 21, 33
'Old Guard' (Bolshevik), 79, 86, 113, 120-1, 123-4

'Oto, Antid', 27-8, 59
Order No. 1, 85, 93
Orlov, Alexander, 183, 186

Party Congresses, 23, 30, 37-40,
   43, 55-9, 63, 90, 98, 102, 107,
   110-11, 113, 115, 117-21, 123,
   128, 130, 132-3, 138-41, 144,
   148, 165, 167
Parvus, Alexander, 40-1, 45, 47,
   58, 75
Paz, Magdeleine, 151
Paz, Maurice, 151
People's Commissars, 94-5
Permanent Revolution, xv, 9, 45,
   48-9, 56, 58-9, 61, 72, 77, 86,
   130-1, 157, 165, 194, 198
Peter and Paul Fortress, 19
Petrograd Soviet, vii, 84-5,
   89-91, 93-4
Pilsudski, Marshal, I., 107, 108
Platform of the Ten, 110
Plekhanov, Georgi, 10, 35-7, 39, 57,
   69, 73, 79
Polish Communist Party, 129
Polish invasion (1920-21), 107-9, 112
Politburo, 107-08, 115, 117-18,
   120-5, 127, 130, 132-40, 150,
   155, 157
Populists (see *Narodniks*,
   Narodnaya Volya)
Potresov, Alexander, 35, 79
POUM (Spain), 166, 184, 216
Power Struggle, 129-31, 135-6, 138
Pravda (The Truth) - Vienna: 60-5,
   68, 74; Bolshevik: 64, 86, 88,
   102, 106, 117, 122-5, 133, 138,
   147, 193
Preobrazhensky, Yevgeni, 112, 121,
   127, 132, 140, 147-8, 155

Pre-Parliament, 90
Prinkipo (Turkey), 152-3, 157, 160,
   162, 168
Provisional Government, 84-90,
   93-4, 98
Pyatakov, Georgei, 112, 120-1,
   127, 130, 132, 136, 144, 148,
   176, 197

Radek, Karl, 68, 71-2, 75, 77, 97,
   101-2, 113, 120, 127, 132, 141,
   143, 147-8, 155, 173, 176
Rakovsky, Christian, 75, 112, 119-20,
   124, 130, 132, 141-3, 146-7
Red Army, xvi, 66, 98-104, 106,
   108, 111, 114, 119, 121-2
Red Guards, 90, 92-3, 99
Reiss, Ignaz, 181-2
Reissner, Larisa, xiv, 101, 180
Revolution of 1905, 42, 48, 52, 57, 68
Riabukhana, Anya, 145, 151
Rivera, Diego, 145, 176, 179, 181,
   183, 187-8
Rosmer, Alfred, 73, 78, 83, 151-3,
   178, 186, 188-9, 191
Rosmer, Marguerite, 151-3, 186,
   188-9, 191
Rubinstein, Genrieta, 168
Rubinstein, Yulia, 168
Russian Communist Party (RCP),
   86, 98, 101, 104-5, 110-12, 115,
   125, 129, 137-8, 146, 148, 154
Russian Civil War, xiv, xvi, 66,
   97-106
Russian Socialist Federated Soviet
   Republic (RSFSR), 95, 118
Russian Social Democratic
   Workers' Party (RSDWP), 21,
   23, 30, 37-9, 41-3, 46, 55, 57-8,
   61, 63-4, 68, 72-3, 76, 78-9, 86

Russkaya Gazeta (Russian Gazette), 45
Russo-Japanese War (1904-05), 39
Ryazanov, David, 60, 75

Samara, 28, 34, 101
Schachtman, Max, 162
Second Congress (1903), 37-8
Second World War, 114, 161, 198
Sedov, Lyova, 48, 51, 53-5, 59, 127,142, 145, 147, 151-4, 157, 159-62, 164, 166, 169-74, 176, 178-9 181-4, 186, 188
Sedov, Sergei, 59, 70, 74, 84, 142, 145-6, 151, 159, 161, 168, 176-7
Sedova, Natalya, xiii-ix, 32-3, 36-7, 41-4, 48, 51, 53-5, 58-60, 68, 73, 75, 81-2, 84-5, 89, 94, 99, 109, 113-14, 121, 126-7, 130, 134, 136, 142, 145-7, 151, 156, 159-61, 163-4, 168, 170, 172, 174-80, 182-3, 188-93, 195
Serge, Victor, 140, 183, 185
Sequeiros, David, 190
Sheridan, Clare, xv, 108-9, 180
Shliapnikov, Alexander G., 107
Shvigovsky, Franz, 12-5, 18-9, 21-3
Show Trials, 170-1, 173, 177-8, 184
Siberian Union, 29, 37
Sklyansky, Efraim, 128
Smirnov, Ivan N., 132, 136, 143, 156
Smirnov, Vladimir, 107, 127
Smolny Institute, 87, 93-5
smychka, 131
Social Democrat, 55
Social Democratic Siberian Union, 29-30, 37
Social Revolutionary Party (SRs), 36, 44-6, 84-5, 88, 91-2, 98-9, 110

Social Democrat (Bolshevik), 73, 76
Social Democrat (Menshevik), 87
social-patriotism, 77, 83
'Socialism in One Country', 131, 134, 138, 198
Socialist Resistance, 199
Sokolnikov, Grigori, 75
Sokolovsky, Grigory, 18, 23
Sokolovsky, Ilya, 17-8, 23
Sokolovskaya, Aleksandra, xvii, 14-19, 22-6, 31-3, 36-7, 48, 60, 85, 99, 132, 145-6, 154, 159-61, 167-8
South Russian Workers' Union, 18, 25
Southern Worker, 34
Souvarine, Boris, 129
soviets, 90, 92 , 112, 141, 167
soviet democracy, 106, 113, 148, 165
Spanish Civil War, 158 184-5
Spentzer, Fanni, 5-8, 10
Spentzer, Moishe, 4-8, 10
Stalin, Joseph, xiii, xv, 27, 29, 32, 40, 52, 58, 64, 84, 93, 99, 102-3, 105, 107-8, 112, 115-21, 123-4, 126-41, 143-4, 147-65, 167, 170-7, 180-1, 184-91, 193-4, 196-200
state capitalism, 106, 112, 165
Stolypin, Pyotr A., 55, 57, 64, 68
Sukhanov, Nikolai, 91, 93
Svyazhsk, 101

Tauride Palace, 88
Tenth Army, 99, 102
Tenth Party Congress (1921), 110-11, 113
The Beginning, 45

The Forty-Six, 122-4, 127
'The 'Great Contest', 200
'The Pen', 27-8, 34
The Proletarian, 61
The Voice (Golos), 73-4
Thermidor, 124, 132, 137-9, 141,
    144, 154, 156, 165, 167, 197
Tolstoy, Leo, 7, 10, 28, 65-6
Tomsky, Mikhail, 110, 120
Trade Union Question, 109-13
Trans-Siberian Railway, 25, 30, 34
'Triumvirate', 115, 118, 120,
    122, 131
Trotsky, Leon: assassination,
    184-93, 189, 198; childhood, 1-14;
    in exile: Alma-Ata, 144-
    6, 149-50; Austria, 59-71;
    Denmark, 156-7; France, 73-
    81; Mexico, 175-92; Norway,
    169-74; Siberia, 24-34, 52-4;
    Spain, 81-2; Switzerland, 71-3;
    Turkey, xviii, 31, 105, 126,
    150-62; USA, 82-4; politics
    (Trotskyism): 46, 48, 86, 123,
    129-31, 133, 138, 144, 151,
    181, 196, 198-200; writings:
    *Declaration of the Eighty-four
    and Our Tasks,* 138; *For New
    Communist Parties and the New
    International,* 163; *History of
    the Russian Revolution,* 153;
    *Leon Sedov - Son, Friend,
    Fighter,* 183; *Lessons of
    October,* 129; *Literature and
    Revolution,* 181; *Manifesto:
    Towards A Free Revolutionary
    Art,* 181; *On Lenin,* 128; *On
    Optimism and Pessimism,* xvi;
    Problems of Everyday Life, 7;
    Results and Prospects, 48-9;
    Siberian Essay, 29; *Stalin's
    Crimes,* 174, 177; *Testament,*
    175, 189; *The Case of Leon
    Trotsky,* 179; *The Class Nature
    of the Soviet State,* 165; *The
    Death Agony of Capitalism
    and the Tasks of the Fourth
    International,* 185; *The Lessons
    of Spain - The Final Warning,*
    185; *The New Course,* 123,
    126; *The Revolution Betrayed,*
    170-1, 177; *The Tragedy of the
    German Proletariat,* 161; *The
    USSR in War,* 187; *The War
    and the International,* 72; *The
    Workers' State, Thermidor and
    Bonapartism,* 167; *Their Morals
    and Ours,* 181, 183; *Towards
    Capitalism or Socialism,*
    131; *What Next?,* 158; *Wise
    Birds,* 39
Trotsky, Nina, 31, 37, 85, 95, 114,
    145-6, 159
Trotsky, Zina, 26, 37, 60, 65, 85,
    95, 114, 146, 151,159-62
Tukhachevsky, General M. N.,
    100, 111

Union of Soviet Socialist Republics
    (USSR), 118, 139, 149-50,
    152-3, 155-6, 159, 162-3, 165-7,
    169-71, 176, 178, 181, 186-7,
    189, 194-6
United Front, 158, 161, 165, 167
United Opposition, 133-7, 139, 144
United States of Europe, 72,
    80, 195
Unity Congress (Stockholm), 55

Uritsky, Moisei, 60, 75, 85, 87, 90
Ust-Kut, 25-6

van Heijenoort, Jean, 154, 162-3, 168, 174, 180
Vatzetis, Supreme C-in-C, Ioakim I., 100, 102
Vienna, 34, 42, 52-71
Volkov, Seva (Esteban), 159-61, 169, 188-90, 192, 218
Voroshilov, Kliment, 99, 102
Vorwaerts, 63

War Communism, 106-7, 112
Weber, Sara, 162-3
White Guards, 99, 101, 106, 108, 112
Winter Palace, 94
Wolf, Erwin, 171-2, 184, 216
Workers' Group, 121

Workers' Opposition, 107, 111, 115-6, 120-2, 135
Workers' Truth, 121
Wrangel, Baron, P. N., 103, 108

Yanovka, 1-2, 4, 14, 44, 67
Yudenich, General, N., 103

Zasulich, Vera, 14-5, 35, 38-9, 41, 79
Zborowski, Mark, 164
Zimmerwald Movement, 76-80, 82, 85-6, 164
Zinoviev, Gregorii, 45, 77, 89, 91-2, 95, 99, 102-4, 110-11, 115, 119-22, 124, 128-44, 147-8, 155-6, 167, 171, 174, 197
Ziv, Grigorii, xviii, 13, 18, 20, 22-3, 50, 83